D0199498

ISLAM AND THE WEST

ISLAM AND THE WEST

BERNARD LEWIS

OXFORD UNIVERSITY PRESS
New York Oxford

Oxford University Press

Oxford New York
Athens Auckland Bangkok Bombay
Calcutta Cape Town Dar es Salaam Delhi
Florence Hong Kong Istanbul Karachi
Kuala Lumpur Madras Madrid Melbourne
Mexico City Nairobi Paris Singapore
Taipei Tokyo Toronto

and associated companies in
Berlin Ibadan

Copyright © 1993 by Oxford University Press, Inc.

First published in 1993 by Oxford University Press, Inc.,
200 Madison Avenue, New York, New York 10016

First issued as an Oxford University Press paperback, 1994

Oxford is a registered trademark of Oxford University Press

All rights reserved. No part of this publication may be reproduced, stored in a retrieval system, or transmitted, in any form or by any means, electronic, mechanical, photocopying, recording, or otherwise, without the prior permission of Oxford University Press.

Library of Congress Cataloging-in-Publication Data
Lewis, Bernard.
Islam and the West / Bernard Lewis.
p. cm. ISBN 0-19-507619-2
ISBN 0-19-509061-6 (Pbk.)
1. Middle East—Relations—Europe.
2. Europe—Relations—Middle East.
3. Islam—Relations—Christianity.
4. Christianity and other religions—Islam. I. Title.
DS63.2.E8L47 1993
303.48'25604—dc20 92-26938

8 10 9

Printed in the United States of America

For
Ophira, Feridey, Zachary,
Jacob, and Rachel

Preface

For more than 1,400 years, since the advent of Islam in Arabia and the incorporation into the Islamic empire and civilization of the formerly Christian eastern and southern shores of the Mediterranean, Islam and Christendom have lived side by side—always as neighbors, often as rivals, sometimes as enemies. In a sense, each is defined and delimited by the other. "God is one, alone, and eternal," says the Qur'ān. "He begetteth not neither is He begotten and He hath no peer." In this and other explicit rejections of Christian positions, Islam clearly distances itself from its predecessor and asserts its own universal message and mission. Yet, at the same time, the scripture and traditions of Islam, and the entire civilization created under their aegis, demonstrate in a thousand ways the profound affinities that link Islam with Christianity and with their common Judaic, Hellenistic, and Middle Eastern antecedents.

Compared with the remoter cults and cultures of Asia and Africa, Islam and Christianity are sister religions, with an immense shared heritage and with a shared—or more often disputed—domain. Each saw itself as the bearer of God's final revelation to humankind, with the duty of bringing that revelation to the rest of the world. Each recognized the other as its principal, indeed, its only, rival in this claim and in this task. The result was a long series of conflicts, beginning with the early holy wars—*jihād* and Crusade, conquest and reconquest—and continuing with the ebb and flow of Muslim empire in Europe and of European empires in the lands of Islam. In this long and—alas—unfinished struggle, the two civilizations have been divided by their resemblances far more than by their differences.

Except by historians, the term "Christendom" is rarely used: the civilization formerly designated by that name has undergone a process of reform and secularization and has come to be known, in various contexts, as Europe, as the free world, and, nowadays, principally as the West. The Islamic world, or as Muslims call it, "the House of Islam," is still known, both at home and abroad, by that name, albeit with regional, national, and—rarely—sectarian subdivisions.

The studies in this volume are concerned with the relations between these two civilizations: the one defined as Islamic, the other at different times as Christian or European or Western. They are grouped according to three main topics: encounters, perceptions, and responses. The first section begins with an historical survey of the interaction—in war and peace, in commerce and culture—between Europe and its Islamic neighbors to the east and to the south. It continues with a discussion of a specific and new issue: the emergence, mainly through immigration, of large Muslim minorities in Western countries. Much has been written in recent years on the latter topic, seen principally as a problem for the majority host societies. In this study I have tried to look at the issue not in a Western but rather in an Islamic context, against the background of Islamic history and law.

The second section is concerned not so much with the encounters between the two civilizations as with the perceptions arising from these encounters. I have dealt elsewhere at some length with Muslim views of Europe. The five studies in this section are principally concerned with Western views of Islam. They deal with the problems of translation from Arabic into a Western language, with the impact on European thought and letters of the centuries-long threat of the Turks, and with Western scholarship on Islamic culture and history. This last theme is discussed in three chapters, looking at the topic from three different perspectives. The first is a case study of Gibbon's chapter on the Prophet Muḥammad in his *Decline and Fall of the Roman Empire;* the second, an examination of the origins, growth, and purposes of Arabic and Islamic studies in the Western world, with some consideration of recent and current controversies about "Orientalism"; the third, a more general discussion of the legitimacy of studying "other people's" history—whether this may be done at all, and, if so, for what purpose and subject to what rules and constraints.

The third and final section is concerned with Islamic responses and reactions in both earlier and more recent times. Four topics are discussed: Islamic religious revival and what is sometimes called fundamentalism; the place in Islamic history of the Shīʿa, whose importance was dramatically brought to world attention by the Islamic revolution in Iran; the introduction and development of the Western idea of patriotism; and, finally, the possibilities of religious coexistence. This last includes some consideration of the rather short history of secularism in the Muslim world.

All the essays contained in this volume have been to some extent revised since their original publication, to correct errors, to avoid overlaps, to establish linkages, and, of course, to take account of more recent literature and developments. Three of them—"The Question of Orientalism," "The Return of Islam," and "The Shīʿa in Islamic History"—have been extensively revised and recast.

There remains the pleasant task of expressing my appreciation and thanks to those who have helped in various ways in the preparation and publication of this volume: to the publishers and editors of the books and journals in which earlier versions of parts of this book were published, who gave perrmission to reproduce them here (the details are set forth in the bibliographical appendix); to Professors Michael Curtis, Halil Inalcık, Charles Issawi, and Hossein Modarressi, for reading parts of my typescript and giving me the benefit of their comments; to Nancy Lane and Irene Pavitt of Oxford University Press, for help and advice in the production of the book; and to my assistant Jane Baun, whose skill, care, and scholarly acumen have both speeded the production and improved the quality of this book. To all of them I offer my thanks for those of their many suggestions which I accepted and my apologies for those that I resisted. From this it will be clear that whatever faults remain are entirely my own.

Princeton, N.J. B. L.
September 1992

Contents

ENCOUNTERS

1

Europe and Islam

Jihād and Crusade

Between these two terms, "Europe" and "Islam," there is, or there would appear to be, a certain asymmetry. The one is a geographical expression, the name of a continent, one of several—the number has varied from two to seven—into which the earth's surface is divided. The other is a religion. One might reasonably speak of Europe and Asia, of Europe and Africa, or one might speak of Islam and Christendom, or of Islam and Buddhism. But what can one say about Europe and Islam?

This asymmetry is more apparent than real. Europe is a European notion, as is the whole geographical system of continents, of which Europe was the first. Europe conceived and made Europe; Europe discovered, named, and in a sense made America. Centuries earlier, Europe had invented both Asia and Africa, the inhabitants of which, until the age of European world supremacy in the nineteenth century, were unaware of these names, these identities, even of these classifications which Europeans had devised for them. Even in Europe, the notion of Europe as a cultural and political entity was relatively modern—a postmedieval secularized restatement of what had previously been known as Christendom.

Islam is not a place; it is a religion. But for Muslims this word, "religion," does not have the same connotation as the word "religion" has for Christians or even had for medieval Christians. "Religion" for Muslims means both more and less than the equivalent term for Christians. The different words used to designate them are indicative. The word "religion," now common to virtually all the languages of European Christendom, both Eastern and Western, derives from the Latin *religio.* This pre-Christian term for the cult and rituals of pagan Rome was first Christianized by Saint Jerome in his Latin translation of the Bible. The Islamic term is *dīn,* originally Arabic but adopted in all the many languages of Islam. The cognate word in other Semitic languages, notably Hebrew and Aramaic, means law.

For Muslims, Islam is not merely a system of belief and worship, a compartment of life, so to speak, distinct from other compartments which are the concern of nonreligious authorities administering nonreligious laws. It is rather the whole of life, and its rules include civil, criminal, and even what we would call constitutional law.

But if the term "religion," in one sense, conveys much more to a Muslim than to a Christian, there is another sense in which it conveys much less. As a building, as a place of worship, the equivalent of the church among Muslims is the mosque. As an institution, as a power, the Church has no equivalent in Islam. Islam has no councils or synods, no prelates or hierarchies, no canon laws or canon courts. In classical Islamic history there could be no clash between pope and emperor, since the caliph, the titular head of the Islamic state and community, combined in himself both political and religious—though not spiritual—authority. There could be neither conflict nor cooperation, neither separation nor association between church and state, since the governing institution of Islam combined both functions.

This well-known difference between Islam and Christendom derives from the different origins—or as some would now put it, the different foundation myths—of the two religions. Muḥammad was not, like Moses, forbidden to enter his Promised Land; still less did he suffer, like Jesus, physical death by martyrdom. Nor were his followers obliged to struggle for centuries as a proscribed and persecuted minority under a hostile government. Muḥammad became a sovereign during his lifetime. He himself founded the first Islamic state and governed it with his Companions. Muḥammad's spiritual mission ended with his death, but his religious and political mission was continued by his successors, the caliphs. Under their rule, Muslims progressed from victory to victory, from triumph to triumph, creating in less than a century a vast realm extending from the borders of India and China to the Pyrenees and the Atlantic, and ruling millions of new subjects, vast numbers of whom came eagerly to embrace the new faith and dispensation. The sacred history, one might even say the salvation history of Islam, related in the Qur'ān and in the traditional biographies of the Prophet and his Companions; the semisacred early history of the Islamic state, which constitutes the core of memory and self-awareness of Muslims everywhere, tell a story of swift and uninterrupted advance, in which the leaders of false and superseded religions were overwhelmed, and the way was prepared for the eventual triumph of the Muslim faith and of Muslim arms, bringing the word of God to all mankind and imposing the law of God on all the world.

It is by now a commonplace that the term "Islam" is the counterpart not only of "Christianity" but also of "Christendom"—not only of a religion in the narrow Western sense but of a whole civilization which grew up under the aegis of that religion. It is also something more, which has no equivalent in Western Christendom and only an approximate and limited equivalent in Byzantium. It is a political identity and allegiance, transcending all others. Always in the ideal, and for a while even in reality, the world of Islam was one polity ruled by one sovereign, the caliph, and even after the decline of the central caliphal power and the emergence of regional monarchies within the extended Islamic realm, the ideal of a single Islamic polity was strong enough to prevent, until comparatively recent times, the emergence of strong regional or dynastic or national powers, such as were beginning to appear in Europe even in the Middle Ages.

This ideal of a single Islamic polity, transcending both country and nation, still has considerable appeal for Muslims, as recent events have demonstrated. Both terms, therefore, "Europe" and "Islam," represent a primary civilizational self-definition of the entities which they designate, and may be seen as counterparts, whose association is not inappropriate. A discussion of the relations between them and of their reciprocal perceptions and attitudes need not therefore be seen as asymmetrical.

Christendom and Islam are, in chronological sequence, the second and third attempts to create a world religion. The first was, of course, Buddhism. From the sixth century B.C., Buddhist missionaries from India carried their faith to South, Southeast, and East Asia, where they won great successes. Buddhist missions to Southwest Asia had much less impact. Though their influence was probably greater than was at one time realized, they failed to win converts to their religion or to set up any kind of Buddhist culture. Among two other ancient peoples, the Jews and the Persians, religious teachers and leaders developed universalist notions which were later to have the profoundest influence and importance, but neither group made any sustained attempt to teach these notions to others or to convert them to their faith. The idea that there is a single truth for all mankind, and that it is the duty of those who possess it to share it with others, begins with the advent of Christianity and reappears with the rise of Islam. Both faiths originated in the Middle East, and they share an enormous common heritage—Jewish ideas about monotheism, prophecy, revelation, and scripture; Greek philosophy and science; Roman law and government; and going back still further, the surviving traditions of the more ancient civilizations of the region. Both shared this new and almost unprecedented idea that they were the unique possessors of the whole of God's truth. They also shared, or rather disputed, a common territory—southwest Asia, northern Africa, and Mediterranean Europe.

In many ways, medieval Islam and medieval Christendom spoke the same language. To some extent and in some places this was true even in the literal sense. In many Mediterranean countries, Muslims and Christians shared not only the local vernaculars but also a knowledge of Arabic. Shared concepts, and shared vocabularies to denote them, made it possible not only to argue, but to translate religious texts. Those medieval monks who translated the Qur'ān into Latin in order to refute it were able to do so because Latin, by that time a Christian language, had the necessary terms. In contrast, when converts tried to translate the Qur'ān from Arabic into Persian and Turkish and Indian languages, they had to take their

Arabic vocabulary with them, because these languages, and the cultures of which they were the expression, did not possess either the concepts or the corresponding terms.

Speaking the same language at least in the figurative sense, using the same methods of argument and reasoning, and adhering to identical or similar notions of what religion is about, Islam and Christendom could disagree meaningfully. Disputations were possible between Christians and Muslims, as between either and Jews, in a way which would not have been possible between Muslim or Christian divines on the one hand and exponents of the religions of further Asia on the other. When Christians and Muslims called each other infidels, each understood what the other meant, and both meant more or less the same thing. In so doing, they revealed their essential similarity.

Christianity and Islam were consecutive, not concurrent, dispensations, with an interval of six centuries between them. For prophets and preachers, for jurists and theologians, there was obviously a crucial difference between a previous and a subsequent religion. This distinction may help to explain the sometimes sharply contrasting attitudes of Christians and of Muslims toward each other, and of both toward the Jews. For Christians, Judaism was a predecessor: an incomplete and superseded religion, fulfilled and replaced by Christianity, but not in itself false. Jews were therefore accorded some measure of tolerance in medieval Europe. This tolerance was always limited, often precarious, sometimes suspended, but somehow Jews managed to survive. Muslims did not, and the reconquests for Christendom of Sicily, Spain, and Portugal were followed, sometimes immediately and sometimes after an interval, by the expulsion or forcible conversion of their Muslim inhabitants. Muslims and Christians alike were convinced that theirs was not only the whole of God's truth—it was also its final expression. Anything subsequent was therefore necessarily false and harmful and could not be tolerated. There was no place for Muslims in the once lost and now reconquered lands of Christendom. Even the republic of Venice, which lived by the Levant trade, had the greatest difficulty in tolerating one small inn for visiting Turkish merchants.

For Muslims, on the other hand, Christianity, like Judaism, was a predecessor, and deserving of the same degree of tolerance. Like Judaism, it was in Muslim eyes a religion which had been true and had possessed an authentic revelation, but was incomplete and now superseded by Islam. True, there were sometimes problems with predecessor religions, whose followers were seen as having falsified or corrupted the authentic revelations which they had once possessed. Muslim theologians had difficulty with such Christian doctrines as the Trinity, and the son-ship and divinity of Christ, which in their eyes were blasphemous absurdities, and are explicitly rejected by the Qur'ān (5:75–76 and 112:1–4). But in general, they were willing to concede the tolerance to the earlier religions enjoined by Qur'ānic law, despite these perceived aberrations.

No such tolerance could be accorded to subsequent religious manifestations which impugned the veracity and finality of their own dispensations and, by their missionary zeal, threatened to mislead the faithful. In the eyes of some medieval Christians, Jews were tolerable as long as they kept to the Old Testament, even if they rejected the New, but they could forfeit that tolerance by following the Talmud, which was in large part subsequent to the advent of Christianity and which therefore in Christian eyes was full of errors. If for the medieval Christian, Talmudic Judaism was falsified, Islam was simply false, and since unlike Talmudic Judaism it sought to convert others, it had to be resisted and overcome. As the Christians feared and persecuted Islam, so did the Muslims fear and persecute such post-Islamic conversionist religious movements as the Baha'is and the Ahmadis. And both Christians and Muslims, Christians more especially, viewed with particular distrust the emergence of deviant forms of their own faith.

For the Muslim, Christianity was an abrogated religion, which its followers absurdly insisted on retaining, instead of accepting God's final word. They could be tolerated if they submitted. If they did not, they were to be fought until they were overcome and either accepted the truth of the Muslim faith or submitted to the authority of the Muslim state. For Christians, Islam was at best a heresy, more usually a false doctrine, founded by one who was variously depicted, at different stages in the evolution of European consciousness, as a heretic, an impostor, and later, in the age of the Enlightenment, an Enthusiast.

Though Christendom and Islam were rivals, indeed, competitors, for the role of world religion, and though both shared so many traditions and beliefs, so many purposes and aspirations, neither was willing to recognize the other as a viable alternative. This unwillingness was expressed in a number of ways, and even these illustrate vividly the essential similarity of the two faiths. Europeans in various parts of the continent showed a curious reluctance to call the Muslims by any name with a religious connotation, preferring rather to call them by ethnic names, the obvious purpose of which was to diminish their stature and significance and to reduce them to something local or even tribal. At various times and in various places, Europeans called the Muslims Saracens, Moors, Turks, or Tatars, according to which of the Muslim peoples they had encountered. "Turk," the name of by far the most powerful and important of the Muslim states, even became a synonym for Muslim, and a convert to Islam was said to have "turned Turk" wherever the conversion took place. Medieval Muslim writers show a similar, indeed, an identical, reluctance, and refer to their Christian rivals and enemies as Romans, Slavs, or Franks, depending on when and where they encountered them. When religious designations were used, they were either wholly negative—such as *paynim, kāfir,* or, more generally, "unbeliever"—or else inaccurate and demeaning. Parallel examples of this are the common Christian practice of referring to Muslims as Mohammedans, and the common Muslim practice of referring to Christians as Nazarenes—in Arabic, *Naṣāra,* from Nazareth. The most common religious term which each applied to the other was, however, "infidel," and it was in the exchange of this insult that they achieved their fullest and most perfect mutual understanding.

These perceptions and the resulting attitudes determined the first encounters between the two religions. They were of course in some respects confirmed, in others modified, by the subsequent realities of the relationship between the two.

At first there seemed every reason why Islam should triumph and Europe succumb. Almost from its beginning, Islam was a world empire and a world civilization extending over three continents, inhabited by many different races, including within itself the seats of the ancient civilizations of Egypt and the Fertile Crescent, to which soon were added Iran and northern India. Muslims had inherited the philosophy and the science of Greece, which Europe did not discover for centuries to come; the wisdom and statecraft of Iran; and much even of the Eastern Christian and Byzantine heritage. While Europe was caught between Islam in the south, the steppe in the east, the ocean in the west, and the frozen wastes in the north, the world of Islam was in contact, sometimes in war but often peacefully, with the rich and ancient civilizations of India and China. From the one, they imported positional, decimal notation of numbers; from the other, paper, with immense effect both on their sciences and on their humanities, as well as on government and business. The Islamic world enjoyed a rich and diverse culture, vast lands and resources, and a complex and flourishing economy. It also had a sophisticated and law-abiding urban society, in such contrast to Europe that as late as Ottoman times, European travelers marveled at the city of Istanbul, where gentlemen and even soldiers walked without swords. The Islamic oecumene was one society and, for a while, one polity, joined in faith and allegiance and linked by a network of land and sea routes, created for the double purpose of trade and pilgrimage.

It was also united by one language and the culture which it expressed. In the Arabic language the Islamic world possessed a medium of communication without equal in premodern Christendom—a language of government and commerce, science and philosophy, religion and law, with a rich and diverse literature that in scope, variety, and sophistication was as unparalleled as it was unprecedented. The ossified Greek, debased Latin, and primitive vernaculars of Europe in the early medieval centuries could offer nothing even remotely comparable.

Of the civilizations that were neighbors of Islam, Christianity alone was, in principle, universal—in belief, in self-perception, in intention. It was not regional like the religions of India or China but aimed at converting all mankind. In fact, however, Christendom, before the great expansion, was coterminous with Europe. There were, of course, exceptions, but they were of no great importance. The Christian populations under Muslim rule possessed no sovereignty and in any case belonged to different churches and cultures. The kingdom of Ethiopia, the one Christian state outside Europe, was remote and little known. As a civilization, Christendom was as European as Confucianism was Chinese. It was the religion of a region, and not a very large one. Its people were all of one race, belonging to a limited number of interrelated ethnic groups with a strong common culture. In other words, it was rather like Hindu India, but smaller and poorer.

Compared with Islam, Christendom was indeed poor, small, backward, and monochromatic. Split into squabbling, petty kingdoms, its churches divided by schism and heresy, with constant quarrels between the churches of Rome and the East, it was disputed between two emperors and for a while even two popes. After the loss of the Christian shores of the eastern and southern Mediterranean to the Muslim advance, Christendom seemed even more local, confined in effect to a small peninsula on the western edge of Asia which became—and was by this confinement defined as—Europe. For a time—indeed, for a very long time—it seemed that nothing could prevent the ultimate triumph of Islam and the extension of the Islamic faith and Muslim power to Europe.

According to Muslim tradition, the Prophet Muhammad during his lifetime sent letters to "all the kings of the infidels"—Chosroes in Persia, Caesar in Byzantium, the Negus in Ethiopia—summoning them to embrace the new faith and submit to its rule and law. Documents survive, purporting to give the texts of such letters. These documents are not accepted as authentic by modern critical scholarship, including much Muslim scholarship, and there is indeed considerable and growing uncertainty concerning the history of the advent and early spread of the new faith. With few exceptions, our information comes exclusively from Arab Muslim sources, orally transmitted for generations before they were committed to writing, and thus inevitably affected, and perhaps distorted, by the bitter factional, sectarian, tribal, and ethnic struggles of the early Islamic state. Modern critical scholarship, by questioning first the accuracy and then the authenticity of a large part of our sources, has darkened rather than lightened the obscurity. All that can be said with certainty is that half a century after the death of the Prophet, Islam had become a new world religion, claiming to supersede Christianity and all other faiths and appealing to all mankind, and that the Muslim polity and community, founded by the Prophet in Medina, had become a vast new empire, advancing—as it seemed at the time with reasonable prospects of immediate success—toward the mastery of the world.

From an early date Muslim law laid down, as one of the principal obligations of the head of the Muslim state and community, the conduct of *jihād,* a term commonly, if inaccurately, translated as "Holy War." The Arabic word literally means striving, and it is often followed by the words *fī sabīl Allāh,* in the path of God. Until fairly recent times it was usually, though not universally, understood in a military sense. It was a Muslim duty—collective in attack, individual in defense—to fight in the war against the unbelievers. In principle, this war was to continue until all mankind either embraced Islam or submitted to the authority of the Muslim state.

Until this purpose was achieved there could theoretically be no peace, though truces were permitted, which in effect and duration did not greatly differ from the peace treaties that from time to time punctuated the almost continuous warfare waged by the princes of Europe against one another.

The obligation of *jihād* was in force on all the frontiers of Islam, beyond which lay the lands of the infidels. The obligation was the same, but between these various groups of infidels there was an important distinction. To the east and to the south of Islam, in Asia and in Africa, there were pagans and idolaters, teachable barbarians who, having no serious religion of their own, were seen as natural recruits to the Islamic faith and realm. Only in one area, Christendom, did Islam encounter sustained resistance, from a genuine rival faith embodied for a while in a rival polity. This gave the *jihād* against Christendom a special character, for it was in these lands that Muslims saw, at different times, the greatest danger and the greatest opportunity. For the Arabs, after their conquest of Iran and Central Asia and their inconclusive ventures into the borderlands of China and India, Europe was by far the most important infidel enemy. Some centuries later, for the Ottoman Turks, there was no other. Local kings and chieftains waged *jihād* against local infidels in South and Southeast Asia and in sub-Saharan Africa, but the great *jihād par excellence*, the major battlefield of the House of Islam and the House of War, was in Europe.

The first barriers to be overcome in the advance of Islam from its Arabian birthplace into the neighboring lands were the two rival empires of Persia and Byzantium, which controlled the region we now call the Middle East. The Persian barrier was overthrown, and the Persian Empire with all its dependencies was incorporated in the new Islamic state, including its capital city and its ruling elite, whose subjection and subsequent adherence to Islam brought incalculable consequences. The Byzantine barrier was weakened and pushed back but remained standing on a new line, roughly equivalent to the southern and eastern borders of Anatolia.

This was the new eastern frontier of Christendom. Elsewhere, the Christian lands of the Fertile Crescent, of Egypt and North Africa, were one by one incorporated in the Islamic realm and served as launching pads for new attacks on Europe itself. In the east, the Muslim attack was halted, and the Byzantines were able to hold the line of the Taurus Mountains and to save the city of Constantinople from repeated siege and attack by the Arab forces. In the west, the swift advance of the Arab Muslim armies took them to the Mediterranean islands and, most important of all, to the Iberian Peninsula. In 710 the first Muslim raiders crossed from Morocco into Spain, invited, so it is said, by a local Spanish ruler with a grievance. By 718 they had occupied most of the peninsula and crossed the Pyrenees into France, where in 732 they encountered and were defeated by the

Frankish leader Charles Martel, in the celebrated battle of Tours and Poitiers. In Western legend and historiography, this is seen as the decisive victory, which turned the tide and saved Europe—Christendom—from the Saracen peril. The Arab historians, if they mention this engagement at all, present it as a minor skirmish. For them, the end of their adventure in France was due to their failure to hold the French city of Narbonne, which they first captured in 715 and finally lost in 759. Muslim armies from Spain attacked the city and neighborhood, without success, in 793 and again as late as 840, but they did not capture it, and in time the Muslim forces withdrew south of the Pyrenees. The battle for Spain continued, and almost eight centuries passed from the first Muslim landing to the defeat and destruction of the emirate of Granada, the last Muslim state in western Europe, in 1492. This was followed, ten years later, by the first of a series of edicts giving the Muslim subjects of the Spanish crown the choice of baptism, exile, or death.

The long struggle for Spain and Portugal and the earlier struggle for southern Italy had ended in Christian victory and Muslim expulsion. Meanwhile a new and devastating Muslim counterattack was gathering force, this time not in the west, but in the east; not from the Arabs, but from a new Islamic power, the Turks. Already in the eleventh century, Turkish armies and migrating Turkish tribesmen had won the greater part of Anatolia from the Byzantines, transforming what had once been Greek and Christian into a Turkish and Muslim land. The eastern bastion of Christendom, which for so many centuries had withstood the Arabs, suffered the first of a series of defeats. In time, these redrew the frontier between Christendom—Europe—and Islam.

First under the Seljuk and then under the Ottoman sultans, the Turks created one of the greatest and most enduring of the Islamic empires. In 1352 a Turkish force, brought over—like the first Arabs in Spain—as allies of a Christian contender for power, occupied the fortress of Tzympe, north of Gallipoli on the European shore of the Dardanelles. A century later, masters of the whole Balkan Peninsula, they were ready to mount the final attack which added Constantinople, as copestone, to their new imperial structure in Europe and Asia. From their new capital in Istanbul, the Ottoman sultans launched a series of further expeditions, which brought them to the plains of Hungary and twice, in 1529 and again in 1683, to the walls of Vienna. For a century and a half, the Turkish armies, operating from their bases in Buda and Belgrade, offered a nearer and greater threat to the heart of Christian Europe than had ever come from the Saracens in Spain.

Nor was the threat limited to central and eastern Europe. Muslim fleets, operating out of North Africa, waged naval *jihād* against the western European states, in the Mediterranean and even in the open seas, attacking shipping and coastal towns and villages. In the early seventeenth century, corsairs from Algeria, now under Ottoman suzerainty, and from Morocco, were raiding the southern coasts of England and Ireland, and once—in 1627—raided as far as Iceland, where their visitation was commemorated in chronicles, sagas, and prayers.

In addition to the Moors and the Turks, there was a third Muslim advance into Europe, often overlooked by Western historians but deeply burned into the consciousness of the East. During the thirteenth century, Mongol invaders from East Asia conquered much of Russia and eastern Europe and established a state known in Russian annals as the Khanate of the Golden Horde. In the third quarter of the century Berke Khan, the grandson of Jengiz Khan and lord of the Golden Horde, was converted to Islam. He entered into relations with the Mamluk sultan of Egypt and began the process by which the mixed Mongol and Turkish people of his realm became a Muslim nation. They are known in eastern Europe as Tatars, after the name of one of the Mongol tribes, and the period of their domination, from the thirteenth to the fifteenth century, is known in Russian annals as "the Tatar yoke." Even after the breakup of the Khanate of the Golden Horde, the successor khanates based in Kazan, Astrakhan, and the Crimea continued to rule—and where they could not rule, to raid—parts of eastern Europe until the extinction of the last khanate, that of the Crimea, in 1783. From 1475, the khans of the Crimea became vassals of the Ottomans. Tatar forces often fought under Ottoman command against European enemies, while Tatar raids on Russian, Ukrainian, Polish, and Lithuanian villages provided merchandise, for centuries, for the slave markets of Istanbul.

There were, of course, periods of European counterattack, notably in the series of wars known—in European historiography—as the Crusades. In recent years it has become the practice, in both western Europe and the Middle East, to see and present the Crusades as an early exercise in Western imperialism—as a wanton and predatory aggression by the European powers of the time against the Muslim or, as some would now say, against the Arab lands.

They were not seen in that light at the time, either by Christians or by Muslims. For contemporary Christians, the Crusades were religious wars, the purpose of which was to recover the lost lands of Christendom and in particular the holy land where Christ had lived, taught, and died. In this connection, it may be recalled that when the Crusaders arrived in the Levant not much more than four centuries had passed since the Arab Muslim conquerors had wrested these lands from Christendom—less than half the time from the Crusades to the present day—and that a substantial proportion of the population of these lands, perhaps even a majority, was still Christian. In the Arabic historiography of the period, incomparably richer than that of the Crusaders, the terms "Crusade" and "Crusader" do not appear at all, and even the notion that these terms represent appears to be missing. The battles against these invaders are described in great detail, but they are usually designated by an ethnic name, the Franks, often simply as the infidels, with appropriate imprecations, rarely as the Christians. With few exceptions, the Muslim historians show little interest in whence or why the Franks had come, and report their arrival and their departure with equal lack of curiosity. This was an age of Muslim weakness and division, and the Muslim world, in East and West alike, was being invaded by barbarians, both external and internal, from every side—nomads from the northern steppes and the southern deserts, Georgians from the Caucasus, Galicians and Normans from Europe. These Frankish invaders, who first appeared as auxiliaries of the familiar Byzantine enemy and then as independent operators, must have seemed no different from the rest. The "Great Debate" between Christendom and Islam, of which Edward Gibbon speaks so eloquently, was, in its verbal aspect, a monologue, from which the Muslim interlocutor was absent and of which he seems to have been unaware.

In the longer perspective of European–Islamic relations, the venture of the Crusades was no more than an episode; its only measurable consequences, within the Islamic world, were an improvement and extension of commercial relations with Europe, and a worsening of relations with local Christians. In the seesaw of attack and counterattack between Christendom and Islam, this venture began with an inconclusive Christian victory and ended with a conclusive Christian defeat.

For almost a thousand years, from the first Moorish landing in Spain to the second Turkish siege of Vienna, Europe was under constant threat from Islam. In the early centuries it was a double threat—not only of invasion and conquest, but also of conversion and assimilation. All but the easternmost provinces of the Islamic realm had been taken from Christian rulers, and the vast majority of the first Muslims west of Iran and Arabia were converts from Christianity. North Africa, Egypt, Syria, even Persian-ruled Iraq, had been Christian countries, in which Christianity was older and more deeply rooted than in most of Europe. Their loss was sorely felt and heightened the fear that a similar fate was in store for Europe. In Spain and in Sicily, Muslim faith and Arab culture exercised a powerful attraction, and even those who remained faithful to the Christian religion often adopted the Arabic language.

It was this fear, more than any other single factor, which led to the beginnings of Arabic scholarship in Europe, to the discipline which centuries later came to be known as Orientalism. In the monasteries of western Europe, studious monks learned Arabic, translated the Qur'ān, and studied other Muslim texts, with a double purpose—first, the immediate aim of saving Christian souls from conversion to Islam and, second, the more distant hope of converting Muslims to Christianity. It took some centuries before they decided that the first was no longer necessary and that the second was impossible.

If that is how the Islamic world looked from Europe, how did Europe look from the Islamic world? Rather, one might say, as central Africa looked to Victorian England. Arabic writings reflect the picture of a remote, unexplored wilderness inhabited by exotic, picturesque, and rather primitive people from whom there was nothing to fear and less to learn. A few intrepid explorers from Muslim Spain and North Africa ventured into darkest Europe and left accounts of their travels; we can hear the same note of somewhat amused disdain in their writings as we sometimes find in European travelers in Africa and Asia many centuries later. The Arabs were, of course, aware of Byzantium. They knew and respected the civilization of the ancient Greeks of Hellas, and also, though to a much lesser extent, of the Christian Greeks in Constantinople. But they had no respect—indeed, there was no reason why they should have any respect—for central and western Europe, which in medieval times was on a significantly lower level of civilization, both moral and material, than the heartlands of Islam.

Yet despite this perception of non-Byzantine Europe as an outer wilderness of barbarism and unbelief, there was at the same time an awareness that the Europeans, even the western Europeans, were not simple barbarians like the other neighbors of Islam in the east and in the south. They were, after all, followers of a real religion, superseded but resting on an authentic revelation and thus vastly superior to the polytheists and idolaters whom the Muslims encountered in other regions. At the same time, unlike those polytheists and idolaters, they were not willing and easily assimilable recruits to Islam but, rather, remained stubbornly attached to their own superseded faith, with an ambition to make it prevail over Islam.

In the second great confrontation, this time between Renaissance Europe and Ottoman Islam, few were tempted to change their faith, and those who "turned Turk" were mostly adventurers in search of a career in the Ottoman land of opportunity. Muslims remained, as always, impervious to the claims of what they considered to be an outdated and superseded religion, and the growing missionary effort of Christian Europe was directed mainly to the Americas and to the remoter peoples of Asia and Africa, east and south of the lands of Islam. The Islamic threat to Europe, in its Ottoman form, was primarily military and political and to some extent social. The challenge and opportunity which it offered to European enterprise was not the conversion of the heathen but the exploitation of the vast markets in the expanding Ottoman realms in Europe, Asia, and Africa.

This new situation is reflected in the continuing and changing study of Islam among Europeans. The main purpose of study was no longer to prevent or to achieve religious conversion, and its centers were no longer in the monasteries. Students of Islam and students of the Islamic world were now pursuing different paths, which only recently have once again come in sight of one another. In the universities that were appearing all over western Europe, scholars imbued with the curiosity and enthusiasm of the Renaissance and disciplined by the philological method of the humanists applied themselves to the study of classical Arabic texts, both religious and other. Practical men of affairs, concerned with the conduct of diplomacy, war, and commerce, sought eagerly for the "news from

Turkey" and made great efforts to collect and to interpret reports concerning the current situation and recent past of this frightening yet tempting neighbor. In time, these studies attracted the attention even of scholars, though not, until centuries later, of professors in universities. Nevertheless, when Richard Knolles, vicar of Sandwich and sometime fellow of Lincoln College, Oxford, published his *General History of the Turks* in 1603, though he knew no Turkish and had never set foot outside England, he was able to draw on a considerable body of literature in several European languages, including translations of Turkish chronicles, to describe, in great detail and with considerable historical depth, "the glorious empire of the Turks, the present terror of the world."

For a long time, Richard Knolles and his numerous European predecessors and informants had no equivalents among Arabs and Turks, who in general showed the same lack of interest as in medieval times. There is evidence that Ottoman officials and officers were from time to time concerned with developments beyond the frontiers, but such concern is rarely reflected in scholarship or letters. There was no attempt to learn non-Islamic languages, and when a knowledge of European languages or conditions was required, Muslim rulers were content to rely on their non-Muslim subjects or on refugees and other Europeans in their service. Nowadays I suppose we would call them defectors. The Christian persecution of the Jews, and the Catholic and Protestant persecution of each other, maintained an ample supply of this important human resource. European advances in weaponry and in naval matters received some attention, and were sometimes—to some extent—adopted, but the arts and sciences, even the politics and economics of Europe, were seen as fundamentally irrelevant to the life and concerns of Islam and were therefore ignored. Such an attitude can be understood—in a sense even justified—in earlier times. By the late seventeenth century, though Turkish pashas still ruled in Belgrade and Buda, and Turkish armies still threatened Vienna, it was becoming dangerously out of date.

Reconquest and Empire

Between 1555 and 1560, Ogier Ghiselin de Busbecq, imperial ambassador to the court of Süleyman the Magnificent, wrote a series of letters in which he expressed his deep pessimism about the prospects of Europe under imminent peril of Ottoman conquest. European Christendom, he lamented, had lost its former dedication, its former valor. Instead of seeking renown on the field of honor and defending Europe against an implacable and dangerous enemy, European Christians preferred to squander their energies "seeking the Indies and the Antipodes across vast fields of ocean, in search of gold." Christian Europe, weak, divided, and irresolute, seemed helpless before the overwhelming power of the centralized, disciplined Ottoman state:

> On their side are the resources of a mighty empire, strength unimpaired, experience and practice in fighting, a veteran soldiery, habituation to victory, endurance of toil, unity, order, discipline, frugality, and watchfulness. On our side is public poverty, private luxury, impaired strength, broken spirit, lack of endurance and training; the soldiers are insubordinate, the officers avaricious; there is contempt for discipline; licence, recklessness, drunkenness, and debauchery are rife; and, worst of all, the enemy is accustomed to victory and we to defeat. Can we doubt what the result will be? Persia alone interposes in our favour; for the enemy, as he hastens to attack, must keep an eye on this menace in his rear.[1]

To Busbecq and his contemporaries, it might well have seemed that Europe was doomed and that the final Ottoman triumph was delayed only by the need to confront another challenge on the far side—the attempt by the Shiʿite shahs of Persia to establish themselves as the leading rulers of the Muslim world and Shiʿism as the dominant form of Islam. But this respite would not last long: "Persia is only delaying our fate; it cannot save us. When the Turks have settled with Persia they will fly at our throats, supported by the might of the whole East; how unprepared we are I dare not say!"[2]

Busbecq was an accurate and perceptive observer of the Ottoman scene, but he was, fortunately for Europe, profoundly wrong in his global perspective. Though the Ottoman power was still to survive for some time, it had already passed its peak. The Ottomans did not in fact "settle with Persia" but continued to fight wars against their Muslim neighbors and rivals until the early nineteenth century, by which time neither Turkey, nor Persia, nor indeed Islam posed a serious threat to Christendom. Contrary to Busbecq's dire predictions, the Ottomans achieved no triumph over Persia, no victory in Europe.

The final defeat and withdrawal of the armies of Islam was no doubt due in the first instance to the valiant defenders of Vienna, but in the larger perspective, it was due to those self-same adventurers whose voyages across the ocean and greed for gold aroused Busbecq's ire. Whatever their motives, their voyages brought vast new lands under European rule or influence, placed great wealth in bullion and resources at European disposal, and thus gave Europe new strength with which to resist and ultimately throw back the Muslim invader.

The sequence of events which Europeans called the Discoveries and others have called the Expansion of Europe inaugurated a new age not only in European but in world history, one that an Indian historian, K. M. Panikkar, named the "Vasco da Gama era," of European penetration, infiltration, influence, and finally domination.

This European encounter with the rest of the world, from the late fifteenth century onward, took a variety of different forms. In some regions, as, for example, northern Asia and North America, Europeans came into uninhabited or thinly inhabited lands, in which they were able to settle and create their own societies. In others, including most of Asia and significant parts of Africa and of Central and South America, they encountered ancient and advanced civilizations—in the eastern hemisphere, specifically, the civilizations of China, India, and Islam.

Between these three there is an obvious difference. China and India are places, and despite their rich and sophisticated cultures, they remained essentially regional. The first universal religion, Buddhism, was decisively rejected in the country of its birth, and had become increasingly local in the Southeast and East Asian countries to which it had been brought. Islam, in contrast, was a universal religion, which never abandoned its universalist aspirations.

There is another profoundly important respect in which the encounter between Europe and Islam differed from the encounters with India and China. When European and Chinese, European and Indian, met, they met as strangers, knowing little or nothing about each other. For the European, India and China were names, with a few, almost forgotten, remnants of classical lore and medieval travelers' tales attached to them. If the Europeans knew little about India and China, the Indians and Chinese knew nothing about Europe. They could therefore meet in a relatively open-minded way.

The European and the Muslim, in contrast, knew—or thought they knew—a great deal about each other. They had been neighbors since the very beginnings of Islam in the seventh century—neighbors in constant contact and communication, often as rivals, sometimes as enemies, and with attitudes toward each other formed and confirmed by centuries of experience and, for the Europeans, of fear. The European image of the Muslim was very different from the image of the Indian or the Chinese. The Indians, after all, had never invaded Spain or crossed the Pyrenees; the Chinese had never conquered Constantinople or besieged Vienna. Neither of them had ever made any attempts to convert Christians to their own religious beliefs, the very nature of which was at that time unknown and probably unintelligible to Europeans. Nor—and this was perhaps what counted most—had they condemned the Bible as obsolete and offered a new scripture to take its place. Europe and Islam were old acquaintances, intimate enemies, whose continuing conflict derived a special virulence from their shared origins and common aims.

Indeed, the whole complex process of European expansion and empire in the last five centuries has its roots in the clash of Islam and Christendom. It began with the long and bitter struggle of the conquered peoples of Europe, in east and west, to restore their homelands to Christendom and expel the Muslim peoples who had invaded and subjugated them. It was hardly to be expected that the triumphant Spaniards and Portuguese would stop at the Straits of Gibraltar, or that the Russians would allow the Tatars to retire in peace and regroup in their bases on the upper and lower Volga—the more so since a new and deadly Muslim attack on Christendom was under way, with the Turkish advance from the Bosporus to the Danube and beyond threatening the heart of Europe. The victorious liberators, having reconquered their own territories, pursued their former masters whence they had come. The same impetus, the same momentum, which enabled the Spaniards and the Portuguese to drive the Moors from the Iberian Peninsula, carried them across the straits into Africa, around Africa, and beyond Africa into undreamt-of lands; the same impetus, the same momentum, carried the victorious Russians from the liberation of Moscow to the Caspian and the Black Sea and ultimately to a large part of Asia. The two movements, of reconquest followed by empire, were almost contemporary at both ends of Europe. It was in 1480 that the Russians finally ended the Tatar yoke and prepared to invade the Tatar homelands; it was in 1492 that the Spaniards destroyed the last Muslim state in Spain and made a spectacular contribution to the voyages of discovery which the Portuguese had already begun. Other European peoples, who apart from slave raids by land and sea had never been subjected to Moorish or Tatar rule, joined in the vast movement which carried Christian Europe from reconquest to empire.

For many, the great voyages of discovery were themselves part of a religious war, a continuation of the Crusades and of the reconquest, against the same Muslim enemy. When the Portuguese arrived in Asian waters, it was Muslim rulers around the Indian Ocean who were their main opponents and who tried without success to stop them. As far away as Ceylon and the Philippines they continued to see and name their Muslim enemies as "Moors."

For a long time, the successes achieved by the Christian counterattack were limited to the periphery—to the Eurasian steppe and to the remoter lands of South and Southeast Asia, while in the center, in the Muslim heartlands around the Mediterranean, the Christian advance was held and, in some areas, reversed. The Ottoman conquest of Syria and Egypt in 1517, followed by the extension of Ottoman suzerainty in North Africa as far as the Moroccan frontier, greatly strengthened Muslim power in the Mediterranean, where even the much-vaunted Christian naval victory at Lepanto in 1571 made little real difference to the balance of power. In the West, the Spanish and Portuguese attack on the North African coast, from Tunis to Morocco, was decisively defeated by Ottoman and Moroccan forces. In the East, Portuguese attempts, from their new bases in India, to penetrate the Red Sea and Persian Gulf were brought to nothing by the Ottomans and the Persians. In the central arena of Christian–Muslim warfare, on the European mainland, the Ottoman threat to Vienna and to the heart of Europe seemed as imminent as ever.

On 12 September 1683, after a siege of sixty days, the Turkish armies encamped outside Vienna began to withdraw. This was their second attempt and their second failure to take the city, but between the two sieges there was a vast difference. In 1529, when the armies of the Ottoman sultan Süleyman the Magnificent first reached the walls of Vienna, they were at the crest of a wave of conquest. The attack failed, but the failure was neither final nor decisive. The retreat was orderly, the defeat inconclusive; the siege initiated a century and a half of stalemate during which the two empires—of the Hapsburgs and the Ottomans—battled for the control of Hungary and ultimately of central Europe.

The second siege and the second withdrawal were quite a different matter. This time, the failure was clear and unequivocal. The withdrawal from Vienna was followed by defeats in the field and the loss of cities and provinces. The victories of the Austrians and their allies were confirmed and established in the peace treaty of Carlowitz, signed on 26 January 1699.

This treaty marked a crucial turning point, not only in the relations between the Ottoman and Hapsburg empires, but, more profoundly, between Europe and Islam. For centuries past the Ottoman sultanate had been the leading power of Islam, representing it in the millennial conflict with its Western Christian neighbors. The real power of Islam in relation to Europe had, in many respects, declined. The advance from eastern Europe across the steppes, from western Europe across the oceans, threatened to enclose the Islamic heartlands in a pincer grip. The pincers were already in place—they would soon be ready to close. And now at the center, the war had shown that the Ottoman armies, once the strongest and best in the world, were falling behind their European adversaries in weaponry, in military science, even in discipline and skill.

The Muslim world was also falling behind Europe economically, notably in the mobilization and deployment of economic power. The rise of mercantilism in the West helped European states and companies to achieve a level of commercial organization and concentration unknown in the Islamic lands. The extraterritorial immunities bestowed on them—as an act of condescension—by Muslim rulers made it easier for them to exploit and, in time, to dominate the open markets of the Islamic world.

For a while, these changes were still hidden from the sight of Christians and Muslims alike by the still imposing panoply of Ottoman military power. After the withdrawal from Vienna and the military and political defeats that followed it, the new relationship became clear to both sides. Europe still had a Turkish problem, because Turkey remained an important factor in the European balance of power, but it was now the problem of Turkish weakness, not of Turkish strength. And Islam, which had long ceased to be regarded by the Christian churches as a serious religious adversary, now ceased to be even a serious military threat.

The change was clear both in the terms of the treaty which ended the war and in the procedures by which it was negotiated. For the Ottomans, this was diplomacy of an entirely new kind. During the early stages of the Ottoman advance into Europe, there were no treaties in the proper sense and very little negotiation. The state of war between the advancing power of Islam and its infidel enemies, conceived as a perpetual religious duty, was from time to time interrupted by truces, dictated in Istanbul by the victorious Turks to their defeated foes. It was not until the Treaty of Sitvatorok, signed in November 1606, that for the first time the Ottoman sultan conceded the title of emperor to the Hapsburg monarch, hitherto dismissively designated in Turkish protocol as "the king of Vienna," and dealt with him more or less as an equal.

The seventeenth century began with a grudging concession of equality; it ended with an unequivocal admission of defeat. For the first time, the Ottomans were compelled to sign a peace after a war which they had unmistakably lost in the field, and on terms which were dictated by their enemies.

The eighteenth century, despite some occasional successes, was a bad time for the Muslim powers, which, far from being able to fulfill their religious duty of expanding the frontiers of Islam, were hard pressed to retain what they already held. The awareness among Muslims of their changed position is indicated in the saying, current at the time, that "this world is the paradise of the unbelievers and the hell of the believers." The Austrians continued their pressure in the Balkans. They were joined by the Russians, whose southward advance against the retreating Tatars brought them eventually to the frontiers—and across the frontiers—of the Ottoman and Persian empires.

For a while both Turks and Persians seemed to be holding their own against their northern enemies, but a new war, launched by Russia against the Ottoman Empire in 1769, ended in total disaster. The Treaty of Küçük Kaynarca of 1774 was rightly described by the empress Catherine II of Russia as a success "the like of which Russia has never had before." Russia's gains at Turkish expense were enormous and brought a decisive change in the power relationships, not only between the two empires, but between the two civilizations.

The war and the treaty which ended it gave Russia three kinds of advantages, all of which served as models for other European powers to follow, and as a starting point for further Russian advances. The first gain was territorial. Though the actual territory ceded to Russia was of small extent, its importance was considerable. Apart from a small foothold which the Russians had seized at the beginning of the eighteenth century, the Black Sea had hitherto been entirely under Turkish Muslim control. The treaty gave Russia two ports on the eastern tip of the Crimean Peninsula and a fortress at the mouth of the Dniester River, effectively breaking the Turkish monopoly. The Crimean peninsula itself, hitherto the seat of a Tatar khan under the suzerainty of the Ottoman sultan, was now declared independent, and the Tatar khan and his territories along the northern shore of the Black Sea were removed from Ottoman control or even influence. This prepared the way for Russian annexation a few years later in 1783. The new Russian seaport of Odessa was founded in 1795 on the ruins of a Tatar village.

Beyond the obvious strategic importance of a Russian naval presence in the Black Sea, these territorial changes had another significance. As a result of their earlier defeats in the Austrian wars, the Turks had been compelled to cede extensive territories to Christian powers. Most of these, however, had been recently conquered lands inhabited by Christian populations. The Crimea was different; these people were Turkish-speaking Muslims whose presence in the Crimea dated back to before the Mongol conquests of the thirteenth century. This was the first cession of old Muslim territory inhabited by Muslim peoples, and it was a bitter blow to Muslim pride.

A second advantage was in trade. By the terms of the treaty, Russia gained freedom of navigation and commerce in the Black Sea and through the straits into the Mediterranean, as well as overland in the European and Asian provinces of the Ottoman Empire. This too marked an important step toward the commercial penetration of the Ottoman Empire, in which all the European powers participated during the nineteenth century.

Associated with this was a third advantage—the acquisition by the Russians, and later by others, of positions of power and influence within the Ottoman realms themselves. These were of several kinds. The most immediately important was the conferment on Russia of a special position in the Danubian principalities. Though these remained under loose Ottoman suzerainty, they now received a considerable measure of internal autonomy and with it of Russian influence. At the same time Russia was given the right to open consulates wherever it pleased in the Ottoman lands—a privilege long sought after by the Western powers—and also to build a Russian church in Istanbul and "make in every circumstance various representations to the Porte in favour of the below mentioned church."[3] Though originally limited to a single Russian church in the capital, this right of remonstrance was, by careful and continuous misinterpretation, expanded into a right of intervention and protection for all the Orthodox Christians of the Ottoman Empire, including many in the Arab lands as well as most of the Ottoman subjects in the Balkan Peninsula. The right of intercession on behalf of the Catholics, long claimed by the king of France, was similarly converted into a right of interference and a virtual protectorate over a smaller but still significant minority among the sultan's subjects.

In this treaty, we can see very clearly the main patterns of European expansion and penetration in the Middle East in the course of the nineteenth and early twentieth centuries. This was the classical age of European domination—a time when the European powers annexed or occupied much of the Middle East and penetrated and influenced the rest.

The most visible form of European expansion was military conquest and annexation, in which, in several successive phases, the Russians took the lead. The annexation of the Crimea in 1783 was followed by a rapid expansion, eastward and westward, along the northern shores of the Black Sea, leading to a series of wars against Turkey, Persia, and local rulers, and to the extension of Russian power, by annexation or by some form of protection, in both the Balkan Peninsula and the Caucasian land bridge between the Black Sea and the Caspian. By 1828 Russia was in possession of the territory now forming the three former Soviet republics of Georgia,

Armenia, and Azerbaijan. The French expedition to Egypt, led by General Bonaparte in 1798, had considerable impact in that country but ended in defeat and produced no territorial change. Anglo-French encroachment on the heartlands began at the extremities, with the British naval presence in the Persian Gulf and the Red Sea, the French annexation of Algeria in 1830, the British seizure of Aden in 1839.

A new wave of advance began in the mid-nineteenth century, with the Russian pacification and eventual annexation of the central Asian khanates. This in turn was followed, in short order, by the French occupation of Tunisia in 1881 and the British occupation of Egypt in the following year.

Another wave began in 1911, with Russian pressures on Persia and a Russian military invasion of the northern provinces of that country. Despite Persian resistance, from this time until the outbreak of the First World War the country was effectively under Russian and British domination. Soon after, the steady extension of French influence in Morocco culminated in the establishment of a French protectorate in that country in 1912. Meanwhile, the Italians, latecomers to the imperial game, declared war on the Ottoman Empire in September 1911 and announced the annexation of the Ottoman provinces of Tripolitania and Cyrenaica, which both became Italian colonies. They were united by Italian royal decree on 3 December 1934 to form a single colony renamed Libya. It has retained that name ever since.

The European pincers around the Islamic Middle East, formed by the expansion of Europe at both ends since the sixteenth century, were coming together. They were finally closed during the First World War, with the defeat and dismemberment of the Ottoman Empire and the partition of its territories between the Allied and associated powers; they were broken and discarded in the aftermath of the Second World War, when all but one of the European empires that had ruled Islamic lands came to an end and were replaced by sovereign independent states. After so long a period of European paramountcy, domination, or rule, their societies, their polities, even their self-perception, were transformed almost beyond recognition.

Less immediately visible, but certainly no less important than the military and political consequences of the rise of Europe, were the economic effects on the relationship between the two worlds.

The European voyages of discovery and, to a much greater extent, the commercial and colonial empires which the Europeans established, brought a dramatic change in the conditions and content of trade between Europe and the Islamic world. In medieval times, Europe had very little to offer in exchange for the rich and varied products of the Islamic lands. Its industry was primitive; its agriculture, barely sufficient for its own subsistence. One of its major exports seems to have been its own people—or, to be more precise, eastern Europeans, sold as slaves (whence the term, from "Slav") and delivered to the Muslim markets across the Mediterranean or through Spain. This traffic continued, despite papal and sometimes even royal bans, until the advancing Turks and Tatars did to the European slave trade what Vasco da Gama had done to the Eastern spice trade: they went to the sources and collected their own.

Another early export from Europe was weapons. This continued throughout the period of the Crusades and into modern times. European powers never seem to have had the slightest compunction in selling weapons of war to enemies who were determined to destroy them. Perhaps they were right—these enemies did not destroy them but instead were themselves destroyed. Apart from European slaves, weapons, and steel, which are often mentioned in Muslim sources and were much appreciated, there were also some minor items, such as coral from the Mediterranean, amber from the northern seas, and fine woolen cloth from Florence, Flanders, and later, England. English scarlet is mentioned by the fourteenth-century Persian historian Rashīd al-Dīn; "London cloth" appears in Turkish customs regulations of the fifteenth century.

With the expansion of Europe into the Western Hemisphere, and the growth of European power in South and Southeast Asia, the situation changed dramatically. As Halil Inalcık has shown, it was the establishment of a strong European presence on both the eastern and western sides of the Islamic world rather than, as was once believed, the circumnavigation of Africa and establishment of direct links which brought the real change.[4] The immediate economic effects of the Portuguese voyages were limited, but with the consolidation of the Dutch and British commercial empires, Europeans had won not only access but control. Moreover, with their eastern and western possessions, they had a much wider range of commodities to sell.

Indeed, they had a great deal to sell, and before long were exporting considerable quantities of colonial merchandise, including some commodities that were first introduced to Europe from or via the Middle East, and which for long were staples of Middle Eastern exports to the West. Coffee, first cultivated and used at the southern end of the Red Sea, in Ethiopia and Yemen, was brought to the Mediterranean lands in the sixteenth century, and by the late seventeenth century was of some significance among Middle Eastern exports to Europe. By the eighteenth century, however, the English, the Dutch, and the French were growing coffee in their tropical colonies in Central America and Southeast Asia, and before long, colonial coffee, cheaper though not better than the local product, came to dominate Middle Eastern markets. Nor was coffee the only commodity which was switched from the export to the import column. Sugar and paper, the one originally from India, the other from China, had long since been accepted and then produced in the Middle East and had been exported to Europe since the Middle Ages. By the late seventeenth century, colonial sugar was being extensively refined in Europe and exported to the Turkish domains. The Ottomans, while refusing to desecrate their holy script with a printing press, nevertheless copied their holy books and wrote their imperial decrees on watermarked paper manufactured in Europe. Perhaps most striking of all was the change in the trade in manufactured textiles, for long one of the most characteristic products and exports of the Islamic Middle East. With the growth of European power in South and Southeast Asia, coupled with the industrialization of western Europe, the Middle Eastern market was now open to textile imports from both sides—cheap cottons brought by European merchants from India, as well as the older trade in manufactured woolens directly from Europe.

In comparison with Europe, both eastern and western, the Middle East had by the nineteenth century become far weaker than it had been in the great days of the sixteenth century. There is some evidence, though this is less certain, that the decline in the economic power of the Middle East was absolute as well as relative.

Several factors, in addition to the new European mercantilism, combined to bring about this change. In their dealings with Europe, the Muslim powers were affected by the increasing complexity and resulting higher cost of armament and war. Their trade and their internal economies were adversely affected by the great inflation of the sixteenth and seventeenth centuries, fueled by the influx of American precious metals and the ensuing rise in prices. Their external trade, as we have seen, deteriorated after the development of European-operated trade routes across the Atlantic, around southern Africa, and into South Asian waters. These processes were accelerated by the technological lag in agriculture, industry, and transport within the countries of the Islamic world. Internal weakness thus contributed significantly to the growing economic advantages gained by European arms, commerce, and industry.

It is not uncommon in history for an economy to be stimulated by the commercial impact of another, more active and technologically more advanced society. What is special in the European impact on the lands of Islam, especially in the Middle East, is that on both sides the agents and beneficiaries of the resulting economic change were aliens. The outsiders were of course Europeans, but even in the Middle East the principal actors were either foreigners or members of religious minorities, seen and treated by the dominant majority society as marginal to itself. The new, evolving middle class thus consisted largely of foreigners and of native Christians and, to a lesser extent, Jews, enjoying the favor and protection of the European powers. As a result of this process, these elements became ever less identified with their Muslim compatriots and rulers, ever more with Europe. It was not until a comparatively late stage that a Muslim bourgeoisie, not inhibited by social separation from the ruling polity and majority society, was able to have some political and social impact.

The predominance of foreigners and members of minorities in financial matters may be illustrated by examples. In 1912, forty private bankers were listed in Istanbul. Not one of them was a Turkish Muslim. Those who can be identified by their names included twelve Greeks, twelve

Armenians, eight Jews, and five Levantines or Europeans. A list of thirty-four stockbrokers in Istanbul included eighteen Greeks, six Jews, five Armenians, and not a single Turk.

Conquest and commerce were not the only factors in the changed power relationship in Europe and Islam. At least equally important was the immense transformation that was taking place within Europe—the upsurge in science and technology, in cultural and intellectual life, in European societies and polities, all of them stimulated by capitalist expansion and by bourgeois demands and contributions. These changes, which, albeit in different degrees, affected all of Europe, had little effect and no parallel in the Islamic world, where, with the partial exception of the armed forces, science and technology, production and distribution, for long remained substantially as they had been in the past.

This new and widening disparity brought significant changes in European attitudes toward Islam and toward the Ottoman and other Islamic powers. In earlier times, it will be recalled, the menace of Islam was seen as something which threatened the souls as well as the bodies of Christian Europe—the threat of Islamic proselytization seemed as great or even greater than the threat of Muslim conquest. After the end of the Middle Ages this was no longer seen as a threat. The number of Europeans embracing Islam was minimal, apart from a handful of adventurers and refugees who sought their fortunes in the Ottoman lands and, as part of their preparation for their careers, embraced Islam and became what Christians called renegades and Muslims called *muhtadi,* those who have found the right path. Islam, for European intellectuals, now became an object of scholarly study, something to be looked at with scientific curiosity, rather than a dangerous adversary to be confronted and refuted. Insofar as European writers of the sixteenth and seventeenth centuries expressed a religious interest, it was in the Eastern Christians more than in the Muslims. In the great struggle between Protestantism and Catholicism in Europe, some in both camps thought that the uncommitted Eastern Christians—uncommitted, that is to say, in relation to the struggles of the Reformation—could bring a useful accession of power.

At about this time there was another change in the European perception of Islam, shown in the increasing use of the adjective "barbaric." This was not a medieval notion; it was very much a Renaissance notion and is common in the European literature of the time, where the struggle against the Turk is no longer presented as one between true believers and infidels but, rather, as a continuation of the ancient struggle between Hellas and Persia—between the inheritors of Greek civilization and the remote Asian successors of the great kings of Persia, whom the ancient Greeks had held back but to whom the modern Greeks had succumbed. These echoes of classical history and literature are frequent in writings of the Renaissance period about the Turks and the Persians, who for this purpose are not very clearly distinguished. The notion of the barbarian comes directly from the Greek classics; with it came related ideas of barbaric splendor and oriental despotism, contrasted with classical austerity and European freedom.

As well as changes in European perceptions of Islam, there were also changes in Islamic perceptions of Europe—though these changes came much later and were at first of limited scope and confined in the main to civil and military officials. In the Muslim perception of Christianity as a religion, there was no significant change. Christianity was still, in Muslim eyes, a superseded revelation. But there was some change in the attitude toward Europe and especially toward the peoples of the West. As the Turks had replaced the Arabs as the rulers of Islam, so the "Franks" had replaced the Byzantines as their principal Christian adversary. There was a continued willingness, as there had always been in medieval times, to acquire, buy, imitate, or adopt the military technology of Christendom—from the Byzantines, Greek fire; from Frankish Europe, artillery. Right through the centuries of Ottoman advance, as well as retreat, Turkish Muslims were ready to adopt, or at least consider, elements of European technology—but not European civilization. Civilization, as Muslims saw it, was defined and determined by religion and by the revelation on which it was based, and that they had no desire to change.

What was adopted therefore was limited to what was recognizably and immediately useful—weaponry, naval construction, the practice of medicine, along with some devices, the most important of which were clocks and watches, eyeglasses and telescopes. But as far as possible, these were stripped of their cultural associations and thus reduced to dead artifacts, without organic roots. There was no desire to learn European languages, no interest in European arts or letters—not even in recent history—which might have had some practical value as political intelligence. A six-volume Ottoman history, covering the period from 1590 to 1660, discusses the Ottoman–Hapsburg wars in great detail, but devotes no more than a couple of pages to the Thirty Years' War, consisting mostly of random and somewhat inaccurate details. One might have thought that Ottoman readers would take some interest in these internecine struggles among their main enemies, not far from their frontiers. Apparently, they did not.

From surviving documents, it would seem that at least some Ottoman statesmen and officials were better informed. From a remarkably early date, some among the Ottomans saw the danger that threatened them and tried to draw attention to it. Lûtfi Pasha, grand vizier to Sultan Süleyman the Magnificent, had, according to his own testimony, warned his imperial master: "Under the previous sultans there were many who ruled the land, but few who ruled the sea. In the conduct of naval warfare the infidels are ahead of us. We must overcome them."[5] In about 1580, an Ottoman geographer, in introducing the first Muslim account of the New World, warned his patron, Sultan Murad III, of the dangers resulting from the establishment of Europeans on the coasts of America, India, and the Persian Gulf, and of the consequent disturbance to Islamic trade and danger to the Islamic lands. Reviving a project already discussed in the 1530s, he advised the sultan to open a canal through the Isthmus of Suez and send a fleet "to capture the ports of India and drive away the infidels."[6]

In 1625 another Ottoman writer, in a comment on the same book, saw the danger in a more acute form.[7] European ships were sailing all over the world and carrying goods everywhere, crowding out Muslim commerce, and earning vast sums of money. Because of this, gold and silver were becoming scarce in the lands of Islam. The only remedy was to control the shores of Yemen and the trade passing that way.

These counsels were not entirely neglected. After their conquest of Egypt in 1517, and of Iraq a few years later, the Ottomans mounted naval expeditions in the Red Sea, the Persian Gulf, and the Indian Ocean to meet the threat of the Portuguese and even sent an expedition as far away as Sumatra to help the local Muslims fight their new Christian enemies. But all these expeditions came to nothing. Ottoman ships, built for the waters of the Mediterranean, were no match for the Portuguese and the Dutch, whose shipbuilders and seamen faced the challenge of the Atlantic. Stouter vessels, heavier armament, and better seamanship crushed the Ottoman attempt to break the pincers and established European Christian naval supremacy in the Indian Ocean. Without naval power, the plan to dig a canal through the Isthmus of Suez was evidently pointless and was abandoned.

In 1569 the Ottomans, now more concerned with the immediate Persian danger than with the remote Russian threat, considered a plan to open a canal between the Don and Volga rivers and thus extend their naval reach from the Black Sea to the Caspian. But this project too was blocked and abandoned, and in time even the control of the Black Sea was lost to the advancing power of Russia.

For the Muslim world, Christendom, at first in the Mediterranean and later in eastern Europe, had been a kind of frontier to which Muslims had looked, rather as Europe had looked to colonial America and as independent America looked to its own west. At first, it was the still unconquered wild west of Islam, offering the alternatives, equally seductive to different minds, of booty, land, or martyrdom. Then, as the west was conquered and settled, it became the land of hope and opportunity, where fortunes could be made and where, in the freer spirit of the frontier, the persecuted, the independent, and the unfortunate might hope to find a home and a refuge. For medieval Arabs, the newly conquered lands of North Africa and Spain for a while met this need—until in time, the Islamic West was sufficiently rich and advanced to throw off the authority of the East and establish independent states, one of which, that of the Fatimid caliphs, for a while became a dominant power even in the East. Some centuries later the Ottomans, in their turn, served as the frontiersmen of Islam, discovering, conquering, and colonizing new lands and bringing the faith and civilization of Islam to the effete and superseded Greeks and to the benighted barbarians of Europe. The closing of the frontier, when the Turks finally came to barriers which they could not cross or remove, posed grave problems to a society and polity that for centuries had been shaped and maintained by a process of continuous conquest and colonization.

The resulting crises caused much heart-searching and gave rise to many discussions on the broad questions of what was wrong and how it could be remedied. For a long time, Ottoman analysts made no attempt to devise or apply new methods but sought, rather, to revive and restore the good old ways that had, in bygone days, brought them success and greatness. While these memoranda make fascinating reading, few reforms of any great importance were attempted, let alone accomplished. For that something more than a halt and a stalemate were needed. The second defeat at Vienna, and the retreat that followed it, provided the necessary stimulus. Muslim Turks—statesmen, soldiers, and scholars—began to confront the bitter fact of their weakness and vulnerability and to compare their own society with that of Europe, in the hope that the latter might provide some of the answers they were seeking. In their references to Europe, there is a change in tone, which passes from amused disdain to alarmed dislike. Ambassadors and memorialists express a growing concern about the states and peoples of European Christendom, no longer seen as a group of picturesque barbarians who in due course would be conquered and incorporated into the divinely guarded realms and introduced to a higher and better way of life but, rather, for the first time, as a source of danger. There had long been an awareness of European wealth; there was now also a growing awareness of European power.

In Muslim eyes, the Christian religion and the culture which was based on it remained negligible, as they had always been. But there was increased respect for the material wealth and armed might of Europe—the one manifested in manufactures and in the changing conditions of trade, the other in the balance of military power—demonstrated in a succession of Muslim defeats.

Defeat on the battlefield is surely the most perspicuous of all forms of instruction, and has a cogency lacking in purely verbal communication. The discussion of the lesson began almost immediately after the Treaty of Carlowitz, and developed in time from specific defects to the larger questions about the state and fate of the empire. There is a rather refreshing quality of self-examination and self-criticism in the writings of these Ottoman memorialists. The Ottomans were after all a sovereign power, entirely responsible for their own affairs; they had long been masters in their own house and indeed in many other peoples' houses. The memorialists did not blame the outside world, occult powers, or secret conspiracies for their setbacks and troubles. Rather, did they ask, Where did we go wrong? and, of course, What can we do about it?

During the last three centuries, these questions came to dominate both debate and policy in the Ottoman Empire and ultimately in the whole Islamic world. The attempt to answer them, and to put that answer into effect, brought profound, indeed, shattering, changes into every aspect of Muslim life.

Retreat and Return

By 1920 it seemed that the triumph of Europe over Islam was total and final. The vast territories and countless millions of the Muslim peoples of Asia and Africa were firmly under the control of the European empires—some of them under a variety of native princes, most under direct colonial administration. Only a few remote mountain and desert areas, too poor and too difficult to be worth the trouble of acquiring, retained some measure of sovereign independence. In the former Russian empire, now called the Soviet Union, revolution and civil war had caused a temporary relaxation of control from the center and had permitted the emergence of independent regimes in some of the former czarist possessions. The Bolshevik victory brought a reassertion of central control. In Europe, the Soviets were constrained to relinquish, for a while, the Baltic, Polish, and Balkan territories which the czars had acquired; in the Muslim territories, the reconquest and reintegration were complete. In April 1920 the short-lived independent republic of Azerbaijan was overthrown by the advancing Red Army, and a Soviet republic, precisely modeled on the Russian Soviet Republic, was installed in its place. This was followed by other similar republics among the Tatars, the Bashkirs, and the Muslim peoples of Central Asia, in which local Communist commissars could play, at best, the role of native princes. The Muslims of the Soviet Union, like those of the British, French, and Dutch empires, were once again part of a political system with its center in a European capital; unlike them, they were also subjugated to vigorous state-sponsored anti-Islamic propaganda, conducted both directly and through such bodies as the League of the Militant Godless and the Institute of Scientific Atheism. This propaganda was certainly not Christian and differed greatly from the much more cautious and tentative work of the Christian missions in the Western empires. It was, however, inspired by a radical secularism of which the intellectual origins, though not the subsequent development, were entirely European.

In the central heartlands of Islam, only two Muslim states, Turkey and Iran, had retained their independence. But Iran, during the First World War, had become a battlefield in which Russian, British, and Ottoman forces operated freely, and the country degenerated into a state of chaos, from which the cessation of hostilities brought no immediate relief. The Ottoman Empire, for centuries first the spearhead and then the shield of Islam, lay prostrate in defeat—its capital occupied, its provinces partitioned between the victorious Western powers and their Greek allies. The dismemberment of the Ottoman Empire was confirmed and itemized in the Treaty of Sèvres, signed by the sultan's representatives on 10 August 1920.

The town of Sèvres is famous for its delicate porcelain wares. The treaty fashioned there by diplomatic craftsmen proved both leaky and fragile, and it was soon shattered beyond repair. The hammer that broke it was wielded by a Turkish general called Mustafa Kemal, later surnamed Atatürk—the last victorious Ottoman soldier and the first president of a secular republic in a nation-state called Turkey. According to a well-known piece of American folk wisdom, "if you can't beat them, join them." Kemal Atatürk did both, and his consecutive actions in rejecting European domination and embracing European civilization mark a turning point, comparable in different ways, with both the victory at Constantinople and the defeat at Vienna.

This was not the first defeat administered by an Asian to a European country. In 1905 the victory of Japan over Imperial Russia and the halting of Russian expansion in the Far East had sent a thrill of joy and hope to all Asia, including the Ottoman Empire. But Russia, though European, was not Western, and Japan, though Asiatic, was remote and little known, particularly in the Islamic lands, where Asianism as a concept had not yet taken root. When Atatürk drove out the Greeks and faced down the mighty British Empire, he gained the first major Muslim victory against a Christian power for centuries, and a wave of exhilaration passed through the entire Islamic world, from French and British West Africa to the Dutch East Indies.

In its early stages, the Kemalist movement in Anatolia expressed itself in almost exclusively religious terms. Its aims, according to its declarations, were to free "Islamic lands" and "Islamic peoples" and to repel and eject the infidel invader. Muslim dignitaries were prominent among the early supporters of the Kemalists, and no fewer than 73 of the 361 members of the First Grand National Assembly, convened in Ankara in 1920, were professional men of religion. In February 1921, a pan-Islamic congress was held at Sivas, to mobilize support. Many delegates from the Arab countries attended, and one of them, the sheikh of the Sanusi religious order in Libya, presided. Those who fell in battle were described as *shahīd,* and the victorious leader himself was hailed as Gazi. Both terms belong to the vocabulary of *jihād*, the holy war for Islam. The one denotes a martyr fallen in the cause; the other, a victorious fighter. An Algerian author, Malek Bennabi, in his memoirs, describes vividly how the reports of the new Muslim hero in Turkey and of his victories against the colonial powers electrified young Muslims in Algeria. All over Asia and Africa, Mustafa Kemal was the shining example whose triumphs others strove, with greater or lesser success, to emulate in their struggle against the alien and infidel imperialist.

In recent years, another myth of Atatürk has begun to appear and in some Muslim quarters has supplanted the earlier shining hero. In the demonology of Muslim radicals and militants of the present time, Atatürk occupies a prominent place—not as the valiant defender of his people, who confronted the Europeans and beat them, but, rather, as the miscreant who, in his moment of victory, joined them and was thus guilty of the ultimate surrender and betrayal. In the thought world of the fundamentalists, Islam is and has for some time been under double attack, from outside and from within. The external enemies are numerous and powerful and include such figures as the imperalist, sometimes also known as the crusader, his ally the missionary, his puppet the Zionist, his rival the Communist. In certain circles, especially those, including some fundamentalists, influenced by European ideologies, these roles may be interchanged. But it is the internal enemy that is both more evil and more threatening; more evil because his enmity is not open but is furtive and treacherous, more threatening because he strikes from within and by his machinations deprives the Muslim community of the religious integrity and divine guidance with which it could otherwise shrug off the ultimately insignificant attacks of these external foes.

These internal enemies are politically heterogeneous; they have included such diverse figures as King Fārūq and President Nasser in Egypt, the shah and his liberal and socialist opponents in Iran, Presidents Hafiz al-Asad of Syria and Saddam Hussein of Iraq. What they all have in common is that they are modernizers; that is to say, in the eyes of resurgent Islam, they are neopagans, whose aim is to weaken and remove Islamic norms, laws, and values and replace them with pagan norms and laws and values imported from the West—to desacralize, to de-Islamize, in a word, to Westernize, the divinely established and divinely guided Muslim polity. And their common predecessor in these evil ways, the pioneer who first presumed to abolish the caliphate, set aside the holy law, and deprive its accredited upholders of the authority which they had for centuries wielded in law and justice, culture and education, was Mustafa Kemal Atatürk.

Kemal Atatürk was certainly the first Muslim ruler to disestablish Islam, repeal the *sharīʿa*, and adopt European practices over the whole range of public and social life, including even such previously sacrosanct matters as marriage, headgear, and the alphabet. By his decrees, Muslim Turks were obliged to write their language in the Latin script, marry only one wife at a time, and abandon their fezzes and turbans in favor of caps and hats. These changes were not mere whims of a capricious autocrat. They were the outward and visible expression—and acceptance—of a profound social and indeed civilizational transformation. Many of his Westernizing reforms have been followed by other Muslim states, including some headed by Islamic militants of both the radical and traditional varieties. But none has pursued them with comparable zeal, consistency, or success. Of late there has been a strong reaction against them in the Islamic world, which has even touched the Turkish republic.

The Kemalist revolution, and the philosophy which inspired it, had a long prehistory, which can, in a sense, be traced back to the first Turkish incursions into Europe. The Turks early realized the vital importance of following the Europeans in weaponry and other military arts and were inevitably brought into contact with the men who made and sold and, to some extent, even operated these weapons. They were, almost from the start, economically involved with many European states, through a great and growing import and export trade in both raw materials and manufactures. But in these and in most other dealings with the infidel West, the Ottomans and other Muslims were preserved from contact and, as they saw it, contamination by a large class of intermediaries consisting in part of the non-Muslim subjects of the Muslim states, augmented by considerable numbers of manumitted slaves and, in part, of refugees and renegades, seeking haven or fortune in the lands of Islam. These intermediaries served as a cushion, or perhaps more precisely as an insulation, protecting the host Muslim society from the culture shock of European impact. Jewish refugees from Europe were allowed to establish printing presses as early as the late fifteenth century, and their example was followed by the Greek, Armenian, and Arabic-speaking Christians. But they were allowed to print only in their own and in European scripts, not in the Arabic script or in the Arabic or Turkish language. It was not until 1727 that an imperial decree was issued authorizing the establishment of the first Turkish printing press in Istanbul. It was initiated by a Hungarian convert to Islam and a Turkish official returning from a diplomatic visit to Paris. Some ascribe this long-standing ban on Arabic typography to the sanctity of the script in which God's book was revealed; others to the vested interest of the guilds of scribes and calligraphers. Either way, the result was the same.

Apart from the enforced travel and restricted access of captives taken by land and sea, diplomatic missions provided virtually the only opportunity for educated Muslims to visit and stay for a while in Christian Europe and to meet and converse, on more or less equal terms, with educated European Christians. Such missions were, however, few and far between, and usually limited alike in purpose, duration, and effect. Some European monarchs, like Francis I of France and Elizabeth I of England, may have flattered themselves that they had won the respect and even the goodwill of the Ottoman sultan and had entered into some form of alliance. There is no evidence of any such perception on the Ottoman side. Since the days when the rival leaders of the Crusade to liberate the Holy Land had set up four contending principalities in the Levant, which promptly began to court Muslim allies against one another, Muslim princes had realized that Christendom, even more than Islam, was divided into petty, warring sovereignties, whose internecine conflicts might be used to some advantage. The Christian merchants who accompanied and followed the Crusaders competed in Muslim markets, buying and selling a variety of commodities, and offered even weapons and other war materials at good prices and with favorable financing. There were also Muslim contacts with the far more numerous European diplomatic missions in Islamic lands, including resident consulates and embassies, and with the active and growing international communities in seaport towns like Alexandria, Beirut, and of course Galata. But on the whole, Muslim rulers seemed to have attached little importance to these contacts, and Muslim intellectuals even less. Ottoman officials were surely aware of the squabbling tribes and "nations" beyond the northwest frontier but were generally content to leave their management to specialized officials, whose duty it was to maintain order in the marches and to keep an eye on the unsubjugated, or not yet subjugated, peoples that lay beyond them.

In diplomatic relations as in so much else, the retreat from Vienna marked the beginning of a new era. For the first time in their long history, the Ottomans were faced with the need to negotiate a peace treaty, and to do so from a position of weakness, as the defeated party in a long and exhausting war. The efficacy of Western weaponry had been demonstrated in battle; the usefulness of Western diplomacy emerged in the course of the negotiations. Britain, France, and the Netherlands, for reasons of their own, were anxious to save the Turks from the full consequences of their defeat or rather, to be more precise, to deprive the Austrians and their allies of the full fruits of their victory. Thanks to the skillful intervention and wise counsel of the British and Dutch envoys in Istanbul, the Turks were able to get rather better terms than they might have been able to achieve through their own unaided efforts.

In the course of the eighteenth century, Ottoman diplomatic missions to Europe had become more frequent, and there is a new tone in the envoys' reports, expressing interest, sometimes even admiration, and occasionally going so far as to recommend certain European practices as worthy of imitation by the Sublime Porte. By the end of the century, the Ottoman sultan Selim III had established permanent embassies in several European capitals, thus following the European practice of continuous diplomatic communication through resident missions. This was a radical departure from the previously universal Islamic practice of sending an ambassador only when there was something to say and recalling him when it had been said. These embassies prepared the way for the integration of a major Islamic state in the European political system; they also provided opportunities for successive generations of young Turkish officials to spend a few years in a European city, learn a European language, and acquire some firsthand knowledge of European civilization.

In the year 1693, at a time when the Turks were still retreating before the advancing Austrians, William Penn published a little book in which he suggested the establishment of an organization of European states to arbitrate disputes and prevent wars.[8] Remarkably, for a man of his time, he suggested that Turkey be invited to join this European association, upon the condition that the Turks renounce Islam and embrace Christianity. Compliance with such a condition was of course then and remains now impossible to the point of absurdity. No such condition was imposed when, by article 7 of the Treaty of Paris of 1856, the European powers formally admitted the sultan to that jangling concatenation of discords known as the Concert of Europe. Nor have religious questions been formally raised in the context of Turkey's application for membership in the

European Economic Community, though there are signs that such considerations are not entirely absent from the debate. In modern secular Europe, inside or outside the community, the idea of imposing a religious condition would seem both offensive and anachronistic. But most Europeans would still lay down an entry requirement, stated in terms not of religion but of civilization—of culture, of social mores, and above all of political norms. Whether Turkey and other Islamic states are willing or able to meet these requirements and whether the states of Europe, after all that has happened, are still entitled and able to impose them are two crucial and interrelated questions.

To play in the Concert of Europe, the Turks, and after them other Muslim peoples, had to acquire and master new instruments and learn new tunes—European tunes, very different from the music of their own culture. Specifically, they had to learn European languages and the unhallowed script in which they were written. In earlier times, this had not been thought necessary or even desirable. For the necessary minimum of communication, Muslims relied on their own non-Muslim subjects or on Europeans who came to them, whether as refugees or adventurers, as merchants or envoys. In early medieval times, a significant proportion of the philosophic and scientific works of pagan Greece, though nothing of Greek literature or history, had been translated into Arabic and had become an important part of the Muslim cultural heritage. There was no comparable movement to translate the products of Christian Europe, tainted as they were with a rival and, in Muslim eyes, a superseded religion. With a very few, unnoticed exceptions, no European books were translated into Arabic or Turkish or Persian; apart from some sailors and traders and other men of low estate, who used a kind of pidgin Italian known as the lingua franca, there were few Muslims who could speak or understand a European language and even fewer who could read a European book.

This too changed in the course of the eighteenth century, the first age of Islamic reappraisal. The first Muslim of rank who is known to have mastered a European language was one Said Efendi, who accompanied his father to Paris in 1720 on a diplomatic mission. He returned speaking, according to a contemporary French witness, "excellent French, like a native" and was, not coincidentally, the co-founder of the first Turkish printing press.[9] One of the first books printed in this press was a treatise describing the states and forms of government existing in Europe; the physical and military geography of the continent; and the armed forces maintained by the European states, with some discussion of their training, their command structure, and their methods of combat.

It was military necessity, even more than the need for political intelligence, that drove Muslims to undertake the distasteful task of learning infidel languages and, even worse, venturing into infidel lands. To hold the advancing European at bay, it was necessary to master European military methods, and for this European teachers were required. In the course of the eighteenth century, several European instructors were employed in training the Ottoman forces—mostly renegades and adventurers who had either learned Turkish or taught through interpreters. At the end of the century, Sultan Selim III asked the government of the recently established French Republic to send a military mission, the first of a long series to which many European states, small as well as great, contributed. In the early nineteenth century, no fewer than three rulers, the pasha of Egypt, followed by the sultan of Turkey, and the shah of Persia, sent groups of young men to Europe as students to study the military and, incidentally, the other arts of the infidel continent. Progress in learning European languages was slow: as late as 1844 an English resident in Istanbul, Charles White, could name only a bare dozen educated Turks who had mastered a European language and had read European books. But thereafter progress was more rapid. The Greek war of independence, and the consequent hanging of the last of the long line of Greek dragomans of the Sublime Porte, persuaded the Turks that they could no longer entrust what had become the vital business of dealing with European states to their Greek subjects, and that they must themselves acquire the necessary skills and knowledge. A language office was set up at the Sublime Porte and later in the various other Ottoman ministries. The acquisition and use of infidel languages was no longer demeaning. On the contrary, it was increasingly seen as acceptable, then useful, finally necessary.

While the study of languages gave a limited number of educated Muslims access to European knowledge and ideas, the development of the translation movement, accompanied and followed by the spread of printing, brought this knowledge and these ideas to a vastly greater audience. Until the end of the eighteenth century, very few European books were translated into Muslim languages, and most of these dealt with such obviously useful topics as geography and medical science, among the latter especially works dealing with the diagnosis and treatment of syphilis, a disease which was introduced by Europeans to the Middle East very soon after its introduction to Europe, and which is still known at the present day—in Arabic, Persian, and Turkish alike—as *firangi,* the Frankish, or European, disease. It has sometimes been used by Muslim authors as a metaphor for the introduction and spread of European ideas and practices.

The first translations issued from the printing presses of Istanbul and Cairo at the beginning of the nineteenth century were still devoted, in the main, to the "practical" sciences, but they included several works on history, among them three on Napoleon, one on Catherine the Great, and, a little later, Voltaire's history of Charles XII of Sweden. Perhaps these too were seen as practical, at the time. The same may be said of a translation of Machiavelli's *Prince,* prepared in 1825 for Muhammad Ali Pasha. It was not printed but survives in manuscript. The translation of literary works—poetry, fiction, and later, drama—dates from the mid-nineteenth century. By the early twentieth century, great numbers of literary works had been translated into Arabic, Persian, and Turkish, and a new literature was developing in all three languages, profoundly affected by European models. By the late twentieth century, traditional literary forms were extinct in Turkish and reduced to insignificance in Arabic and, to a lesser extent, in Persian.

In the arts, Europeanization began earlier than in literature and went much further. For artists the European impact was direct and immediate, unimpeded by the barriers of language and learning. From an early date Turkish and Persian painters revealed the influence of European pictures which they had seen, and by the eighteenth century, European decorative motifs appear even in mosque architecture. In the course of the nineteenth century, the traditional high arts—architecture, minature painting—were in effect supplanted, surviving only in the work of a few diehard and for the most part neglected traditionalists and, later, in the form of a rather mannered neoclassical revival. In contrast, European art music had a cooler, slower welcome. Though enjoying the same advantage of immediacy, and in addition, at certain times, of vigorous state patronage, the composition, performance, and even appreciation of Western music have made far less progress in the Islamic lands than in other, much remoter non-Western societies, such as China, Japan, and India.

The speed and scope of Europeanization, notably of the Muslim view of the world and of recent and current events, were enormously increased by the introduction from Europe of the mass media. The first newspapers published in the Middle East were a gift of the French Revolution—first a newspaper printed and published in the French embassy in Istanbul and then others published by the French occupying authority in Egypt. All these were in the French language and therefore had very limited effect. The first indigenous newspapers appeared in the early nineteenth century, in Cairo and in Istanbul, in Arabic and in Turkish, and were published under the authority of the pasha and of the sultan. An early editorial in the Ottoman official journal, published in 1821, explains their purpose. The journal, it said, was a natural development of the office of the imperial historiographer; its purpose was to make known the true nature of events and the real content of the laws and orders of the government, so as to prevent any misunderstanding and preclude any ill-founded criticism. Another purpose was to provide useful knowledge of commerce, the sciences, and the arts.

The first nonofficial newspaper was founded by an Englishman, William Churchill, in 1840 and devoted some attention to news from home and abroad. But the real development of newspapers began with the Crimean War, when, for the first time, Turkey was involved in a major war with two western European powers as allies. The presence of British and French armies on Turkish soil, the activities of British and French war correspondents at the battlefronts, and the bringing to Turkey of the telegraph encouraged the development of an appetite for daily news and provided the means of satisfying it. Thereafter, the spread of the newspaper press was rapid and reached not only the literate population but many others who had newspapers read to them by neighbors and by friends.

The advent of the newspaper in the lands of Islam created a new perception and a new awareness of events, notably in Europe, where the decisive events, at that time, were taking place. The need to discuss and explain these events led to the creation of new languages, from which modern Arabic, Persian, and Turkish have evolved. They also led to the emergence of a portentous new figure, the journalist, whose role in the development of the modern Islamic world has been profoundly important. The period of Anglo-French rule in the Middle East gave the newspapers an interlude of relative freedom, which contributed significantly to their maturing. In 1925, Turkey, followed by most other countries in the Muslim world, initiated radio broadcasting. Television was introduced in the 1960s, and this too has become universal in the Islamic world. Radio and television broadcasts, unlike newspapers, cannot be stopped and confiscated at frontiers. Though many journalists and their employers still adhere or have returned to the purposes laid down by the Ottoman editorialist of 1821, the listener or viewer at the present time at least has the option of choosing between various authoritarian and foreign messages. The possibility and exercise of such choices may also be counted as part of the Europeanization of the Islamic world.

Along with the journalist, another new and portentous figure, also derived from a European prototype, entered and helped to transform the Islamic world—the lawyer. In the traditional Islamic order, there is in principle no secular law but only the God-given Holy Law of Islam. In practice this was not always so, and secular laws were in fact recognized and administered. But there was no secular jurisprudence, and there were no secular jurists to challenge the monopoly of the doctors of the Holy Law. The change began when the Turkish, Egyptian, and eventually other Muslim governments promulgated sets of rules, which in time became codes of law. These dealt primarily with commercial matters and were necessitated by the growing extent and variety of European commercial activities in the Islamic lands. There were also new provisions in other matters, notably in criminal law. The new laws required new courts and new judges, different from the qadis and the muftis of the Holy Law. In time they produced a new profession, that of the advocate, previously unknown to either the theory or the practice of Islamic jurisprudence, and another non-Islamic innovation, the court of appeal, with all the complications and delays which that involves. In traditional Islam, there is no appellate jurisdiction, either in this world or in the next.

Schools and, a little later, colleges were a central part of the classical Islamic order, dating back almost to the beginning. The education they provided was dominated by religion and was in the main conducted and administered by professional men of religion. The new army, the new courts, the new administration of the age of reform required a new kind of personnel and new schools to train and educate them. These schools were manned by schoolmasters and professors, who came increasingly to resemble their European equivalents and who joined the journalists and the lawyers in a new secular, activist intelligentsia. By the modernization of justice and of education, two areas in which their control had previously not been challenged, the ulema lost a great deal of their power. Even in their last stronghold, the *sharīʿa* law of personal status, their influence was whittled down by modernizing regimes and, in the Turkish republic, formally abolished.

Lawyers and journalists were wholly new professions, with a vested interest in modernization. But even the older pillars of the state—the soldiers, the civil servants, the men of learning—played their part in the process of change. For all these, the ultimate purpose of their work was to preserve the Islamic state and society from destruction by their enemies; a significant proportion of these had come to the conclusion that the only way to resist the European enemy was to meet him on his own terms and fight him with his own weapons. In the course of the nineteenth and twentieth centuries, the state, the administration, the armed forces, the schools and colleges were reshaped and redirected and given the appearance, and sometimes more than that, of their European models. Some went even further. Seeing in constitutional and parliamentary government the secret talisman of Western wealth and power, they tried to obtain these advantages for their own societies, if necessary by opposing and overthrowing the autocrats who ruled over them.

Along with these reforms, the countries of the Islamic world also adopted a number of other changes, in the direction of a greater resemblance to Europe. Some of them were symbolic but nevertheless important, such as the adoption of European attire, first by the bureaucratic and military servants of the state, then by other urban males. The change in headgear, the last bastion of Muslim conservatism, was inaugurated, against considerable resistance, by Kemal Atatürk; it has since been accepted, at least partially, in most other Muslim countries, notably in the armed forces. In the armies of even the most radical Islamic states, officers wear slacks, belted tunics, and even peaked caps, European style. The Westernization of weaponry may be ascribed to simple military necessity; the Westernization of uniforms marks significant cultural change. But the change was limited. The Europeanization of female clothing came much later, was more strongly resisted, and affected a much smaller proportion of the population.

Some of the changes were primarily social, such as the abolition of chattel slavery, the emancipation of women and restriction of polygamy, and the granting, in principle, of equal legal rights to non-Muslims. There were other major changes, which transformed even the infrastructure of society, through the introduction of street lighting and other municipal services, of gas and electricity, of a network of modern communications on land, sea, and air, and, increasingly, the factory system of production. All these furthered and facilitated the incorporation of the Islamic world into the world economy that had been created by, and was for a long time dominated by, Europe. They also generated increasingly dangerous tensions with Islamic society, which became more visible and more audible when television brought the sight and sound of innovation and inequality to the remotest places and the deepest layers of the social pyramid.

For a long time, the ideologies for change, by reform or by revolution against native or foreign oppressors, came mostly from Europe and were imported by returning students, diplomats, and, as the changes began to work, exiles. In the nineteenth century the most important new ideas came from western Europe, especially patriotism and liberalism—patriotic loyalties defined by country and liberal aspiration to a freer and more open society. In the twentieth century, with the fragmentation of patriotic identities and the failure of liberal experiments, new ideologies were found, this time in central and eastern Europe: fascism in the 1930s and early 1940s, communism from the 1950s to the 1980s, and the rise in ethnic nationalism throughout the period.

But not all the movements of opposition were of European inspiration or expressed in European terms. Some Muslims opposed foreign domination and domestic change in the name not of their nation or country or class but of their faith, and saw the real danger as the loss of Islamic values and the real enemy, at home even more than abroad, as those who sought to replace Islamic laws and obligations by others derived from secular or, as they would put it, infidel sources. There have been several such movements of Islamic defense and renewal—the Wahhābī rising against the Ottomans at the turn to the eighteenth and nineteenth centuries; the resistance of the religious devotees of Ahmad Brelwi to the British in northern India (1826–1831); of Shāmil to the Russians in Daghestan (1830–1859); of ʿAbd al-Qādir to the French in Algeria (1832–1847); the pan-Islamic movement against the European powers in the late nineteenth and early twentieth centuries; the resistance of the Basmachis and other Islamic rebels against Soviet power in the 1920s; the brief upsurge of radical Islamic movements in the Arab lands and Iran in the late 1940s and early 1950s. All of these were crushed and their leaders killed or rendered innocuous. The first to achieve success and to gain and retain power was the Islamic revolution which began in Iran in 1979. The impact of that success was felt all over the Islamic world.

It is easy to understand the rage of the traditional Muslim confronted with the modern world. Schooled in a religious culture in which, from the beginning, rightness has meant supremacy, he has seen that supremacy lost in the world to Western power; lost in his own country to foreign intruders, with their foreign ways and their Westernized protégés; lost in his own home to emancipated women and rebellious children. Brought up in a complex but functioning system of social loyalties and responsibilities, he finds those loyalties, defined by faith and kin, denounced as sectarian and nepotistic, and those responsibilities derided and abandoned in favor of capitalist acquisitiveness or socialist expropriations. Impoverished by real economic and demographic problems aggravated by mismanagement and misgovernment, he is made painfully aware, by the now ubiquitous mass media, of the discrepancies between rich and poor, now richer and poorer, and more visibly so than ever before in history. And he does not fail to notice that the way of life of the rich and tyrannical—their homes, their clothing, their style, their food, their amusements—are modeled, at least in appearance, on those of the infidel West. The Westerner may think, and sometimes dare to say, that these resemblances are in fact no more than appearance and that the underlying reality, though it has ceased to be Islamic in any meaningful sense, has not become European. Traditional Muslims who up until now have had little opportunity to observe European realities could hardly be expected to accept such fine distinctions, and it is not surprising that so many of them have found in the idea of resurgent Islam a new identity and dignity and an ideology for the critique of old and the devising of new regimes.

The movement inspired by the charismatic leadership of Khomeini and led by the mullahs of Iran was by far the most effective of these Islamic movements—if not perhaps in the attainment of its ultimate objectives, then surely in the mobilization of support. But it was far from being the only such movement. In virtually every country in the Islamic world, as well as among Muslim minorities elsewhere, there were powerful and passionate movements of Islamic resurgence. Some of them were sponsored and directed by governments, as instruments of state policy; others—including some of the most important—arose from below and drew their strength from the mass of the common people. But all of them were driven by the same feelings of revulsion against the West, of frustration at the whole new apparatus of public and private life, inspired by or derived from or mimed after Western originals, and all of them were drawn by the same vision of a restored and resurgent Islam, through which God's law and those who uphold it would prevail over all their enemies.

The victories of Kemal and later of Kemalism were in a sense a paradox—the first decisive victory and the defiance of European power, the final decisive steps in the acceptance of European civilization. Muslim radicalism today presents a rather similar paradox—the denunciation and rejection of European and more generally Western civilization, coupled with a new and massive Muslim migration to Europe, and also to America.

The resulting Muslim presence represents a major change in attitude and action, entirely without precedent in the Islamic past. Muslim law and tradition devote much attention to the legal situation of the non-Muslim under Muslim rule, which is discussed at great length and regulated in great detail. Very little, however, is said about the corresponding problem of the Muslim under non-Muslim rule. This is not surprising. During the early centuries of Islamic history, when Muslim traditions were collected and committed to writing and the basic rules of Muslim jurisprudence laid down, the Muslim state and community were expanding almost continuously, and great numbers of non-Muslims were brought under Muslim rule. In contrast, virtually no Muslim territories were lost to non-Muslim invaders, and apart from occasional tactical withdrawals along the

Byzantine frontier, usually of limited extent and brief duration, the loss of Muslim territory was for several centuries unknown and therefore inconceivable. It was not until the eleventh century that the reconquest in Europe, the irruptions of the Christian peoples of the Caucasus into the Middle East, and the invasions of the Crusaders and, later, of the heathen Mongols created an entirely new situation. But by then the basic norms of the *sharī'a* had long since been established.

The initial assumption of the jurists in discussing this matter is clearly that for a Muslim to live under non-Muslim rule is undesirable and, according to some, forbidden, and only dire necessity could lead a Muslim to do such a thing. Until modern times, the entire discussion of the position of the Muslim under non-Muslim rule was considered in relation to two situations—the practical needs of the short-term or long-term visitor to an infidel land, and the sad predicament of a Muslim community conquered by infidel invaders. What never seems to have occurred to any of the classical jurists was that great numbers of Muslims, of their own free will, would go and live under the rule of non-Muslim governments, subject themselves and their families to non-Muslim personal law, and send their children to be educated in non-Muslim schools. But this is precisely what has happened. This is the situation in which many millions of Muslims from North Africa, the Middle East, South and Southeast Asia, and elsewhere now find themselves in every country in western Europe. These special problems, of Islam without authority, without the law of personal status, without separate education, especially for their girls, are the more acute in that the vast majority of these immigrants come from the more traditional social classes and from the more traditional regions of their countries of origin. It is clear that many of them still feel that it is their God-given duty to command what is good and forbid what is evil, in their new no less than in their old homes.

There are other changes in the relationship between Europe and Islam, some of them a reversion to earlier patterns, some of them entirely new. Once again, as in the days before the imperial expansion of Europe, the Middle East offers an attractive market in which European merchants and their governments compete to sell their wares. The imbalance in favor of Europe in military and industrial resources and capacity and in the production and, to a lesser extent, the use of technology remains and is, indeed, if anything wider. But the financial situation, and to some extent even the military situation, is reversed. Between 1939 and 1945, probably for the last time, European states fought out their wars on Middle Eastern soil, with little concern for the Middle Eastern peoples. Now it is Middle Eastern powers that, using different weapons and military techniques, sometimes fight out their wars on European soil, with similar unconcern. And in the financial markets, it is now Muslim governments and individuals that invest and lend vast sums and dispose of immense assets in Europe.

Some have even described the present situation as the third Muslim invasion of Europe, more successful than either the first or the second.

According to this view, capital and labor have succeeded where the armies of the Moors and the Turks both failed. There are now close to 2 million Turkish and other Muslims in Germany, similar or greater numbers of North Africans in France, and of Indians, Pakistanis, and Bangladeshis in the United Kingdom, as well as others in Belgium, Holland, Switzerland, Austria, Spain, Italy, and the Scandinavian countries, establishing, for the first time since the retreat across the Straits of Gibraltar in 1492, a massive and permanent Muslim presence in Europe. These communities are still bound by a thousand ties of language, culture, kinship, as well as religion, to their countries of origin and yet, inexorably, are becoming integrated in their countries of residence. Their presence, and that of their children and grandchildren, will have incalculable but certainly immense consequences for the future both of Europe and of Islam.

2

Legal and Historical Reflections on the Position of Muslim Populations Under Non-Muslim Rule

One of the earliest Muslim visitors to western Europe in modern times was a certain Mīrzā Abū Ṭālib Khān, an Indian of Perso-Turkish background, who traveled in England and France between 1798 and 1803 and wrote an extensive and detailed account of his journeys, adventures, and impressions. During his stay in London he was taken several times to the Houses of Parliament. He was not impressed by what he saw, remarking that their oratory reminded him of the squawking of a flock of parrots. He was, however, astonished when he found that this was a legislative assembly, with the duty of enacting laws to regulate both civil and criminal matters—defining offenses and prescribing penalties. Unlike the Muslims, the English, he explains to his readers, did not accept any divinely revealed holy law to guide them and regulate their lives in these matters and were therefore reduced to the pitiable expedient of making their own laws "in accordance with the exigencies of the time, their own dispositions, and the experience of their judges."[1]

In this comment, Mīrzā Abū Ṭālib Khān was revealing an essential difference between the classical Islamic and the modern Western views on the nature of law and authority and therefore of the functions and jurisdiction of the state. For the Muslim, law is an essential, indeed a central, part of his religion, which would be inconceivable without it. The law in all its details is divine not human, revealed not enacted, and therefore it cannot be repealed or abrogated, supplemented or amended. It deals equally—deriving from the same authority and sustained by the same sanctions—with what we would call public and private, civil and criminal, ritual and even dietary matters. Its jurisdiction is in principle universal, since God's revelation is for all mankind, but it is in practice personal and communal, since its enforcement is limited to those who accept it and submit to its authority. For them, its authority is absolute and applies to every aspect of human life and activity. In theory, therefore, there is no legislative power in human society, since the making of laws is for God alone. According to a frequently cited Muslim dictum, to forbid what God permits is no less an offense than to permit what God forbids.[2] This principle is of obvious relevance to certain contemporary situations in which modern social mores conflict with traditional Islamic practice.

While in principle there is no legislative function in the Islamic state, in practice Muslim rulers and jurists, during the fourteen centuries that have elapsed since the life of the Prophet, encountered many problems for which revelation provided no explicit answers, and found answers to them. These answers were not seen as enactments or presented as legislation. If they came from below, they were called custom. If they came from government, they were called regulation. If they came from the jurists, they were called interpretation. And Muslim religious lawyers, like lawyers everywhere, could accomplish many changes by reinterpreting even the most sacrosanct texts.

For Muslims, the most sacred text—indeed the only text to which that adjective can properly be applied—is the Qur'ān. This book is the primary source of holy law, and where it contains a clear and unequivocal statement, this is accepted as an eternal commandment equally valid for all times and all places. The clearer and more explicit the statement, the less room there is for interpretation. But where, as often, the statement is elliptic or allusive, there is a need for interpretation and an opportunity for creative ingenuity.

The scope for interpretative ingenuity is correspondingly greater in dealing with the second major source of Islamic law, the corpus of traditions, transmitted through the generations and describing the actions and utterances of the Prophet. Such traditions are known as *ḥadīth*. While *ḥadīth* is also binding and in principle equally so,[3] it differs from the Qur'ān in an important practical respect. Whereas there is a single Qur'ān with an undisputed text, there are vast numbers of different and sometimes contradictory *ḥadīths*, some of them surviving in variant versions and many of them regarded as questionable or even false by respected authorities. The collection, transmission, study, and authentication of such traditions became a major branch of Muslim religious scholarship. In time, scholars assembled a considerable body of traditions that were widely accepted among Muslims as authentic. But even these were subject to a variety of interpretations, often differing considerably. To regulate this, certain principles of interpretation were accepted, involving analogy and other forms of reasoning and even, within limits, the exercise of independent judgment. The dominant principle accepted by the vast majority of Muslims was the *sunna*, a word meaning practice or precedent and specialized to mean the practice of the Prophet and his Companions and other revered early Muslims, sanctified by tradition. The need for an authority to scrutinize, verify, and interpret the immense body of traditions was met by the acceptance of the doctrine of consensus (in Arabic *ijmāʿ*), which might be approximately translated as the climate of opinion among the powerful, the learned, and the pious. Following precedent was *sunna* and was good. Departure from precedent was *bidʿa,* innovation—the nearest Muslim equivalent to the Christian notion of heresy.

The principle of consensus made it possible for jurists over a period of time, in one or another part of the Muslim world, in practice though never in theory, to modify and adapt the law to meet changing circumstances. They were further helped in this by another principle laid down by the jurists, that of *ḍarūra,* necessity. Even in the Qur'ān there are verses that sometimes implicitly and sometimes even explicitly permit, on ground of necessity, what would otherwise be forbidden. As developed by the jurists, the principle of necessity applied in two forms. The first, relating to individuals, deals with the dire constraints under which a person might find himself. A Muslim may, for example, eat pork or carrion rather than starve to death. A seafarer may throw another seafarer's goods into the sea if their boat is overladen and about to sink. In the second sense, necessity no longer refers to individual constraint but, rather, to the exigencies of social and economic—and some would add political—life. But the principle of *ḍarūra* has limits. For the individual, these are clear and unequivocal: Thus, for example, to save his life, a Muslim may eat pork, but he may not commit murder. The social limits are more subtle, more debated, and, of course, more relevant.

The most important among those who rejected the Sunni view are the Shīʿatu ʿAlī, the faction or party of ʿAlī, the major breakaway group in Islam. In the classical Sunnī perception, the Muslim community is guided by God; its ruler is ordained and approved by God; and its history reveals the working out of God's purpose for mankind. For the Shīʿa, all the sovereigns of Islam since the abdication of Ḥasan—the son of ʿAlī, the founder of their sect—in the year 41 of the *hijra,* are usurpers. The Muslim world is living in sin, and history has taken a wrong turning. In practice, the two differed rather less from each other than their doctrines would appear to require. The Shīʿa found themselves obliged to make a series of compromises and live at peace under rulers whom they theoretically regarded as tyrants and usurpers. For their part the Sunnīs were obliged to compromise on their definitions of what constitutes a legitimate and just ruler and to accept a series of usurpers and tyrants whose only claim to power was the possession of sufficient military force to seize and hold it. Accepting them meant recognizing their legitimacy in terms of *sharīʿa,* and this in turn meant that obedience to them was a religious obligation, disobedience a sin as well as a crime. Tyranny, according to a common saying, is better than anarchy. The reason was eloquently set forth by the eleventh-century theologian and philosopher Ghazālī:

> Which is better, to declare that the qāḍīs are revoked, that all authorizations are invalid, that marriages cannot be legally contracted, that all acts of government everywhere are null and void and thus to allow that the entire population is living in sin—or is it better to recognize that the imamate exists in fact and therefore that transactions and administrative actions are valid, given the actual circumstances and the necessities of these times?[4]

Other scholars go even further and say that any ruler who can seize power and maintain order—even if he is barbarous or vicious—must be recognized and obeyed "for the welfare of the Muslims and the preservation of their unity [i.e., their social cohesion]." From a barbarian and a tyrant to an infidel it was only one step, but a very difficult one. Some writers were willing to take even that step, and from the eleventh century we find Arabic and Persian authors quoting a maxim, and sometimes even—absurdly—attributing it to the Prophet, that a just infidel is preferable to an unjust Muslim ruler—or as some put it, government can exist with unbelief but not with injustice.[5] The more usual view among the jurists, for whom justice is defined by the holy law of Islam, is that the worst of Muslims is preferable to the best of infidels.

Over time, different schools of jurisprudence arose among the Muslims. The Shīʿa, of course, have their own, but even among the Sunnīs several different schools emerged in the Middle Ages, four of which have survived to the present time. These are the Mālikī school, which predominates in almost the whole of Muslim Africa outside Egypt; the Shāfiʿī school, which is found principally in the eastern Arab countries and among the Muslims of South and Southeast Asia; the Ḥanafī school, in Turkey, Central Asia, and the Indian subcontinent; and the Ḥanbalī school, in Saudi Arabia. Although these differ from one another on many minor and a few major points, all recognize the others as Muslim and within the limits of permitted difference of opinion. There is indeed a dictum, first cited by Abū Ḥanīfa, founder of the Ḥanafī school, and later ascribed to the Prophet, that "difference of opinion within my community is a sign of God's mercy."[6]

In most systems of law, actions are divided into two categories, permitted and forbidden, or, in religious matters, commanded and forbidden. Islamic law, dealing with both religious and worldly matters, divides actions into five categories which one might render as (1) required, commanded; (2) recommended; (3) permitted; (4) disapproved; and (5) forbidden. The first category is subdivided into individual and collective commandments. Thus, for example, the duty of fighting in *jihād,* the holy war for Islam, is a collective duty on the community as a whole in offense but becomes an individual duty of every able-bodied male Muslim in defense.

It is under the heading of *jihād* that the Muslim jurists normally discuss the various legal problems arising from relations between Muslims and non-Muslims: authorities, communities, individuals. The reason for this classification is clear. Like Christians, Muslims believed that the revelation that had been given to them was for all mankind and that it was their sacred duty to bring it to those who were not aware of it or had not yet accepted it. This obligation is known in the language of the holy law as *jihād,* usually translated as holy war but literally meaning striving. In later times this was sometimes interpreted in a moral sense. In classical juristic literature it is invariably interpreted in a military sense, and the jurists go into great detail on such questions as the opening, conduct, and termination of hostilities, the treatment of prisoners and noncombatants, and the definition and division of booty.

Islamic teaching, and with few exceptions Islamic practice, rejects forcible conversion. The power of the Islamic state and therefore the jurisdiction of Islamic law were, however, extended in the early centuries of the Islamic era over vast territories and populations, and the literature of the time clearly reflects the belief that this process would continue without interruption until, in a not too distant future, the whole world would either accept the Islamic faith or submit to Muslim rule. In the meantime, the world was divided into two, the Dār al-Islām, the House of Islam, in which Islamic government and Islamic law prevailed, and the Dār al-Ḥarb, the House of War, in which infidel rulers for the time being remained in power. The denizens of the Dār al-Ḥarb were known as *ḥarbī.*

The swift, vast conquests achieved by the early Muslims brought great numbers of non-Muslims into the Islamic empire, of which for some time they constituted the majority of the population. Even after their majority status was ended by conversion and assimilation, they remained in significant numbers as minorities living among the Muslim majority. Later, when the first great wave of conquest was spent and a more or less stable frontier was established between the House of Islam and the House of War, other non-Muslims from the House of War came to the Islamic lands as visitors or temporary residents, sometimes as students or diplomats, but most commonly for purposes of trade.

Muslim law deals at some length and in great detail with the first group and also devotes some attention to the second.

Non-Muslims who were permitted to live as permanent residents under Muslim rule were called *dhimmī,* that is, members of a community that had been granted a *dhimma,* a pact, by the Muslim authorities. Under the terms of the *dhimma,* the non-Muslim subjects agreed to recognize the primacy of Islam and the supremacy of the Muslims and to symbolize their submission by paying a poll tax and accepting certain social disabilities, notably withholding from them the right to bear arms. In return, they were allowed to practice their religion and to maintain and, when necessary, repair their places of worship (a ban on the construction of new churches and synagogues was rarely enforced). In general they enjoyed a large degree of autonomy under their own religious chiefs, to whom they owed obedience and who exercised jurisdiction over them. Apart from the measures necessary to protect the security of the state, maintain public order and decency, and safeguard the primacy of Islam, they lived by their own and not by Muslim law. In most civil matters, including marriage, divorce, inheritance, and the like, as well as disputes between members of the same community, their disputes were heard before their own courts and decided by their own judges according to their own laws. Their education also was the responsibility of their community chiefs, who controlled schools, teachers, and curricula.

The visitor or temporary resident from abroad was called *musta'min,* the holder of an *amān,* or safe conduct. This might be personal or might be granted to the ruler of whom the visitor was a subject. The *musta'min* was exempt from the poll tax and many of the other disabilities imposed on the *dhimmī* but enjoyed the same right of living by his own laws and under his own chief, in this case usually the consul of his city or country. The *amān* was normally granted for a limited time and could be renewed. If the *musta'min* overstayed his *amān,* he became a *dhimmī.* The foreign communities under the authority of their consuls functioned as autonomous states within the state. In later centuries, when the changing balance of military and economic power transformed the relationship between the West and the Islamic world, what had originally been a voluntary concession granted by Muslim governments in accordance with the logic of their own laws became a ruthlessly enforced and bitterly resented extraterritorial privilege imposed by the now-dominant Western powers.

In the early centuries of Islam, when the juristic schools were formed and the major legal treatises were written, the position of the non-Muslim, temporary or permanent, under Muslim rule was a current and almost universal issue and therefore needed elaborate consideration and regulation. The corresponding problem of the Muslim under non-Muslim rule hardly arose and, where it did, received only minor and fleeting attention. In an age when the frontiers of Islam were continually expanding and when such losses of territory as occurred were tactical and temporary, it was hardly likely that the jurists would devote much attention to what was largely a hypothetical question.

When the question is discussed at all it is, naturally enough, under the same general heading, *jihād,* and in the same categories, permanent resident and temporary visitor, as is the status of the non-Muslim under Muslim rule. In the earliest juristic literature, the position of a Muslim permanently resident in a non-Muslim land is considered only in one contingency, that of an infidel in the land of the infidels who sees the light and embraces Islam—surely a rare occurrence. The question they discuss is whether he may remain where he is or must leave his home and migrate to a Muslim country. The Shīʿa jurists, more attuned to the idea of surviving in a hostile environment and under a hostile authority, allow him to stay and indeed see him as an outpost and beacon of Islam. The majority of Sunnī jurists, accustomed to the association of religion and authority, insist that he must leave and remove himself to a Muslim land where he can live in accordance with the holy law of Islam. In this he would be following the sacred precedent set by the Prophet and his Companions when they left their homes in pagan Mecca and undertook the migration (*hijra*) to Medina, where they established the first Muslim state and community. Some jurists even go so far as to say that if he remains where he is and his country is subsequently conquered by the Muslims, then his non-Muslim family and his property are liable to be treated as booty by the conquerors in the same way as those of his infidel neighbors and compatriots.[7]

Two cases of such conversion cited in the biographies of the Prophet indicate that the departure of a convert would be an act of expediency as well as of piety. The Byzantine governor of Maʿān in south Jordan embraced Islam and wrote to the Prophet. When he refused to recant, he was executed by the Byzantine authorities. Another story tells of a churchman at the court of Byzantium who responded to the Prophet's summons and publicly recited the Muslim profession of faith, whereupon he was beaten to death by the crowd.[8]

The question of a Muslim traveler to the lands of the infidels for a voluntary or involuntary, brief or protracted visit was of more practical concern and receives more attention. Prisoners, captured in war or at sea, had no choice, and the jurists offer guidelines on how a Muslim who suffers this misfortune should conduct himself until he is ransomed or exchanged or he escapes. As regards voluntary visitors, the first question to be decided was whether such visits are permissible at all in law and, if so, under what circumstances and subject to what rules. Mālik, the founder of the Mālikī school, allows Muslims to visit the lands of the infidels for one purpose only—to ransom captives. It is significant that almost all the reports of the Moroccan ambassadors to the various courts of Europe are headed "Report of a Mission for the Ransoming of Captives"—no doubt in order to avoid possible legal difficulties for themselves or their sovereign.

There was lively discussion among Mālikī jurists as to whether it was permissible to travel to the lands of the infidels for purposes of trade and specifically in order to buy foodstuffs at a time of dearth in the lands of Islam. Juristic answers to this question fall into three main groups. According to one group, it is forbidden in all circumstances to trade with the infidel, since they would use their profits to make war against Islam. If this means famine, then it must be endured. A second group, invoking the principle of *ḍarūra,* necessity, allows trade and travel only in order to secure supplies of foodstuffs in times of shortage. A third group is more willing to extend a general tolerance to Muslim travel and temporary residence abroad and allow a Muslim to accept *amān* from a non-Muslim government and stay for a while in a non-Muslim country, with the status of *mustaʾmin*. The assumption is that he would enjoy the same privileges and accept the same duties as applied to an infidel *mustaʾmin* in a Muslim land. The acceptance by a Muslim of a non-Muslim *amān* is subject to certain conditions from the Muslim side, the most important of which is that he be able to "manifest the signs of Islam." This phrase, which occurs frequently in discussions of Muslims *in partibus,* will need some further consideration.

The presence of Muslims, in groups or even as individuals, in the House of War raised the question of jurisdiction, to which the juristic schools give different answers. Are such Muslims still subject to Muslim law? Of more practical importance, are Muslim judges empowered to deal with persons living, or actions committed, under infidel rule? The Shī'a say yes, the Ḥanafīs usually say no, and the others adopt a variety of intermediate positions.[9]

Muslim discussions of these matters were concerned almost exclusively with Christendom, seen as the House of War *par excellence.* The jurists were much less worried about the colonies of Muslim merchants established from early times in India, China, and other parts of Asia and Africa. These were, so to speak, religiously neutral zones, offering no threat to Islam in either the religious or the political sense. On the contrary, their peoples were seen as potential recruits to the Islamic faith and their lands as potential additions to the Islamic domains. This expectation proved historically justified. Only in Christendom did Muslims encounter a rival and in many respects a similar religio-political power, challenging their claim to both universal truth and universal authority.

The first recorded agreement between the Muslim state and a Christian state was with the Christian kingdom of Nubia, to the south of Egypt. Modern critical scholarship has cast doubt on both the modalities and the chronology of this agreement as reported by the chroniclers, but from the point of view of the jurists what matters is not the reconstituted reality but the traditional narrative. According to this, in the year 31 of the *hijra,* corresponding to 652 of the common era, a pact was concluded with the king of Nubia stipulating, among other things, that the king would "protect those Muslims . . . who tarry or travel there until they leave . . . maintain the mosque that the Muslims have built in the center of [his] city and not hinder anyone from praying there . . . and keep it swept, lit and treated with respect."[10] The Nubian pact served as a starting point for some later juridical theories—and arrangements—whereby certain territories were regarded as falling into an intermediate category between the House of Islam and the House of War, variously designated as Dār al-Ṣulḥ, the House of Truce, or Dār al-'Ahd, the House of Pact or Covenant. Such arrangements existed in both medieval and Ottoman times, and the countries in question were usually in a tributary or subordinate relationship to the Islamic state. Agreement with these states normally provided for Muslim travel and even residence in their territories, with virtually extraterritorial privileges. No such arrangement was possible with those Christian states that remained fully independent and were therefore presumed hostile.

The tenth century saw the beginning of a Christian recovery and counterattack, which in time forced the retreat—sometimes temporary, sometimes permanent—of the Muslims from many of the former Christian territories that they had conquered and dominated. Already in the tenth century, a Byzantine advance brought much of northern Syria back under Christian rule for a while. In the eleventh century, the Norman Conquest recovered Sicily for Christendom, and shortly afterward, the Crusaders established four Christian principalities in the Levant, between Taurus and Sinai, in lands that had been held by Islam since the seventh century. Most important of all, the long struggle for the reconquest of the Iberian Peninsula gained significant victories in the eleventh and succeeding centuries and was finally completed with the fall of Granada, the last Muslim principality in western Europe, in 1492.

Even greater disasters struck the Muslims in the East, when the great Mongol conquests of the thirteenth century brought Central Asia, Iran, and Iraq under pagan rule and, for a while, seemed to threaten Syria and even Egypt. Muslim historians did not fail to note that there were Christians among the Mongols and that they seemed to enjoy some favor. They tell in particular of a dramatic incident in 1260 when the Mongol forces entered the city of Damascus. Their commander was a Nestorian Christian from the East, and he rode through the city flanked by two other Christian princes, one an Armenian and the other a Crusader.

With the decline of Muslim power and the rise of modern Europe, the problem was compounded a thousandfold, as province after province, country after country, was conquered and annexed to the great European empires—first Austria and Russia, then the maritime powers of western Europe. All these Christian advances brought large Muslim populations under Christian rule and confronted them with a new and agonizing problem.

The problem, as usually formulated in the juridical literature, is as follows: "If their country has been conquered by the Christians, may Muslims stay or must they migrate to a Muslim land?"

The term that they use—migration, in Arabic *hijra*—indicates how the problem is seen in terms of Islamic jurisprudence. According to Muslim teaching, the Prophet was a model to be followed by the Muslims in almost all respects. The Prophet himself had set the example of migration by leaving pagan Mecca and enjoining his followers to accompany or precede him in the migration to Medina, where they would be able to live a Muslim life. The obligation of Muslims to migrate to a place where they can practice their religion freely is based on a passage in the Qur'ān (4:97–100) supported by a number of *ḥadīths*. In a characteristic and frequently cited saying, the Prophet denounces and rejects any Muslim who chooses to live among the polytheists.

In the early centuries of Islam, the question of *hijra* was purely theoretical, and some jurists, notably of the Hanafī school, argued that the obligation of *hijra* ceased to operate after the Muslim conquest of Mecca. They even adduced a *ḥadīth* to this effect: "There is no *hijra* after the conquest [of Mecca]." The tide of Christian reconquest gave the question a new relevance and urgency, and the Mālikī jurists of the West, confronted by the subjugation of extensive Muslim territories in Sicily, Spain, and Portugal, gave a different answer. The obligation of *hijra,* they declared, has not lapsed but will remain in effect until the Day of Judgment. The only questions are when and in what circumstances it applies and when and for whom it may be remitted.

Some jurists find authority in the Qur'ān and *ḥadīths* for exemption on the ground of physical or financial incapacity; some invoke the principle of *ḍarūra,* necessity, both personal and communal, to allow significant postponements of the inevitable departure; and some allow Muslims to stay, in the hope of "guiding the people of unbelief to the truth and saving them from error." But all agree that it is a bad thing for Muslims to remain under non-Muslim rule, the principal disagreement being whether such as action falls under the heading of disapproved or forbidden—or, to put it the other way around, whether emigration is commanded or merely recommended. The key question is whether they are permitted to practice their religion or, more precisely, to "manifest the signs of Islam." If they are not, then all agree that they must leave. If they are, then the moderates see their continued presence as disapproved, and the more rigorous jurists insist that even then they are bound by religious law to leave. The Moroccan jurist Aḥmad al-Wansharīsī, writing in the final stages of the Christian reconquest of Spain, insists that even if the Christian conquerors are both just and tolerant, the Muslims are still required to leave—indeed, even more so, since under such a regime the danger of apostasy would be correspondingly greater.[11]

In that particular case, the question was entirely hypothetical, since the Christian conquerors were neither just nor tolerant, and the Muslims were obliged to leave irrespective of their own choice or preference. Other Muslims conquered by Christian European powers were more fortunate, and the choice was their own, whether to stay or to go. Into modern times the term *muhājir,* one who performs *hijra,* has been used of Muslims who migrated from the lost provinces of the Ottoman Empire to Turkey and from secular India to Pakistan.

The choice they made and the juridical ratification of their choice depended largely on how far they were free to practice their religion and how in fact they understood that freedom. For the modern Westerner, religious freedom is defined by the phrase "freedom of worship" and means just that. But the practice of Islam means more than worship, important as that may be. It means a whole way of life, prescribed in detail by the holy texts and treatises based on them. Nor is that all. The primary duty of the Muslim as set forth not once but many times in the Qur'ān is "to command good and forbid evil." It is not enough to do good and refrain from evil as a personal choice. It is incumbent upon Muslims also to command and forbid—that is, to exercise authority. The same principle applied in general to the holy law, which must be not only obeyed but also enforced. Thus, in the view of many jurists, a Muslim not only must abstain from drinking and dissipation, but also must destroy strong drink and other appurtenances of dissipation. For this reason, in any encounter between Islam and unbelief, Islam must dominate. That is why mosques must overtop non-Muslim places of worship and never be overtopped by them, and why—on this point the jurists are unanimous—a Muslim man may marry a non-Muslim woman, but a non-Muslim man may not, on pain of death, marry a Muslim woman. In marriage, so the jurists believed, the husband is always the dominant partner.

A similar asymmetry appears in the law concerning proselytizing. It is the duty of a Muslim, wherever he may be, to bring the faith to the unbelievers. Islam, unlike Christianity, has no professional missionaries but assigns this task to all Muslims alike. It is, however, strictly forbidden for a *dhimmī* to try to convert a Muslim to his religion, and if by any mischance he succeeds, the penalty for apostasy is death. From a Muslim religious point of view, this discrepancy is both logical and proper. To promote the true faith is a divine commandment. To abandon it, or to persuade another to do so, is both a mortal sin and a capital crime.

There are some who followed this argument to its logical conclusion and maintain that an authentic Muslim life is possible only under a Muslim government. There are others who reject this extremist view and admit the possibility of living a Muslim life under a non-Muslim government, provided that that government meets certain specific requirements. The Ḥanafi school, in this as in most other matters inclined toward moderate positions, was satisfied with basic tolerance, and imposed migration only when Muslims suffered forced conversion or were prevented from performing their religious duties. Even then, emigration was obligatory only for those who had the necessary means. The Mālikī school, as well as other eastern schools, was more rigorous and regarded emigration as being at the very least recommended and in most cases obligatory.

A key question in deciding whether staying in their homeland is forbidden or merely disapproved is the application of Muslim holy law. If the affairs of the Muslims are conducted in accordance with the holy law and are adjudicated by Muslim qāḍīs in courts administering that law, then according to some of the jurists they may remain, and the actions of such qāḍīs, even if they are appointed by infidel authorities, are valid. For a significant number of jurists, remaining where one is in such circumstances is disapproved but not forbidden. For the most rigorous, even in the most favorable circumstances, Muslims are forbidden to stay and are required to leave.[12]

Nevertheless, in spite of these strictures, many did stay, and during the centuries of the *Reconquista* in Spain there were times when considerable Muslim populations lived under the newly established Christian governments, to which they paid tribute in return for tolerance. They were despised by both the emigrants and the unconquered, who saw them as *dhimmīs* of the Christians. They were known by the Arabic terms *ahl al-dajn* or *mudajjan,* a word used to denote tame or domesticated, as contrasted with wild and free, animals. The word passed into Spanish in the form *mudejar.*[13] The steady worsening of the condition of the *mudejar* subjects of the Christian states gave added strength to the rigorist point of view, and a series of *fatwās* by Andalusian and North African jurists reiterated that it was the duty of the Muslims of Spain to leave their conquered homelands and seek refuge under the rule of Islam. No less a person than Ibn Rushd, qāḍī and imām of the great mosque of Cordova and grandfather of the philosopher known in Europe as Averroes, laid down that the duty of *hijra* is eternal and that a Muslim must not remain where he is subject to the jurisdiction of the polytheists but must leave and go to the lands of the Muslims, where he will be subject to Muslim jurisdiction. Just as the Companions of the Prophet were permitted to return to Mecca after it was conquered, so the *muhājir* will be permitted to return to his homeland when it is restored to Islam.[14]

The dilemma of the Muslim populations of Iberia and Sicily was resolved by their voluntary or enforced departure. Centuries later, the Muslim populations of the lost Tatar and Turkish lands in Europe had a freer choice. Many left voluntarily; others stayed for a somewhat problematic existence as minorities in Russia and the newly independent Christian states. The dilemma arose in a more acute form with the establishment of European imperial rule in countries of predominantly Muslim population—the French in North Africa, the Russians in the Black Sea and Caspian regions and in Central Asia, and the British and the Dutch in South and Southeast Asia. At first, some Muslim leaders and jurists applied the rule of emigration even in these places, and there were Muslims in significant numbers who went from North Africa to Turkey, from the Russian Empire to Turkey and Iran, from India to Afghanistan. But the vast majority perforce remained, and both they and their leaders and teachers had to adapt themselves to a new reality.[15] With the exception of the state-imposed secularism and atheism of the Soviet era, the imperial regimes in general were, for good reasons of their own, tolerant in religious matters and allowed the Muslims not only the free practice of their religion in the limited Western sense of that word but also the maintenance and enforcement of their own laws, through their own judges and courts, over a wide range of social, personal, and even to some extent economic matters. Muslim jurists responded to this, and some were even willing to rule that a country where Muslims live and where Muslim law is enforced may be considered part of the House of Islam, even if the sovereign authority is in the hands of infidels. Others, though not prepared to go that far, accepted a variety of compromises, mostly justified by necessity—*ḍarūra.*

In the last analysis, the real test of whether Muslims may stay or go is the holy law by which they must live. The primary concern of the classical jurists was to maintain that law; the main aim of the modern fundamentalists is to restore it where it has been neglected or set aside. For some, including most of the Mālikī school, no place conquered by infidels can be considered under Muslim law, and Muslims must sooner or later leave when they have the means and the capacity. For others, the mere fact of conquest by infidels does not make a country part of the House of War. If the holy law is still maintained and enforced, even under infidel authority, that country may still be considered, for legal purposes, as part of the House of Islam. Jurists are, in particular, concerned with the validity of legal actions and documents and the legitimacy of the qāḍīs who validate them. They give primary importance to the laws relating to marriage and divorce and to inheritance and other matters of property. Without the one, Muslims may find that they are living in sin; without the other, they cannot be sure of the lawful enjoyment of their worldly goods.

The colonial empires had allowed this kind of communal, legal autonomy to the Muslims living under their rule. And before that, Muslim rulers from the first Arab caliphs to the last Ottoman sultans had allowed the Christian communities to live by their own laws of personal status and to provide for their own schooling and higher education. To many Muslims, it seemed not unreasonable to expect the same courtesy from the governments of their new homes abroad. In fact, they received far more personal freedom, but far less communal autonomy, than had been accorded to the Christian subjects of Muslim states.

The resulting dilemma is epitomized in the no-doubt apocryphal complaint of a recent Muslim immigrant to Europe: "We allowed Christians to practice and even enforce monogamy under Muslim rule, so why shouldn't you allow us to practice polygamy under Christian rule?" The difficulty arises not only from conflicting social mores, as in this and similar cases, but also—more especially—from an understanding of identity and jurisdiction that is clearly out of accord with the accepted practice of most of the modern world, including some of the Muslim states. In Turkey, *sharī'a* law has been legally abolished but was for long in fact unofficially maintained in remote rural areas. As a result, many children born of polygamous "marriages" were legitimate under *sharī'a* law but illegitimate under state law. What the jurists principally fear when Muslims live under non-Muslim law is the reverse—a disastrous process that could destroy the very fabric of the Muslim family and therefore of Muslim society.

Today, all the colonial empires that once governed a large part of the Islamic world have ended. The last—the former Soviet Union—is in process of dissolution. Most of its 50 or 60 million Muslims live in six independent republics where, for the time being at least, they are still subject to social and legal systems that are very remote from Muslim holy law. Many remain as minorities in Russia and other non-Islamic republics. Even after the breakup of the empires, by no means all Muslim populations are under Muslim rule. Two non-Muslim countries, China and Ethiopia, have ruled over Muslim populations for many centuries. Among the new states established after the fall of empire, several non-Muslim countries retain significant Muslim populations, notably India, Sri Lanka, Israel, and a number of sub-Saharan African states. Most, if not all, of these have been willing to maintain the system of devolution and legal autonomy, at least in matters of personal status, bequeathed to them by the empires. Their position in this is significantly different from that of the Muslim remnant in ex-Ottoman southeastern Europe.

To these one must now add an entirely new category—Muslim minority communities formed by voluntary migration from Muslim lands to predominantly Christian countries that have never at any time formed a part of the House of Islam. For such an action by Muslims, there is no precedent in Islamic history, no previous discussion in Islamic legal literature. The jurists, ancient and modern, discussed the predicament of the Muslim under a non-Muslim government under several headings: the new convert alienated from his previous coreligionists, the temporary visitor taken as a captive or traveling as an envoy or a trader, the unhappy inhabitant of a Muslim country conquered by unbelievers. Not surprisingly, the possibility never seems to have entered their minds that a Muslim would voluntarily leave a Muslim land in order to place himself in this predicament. There have always been individuals and even small groups—students, political exiles, as well as traders, but until recent years these were infinitesimally few in number and not remotely comparable with the unending flow through the centuries of travelers of every kind from Christendom to the lands of Islam. A mass migration—a reverse *hijra*—of ordinary people seeking a new life among the unbelievers is an entirely new phenomenon, which poses new and major problems. The debate on these problems has only just begun. The most common argument offered in defense of such migration is *ḍarūra,* necessity, interpreted in economic terms. Some have tried to adduce a prophetic precedent for their action by citing the example of the Prophet, who, before the *hijra,* authorized some of his Muslim followers in Mecca to seek refuge in Christian Ethiopia. The Prophet himself, that is, had authorized the migration of Muslims to a Christian country. Others reply that they were leaving a pagan, not a Muslim, city and that no Muslim state existed at that time. The flight to Ethiopia does not therefore set a precedent for voluntary migration from a Muslim to a Christian country.

One may wonder how far the new Muslim immigrants to Christian and post-Christian lands—many of them men of limited education—are aware of these juridical arguments and of the legal and theological texts on which they are based. It does not greatly matter. These texts are evidence of the concerns, beliefs, and aspirations of the community from which they came. For the outsider, they are the most accessible, the most reliable, and often the only source of information. For the insider, these texts, and the simpler tracts and homilies based on them, are one of the channels through which the living tradition of the community is transmitted to him; there are many others, in the home, the school, the mosque, the marketplace, and the company of his peers. And one of the lessons to be learned from these texts is the capacity of the tradition in the past to confront new problems and to respond to them in unexpected ways.

Last year, while I was in Paris, I was invited to participate in a television program discussing books. The following day, a young man in a shop where I went to make a purchase, recognizing me, remarked that he had seen me on television talking about Islam. He then made an observation that has been puzzling me ever since. "My father," he said, "was a Muslim, but I am a Parisian." What, I wondered, did he mean—that Islam is a place? Or that Paris is a religion? As stated, neither proposition, obviously, is true. Yet as implied, neither is completely false. Their interacting implications reflect the dilemma of a minority, most of them from the less modernized parts of their own societies of origin, who now find themselves in a situation in which they differ from the majority among whom they live, not only because they profess a different religion, but also because they hold a radically different conception of what religion means, demands, and defines.

STUDIES AND PERCEPTIONS

3

Translation from Arabic

Until the Renaissance and the Reformation, that is, until the period when the great wave of translations from scriptures and classics began in the West, Arabic was probably the most widely translated language in the world, both in the number of books translated and in the number of languages into which these translations were made. Arabic was therefore also the language in connection with which the problems of translation had been most carefully and systematically considered. It may be noted in passing that the first book ever printed in England was the *Dictes and Sayings of the Philosophers,* printed in 1477. This was an English version of an Arabic original, the *Kitāb Mukhtār al-Ḥikam wa-Maḥāsin al-Kilam,* written in about the middle of the eleventh or early twelfth century by a certain Mubāshir ibn Fātik. The first critical edition of the Arabic text appeared in 1958.

Arabic has since the seventh century been a scriptural language—the language of the Qur'ān, the holy book of the Muslims, and also of the major works of Muslim theology and law; a classical language, the medium of a body of literary, philosophic, and scientific writing which was regarded as exemplary and authoritative not only by the Arabs themselves but by other Muslim peoples; a practical language, widely used in government, society, and commerce. It was thus the equivalent in the medieval Islamic world of Latin, Greek, and Hebrew in the West, as well as of the literary vernaculars until the beginnings of the modern period. It has a literature of immense richness, created over a vast area by an enormous diversity of peoples in a great variety of contexts. Hence some of the peculiar difficulties of the language, and of translation from it.

Translations from Arabic began in the Middle Ages and fall into two main groups, both selected for the content rather than for the artistic or literary merits of the work translated. The first group consists of translations from Arabic into other Islamic languages—first into Persian, then into Turkish, and later into the remoter languages of Islam. This group consists chiefly of books on religion, with some on law and history.[1]

The second group consists of translations from Arabic into non-Muslim languages—first into Hebrew, then directly or indirectly into Latin, and later into other European languages.[2] These to begin with were principally works on philosophy, theology, science, and medicine—in a word, the useful sciences, philosophy and theology being at that time considered as such. An early Latin translation of the Qur'ān was produced entirely for the purpose of enabling missionaries to refute it.[3]

Of literary translations there were surprisingly few. It is rather striking that despite the great wealth and high prestige of Arabic literature, very little of Arabic poetry or belles lettres was translated into other Muslim languages, even less into non-Muslim languages. We do not, for example, find any equivalent in Persian or Turkish of the Latin translations of Greek plays or of the vernacular translations of classical works, both Latin and Greek, in Europe. The one outstanding exception, perhaps because of its extreme difficulty which challenged the ingenuity of translators, is the peculiarly Arabic art of the *Maqāma*. Many *Maqāmāt* were rendered—adapted rather than translated—in Persian, in Hebrew, and in other languages.[4]

Compared with his modern successor the medieval translator had a relatively simple task. For Muslims translating from Arabic into Persian or Turkish, it was possible to a very large extent to use the same lexical material. An Arabic word could simply be transferred from the Arabic text into the Persian or Turkish text and used in a Persian or Turkish syntactical combination—sometimes with slight changes but not always. Translators concerned with scholarly and scientific texts and translating them from Arabic into other Muslim languages had, that is to say, no greater problem than is encountered by the modern translator of similar works from one European language into another, within a common universe of discourse expressed in common lexical material. We can translate the English word "revolution" into French *revolution,* German *Revolution,* Italian *revoluzione,* Spanish *revolución*, or Russian *revolutsia* with perhaps some differences but without loss of communication. The same facilities, with the same limitations, existed between Arabic, Persian, and Turkish.

For the early translators from Arabic into Hebrew the problem was a little but not much more difficult. They could not simply borrow and transfer Arabic words but they could and did calque—form Hebrew words from cognate roots in imitation of Arabic words. Thus, the Arabic *murakkab,* complex, gave rise to the Hebrew *murkav;* the Arabic *kamiyya,* quantity, to the Hebrew *kāmūt,* etc. Incidentally, much of the scientific and philosophic vocabulary of early modern Hebrew originated in this way.

The problem became very much more difficult when the translator had to cross the cultural boundary between Islam and Christendom, but even here the medieval translator was helped by the common biblical and Hellenistic background of the two civilizations on the one hand, and by the limited range and vocabulary of the material on the other.

Problems of translation were discussed quite explicitly at an early date. The question arose for Muslims on the theological issue of the translatability of the Qur'ān.[5] According to common Muslim belief, one of the proofs of the Qur'ān is its miraculously beautiful and inimitable style. Some theologians therefore argued that the Qur'ān could not be translated into other languages and that the mere attempt would be a desecration, a form of blasphemy. Others argued that the Qur'ān might be translated within certain limits. In fact, translations were made, though usually disguised as commentaries. They were however never recognized or given status of a religious character like the Vulgate, the Peshitta, the King James Bible, or other more recent efforts to present the Jewish and Christian scriptures in contemporary idiom.[6]

I should like to quote one medieval comment on translation which appears in a letter written by Maimonides to his translator Ibn Tibbon in about 1199. Ibn Tibbon was translating a philosophic work by Maimonides from Arabic into Hebrew and sought the author's advice. This is part of the answer sent to him:

> Let me premise one rule. Whoever wishes to translate and aims at rendering each word literally and at the same time adheres slavishly to the order of words and sentences in the original will meet with much difficulty and his rendering will be faulty and untrustworthy. This is not the right method. The translator should first try and grasp the sense of the passage thoroughly and then state the author's intentions with perfect clearness in the other language. This, however, cannot be done without changing the order of the words, putting many words for one, or one for many, and adding or taking away words so that the subject may be perfectly intelligible in the language into which the translation is made.[7]

This is good advice, and although it has been on offer for almost seven hundred years, it is not always followed.

Modern translation in the West began with the great movement of Orientalist scholarship from the Renaissance and Reformation onward. A whole group of famous translators rendered Arabic texts into the clerkly Latin which was in use among scholars of that time and then, initially with some disdain, into the languages which they spoke. One of the most famous was the German scholar Reiske, whom Victor Hugo called "ce bon allemand de Reiske, qui preferait si energiquement le chameau frugal de Tarafa [an early Arabic poet] au cheval Pégase." The texts selected for translation were at first usually philological or theological. They included some historical works, a few of which were used by Gibbon and before him by the authors of the *Grande Encyclopedia* and thus found their way into the European mainstream.

Translations of other historical texts came a little later, and in themselves also constituted an important contribution to Western historical studies. There were few before the nineteenth century, and these mostly of Oriental Christian texts; many more appeared from the early nineteenth century onward, chiefly in connection with those subjects which most interested the rather ethnocentric historians of western Europe, that is to say the Crusades and the Muslim occupation of Spain, Sicily, and parts of France.[8] These early translations, with all the errors, misunderstandings, and misrepresentations which they contain, have become part of the common stock of accepted knowledge in the West.

The vogue of literary translation began with the famous French version of the *Thousand and One Nights* by Antoine Galland, completed in 1704, and followed by a whole series of others, including translations by such eminent scholars as Sir William Jones and such gifted writers as the German poet Friedrich Rückert.

Until the end of the eighteenth century, interest in Arabic was almost exclusively scholarly and to a much lesser extent literary. It was rarely practical. For the practical purpose of dealing with the Muslim lands Persian and Turkish, the languages of the rulers of the Middle East at that time, were far more important. A new phase began with Bonaparte's expedition to Egypt and the consequent direct involvement of Europe in the affairs of the Arabic-speaking lands. Translation now also became the concern of dragomans, diplomats, and others concerned with official documents, their rendering, and their interpretation. This is not my immediate concern at this time, but the whole question of authorized translations and abstracts raises profound doubts. Some time ago I had occasion to look at some documents at the Public Record Office in London received from Muslim monarchs by the kings and queens of England, with contemporary translations in English, French, Italian, or Latin. Some of the translations are quite remarkably inaccurate, often tendentiously so. This throws a sidelight on some aspects of the history of diplomacy which deserve a closer look.

I turn now to my main theme, the problem of a modern translator trying to put an Arabic text into accurate and intelligible English. Assuming that he possesses the necessary skills—to read Arabic and to write English—he must guard against the two major sources of error, which we might call subtraction and addition; that is to say, omitting something which is in the text and inserting something which is not.

There are three main aspects to this problem of translation, the linguistic, the cultural, and the stylistic—that is, the task of finding an appropriate form of English.

We may begin with a very practical and pressing problem for Arabists and would-be Arabists; the lack of tools. The inquirer can if he wishes arrive at a very simple measure of the difference between the study of Arabic and Islamic civilization and the study of Latin and Greek and ancient civilization, by going into a reference library and comparing the Pauly Wissowa lexicon of classical antiquity with *The Encyclopedia of Islam.* Such a comparison would give an indication of the difference between a well-established, sophisticated academic discipline, cultivated by many scholars in many places for a long period, with a high standard of entry, performance, and preferment, as compared with the discipline of Middle Eastern studies, in which unfortunately these conditions do not prevail. We have no really adequate dictionary for classical Arabic, no historical dictionary at all, and no historical grammar. Most of the dictionaries at our disposal are based on the lexica made by Arabs and other Muslims in classical times, using their material and following their methods. These are works of the greatest importance and represent an immense achievement. They are not, however, adequate for the needs of modern scholarship. For one thing, the purpose of the medieval Muslim lexicographers was not that of their modern successors, that is to say, to fix the usage of educated speakers in their own time. Their purpose was to explain words which were already rare or obsolete and therefore obscure in their time; this means of course that they were often mistaken in their explanations. Another drawback is that the medieval lexica are in the main confined to poetic and literary usage, and pay little attention to more practical matters. They are furthermore vitiated by methods of inquiry and deduction which, though advanced in their day, would not be acceptable by modern standards. They are full of ghost words and ghost meanings which have no existence outside the dictionary. Every student of Arabic has at one time or another been daunted by the long ranges of alternative meanings which overshadow Arabic words in the dictionary and has wondered how anyone could possibly operate with such a language.

The answer is very simple. No one did. A good proportion of the meanings listed in the dictionary are quite mythical and are simply translated and transferred by modern dictionary makers from the classical lexica. Many of them are chance rhetorical figures found in some line of poetry and duly incorporated in the dictionary as a valid meaning of the word; some are due to scribal errors, to misreadings, to false analogies, to differences of opinion between scholars, and, worst of all, to etymological deductions, a bad habit into which the lexicographers frequently fall. Yet on the other hand, these lexica omit nuances of meaning which were certainly felt in the living language as well as differences of usage by dialect, social origin, age group, status, occupation, religion, and many other variables. Above all, they pay no attention to the evolution of the language, to changes in the usage and meaning of terms over the very long period and in the very broad area in which classical Arabic has been used. When I was a young student, just beginning Arabic, I remember encountering, in the reader which we used, the word *baḥīra*. I looked this up in my vocabulary and was duly instructed that a *baḥīra* was a she-camel with one ear split in half lengthwise. This troubled me rather and I sought the guidance of my teacher. He explained there was no problem—*baḥīra* came from the verb *baḥara,* which among other things means to split the ear of a she-camel in halves lengthwise.

Words like this—the terms of art of ancient camel-breeders—are easy. The lexicographers delight in them and offer them in great numbers, both real and ghostly. They are obviously related to the society which needed to create such terms, and once their connotation is known, they present no problems of understanding or interpretation.

What is much more difficult is the apparently familiar word, the superficially easy word which we do not even bother to look up in the dictionary because we know it—and if we do bother to look it up in the dictionary we in fact find no more than we already know—but which in a text can convey a meaning quite different from the knowledge which we and the dictionary share.

Let us take one or two simple examples. A typical one is the word *malik*. Any Arabic–English and English–Arabic dictionary will tell us that *malik* equals king and king equals *malik*—almost like a mathematical equation. But the word *malik* in Arabic has been used at different times with many different meanings. In the Qur'ān it appears as a divine epithet, and yet at about the same time it also appears as a term of disapproval indicating a tyrant, a bad ruler, an autocratic ruler, a nonreligious ruler. In the period of the early caliphate, it seems to have gone out of use for human monarchs except as an occasional term of abuse. It was later revived by Iranian dynasties, the Samanids and Buyids, apparently as an Arabic cover for the Persian term *shāh*, and was used as a sub-royal rather than as a royal title, that is to say, as a claim to sovereignty less than supreme sovereignty. A ruler called himself *malik* when he was admitting that there was a sultan or caliph above him. This is the sense in which the title *malik* is used by Saladin and his successors, who all had composite titles including the word *malik* but recognized the suzerainty of the caliph. *Malik* thus means something less than a supreme sovereign—clearly not the normal English meaning of the word "king," a sovereign who admits to no superior. It went out of use again in the later Middle Ages but reappeared in the twentieth century, when it was adopted by Muslim rulers as representing something better, because more Western sounding, than the title *sultan,* by then somewhat tarnished. Thus in 1916 when the ruler of Egypt wished to indicate his increased status, he changed his title, which he had previously augmented from Khedive to sultan, from sultan to king. The title *malik* was later adopted by such other Muslim rulers as those of the Hijaz, of Saudi Arabia, of Morocco, Libya, and elsewhere. At the present time, with the growth of various forms of Islamic radicalism, the word *malik* is acquiring fresh overtones and recovering some of its earlier implications.

Siyāsa is another instructive example. In modern Arabic *siyāsa* means politics or policy. It is connected with an ancient word meaning a horse and derives from the Arabic verb *sāsa,* meaning to attend or care for a horse. The active participle, *sā'is,* a groom, has penetrated via India into English in the form "syce." The image is of course a familiar one. Our word "government" comes from a Greek word meaning a rudder and indicates our maritime image of leadership and authority. The image of the state as a ship and of its leader as a helmsman is common among the maritime peoples. Among land-bound peoples, it is equally natural that they should use a word with a connotation of horsemanship, leading by analogy from the management of horses to the management of men—statecraft, government, and politics. This was the normal meaning of the Arabic word *siyāsa* and of its loan equivalents in Persian, Turkish, and other Islamic languages.

Does *siyāsa* always mean politics? If we are to believe the dictionaries, then the answer is yes. But let us look at a famous thirteenth-century text, the *Fakhrī* of the Iraqi historian Ibn al-Ṭiqṭaqā, in which we read: "*Siyāsa* is the chief resort of the king on which he relies to prevent bloodshed, defend chastity, avert evil, suppress evil doers and forestall misdeeds which lead to sedition and disturbance."

This is surely a tall order for politics, even allowing for local variations in political style and usage. In fact *siyāsa,* at that time and in that place, does not mean politics at all. It means punishment. There is of course a connection between politics and punishment, but the two terms are not as yet synonymous. *Siyāsa,* in late medieval Islam, more commonly means punishment than politics, more specifically discretionary punishment administered at the will of the ruler in contrast to legal punishment prescribed in accordance with the holy law of Islam. Often it is specialized to mean physical punishment, more particularly capital punishment. If we look again at the passage from Ibn al-Ṭiqṭaqā and interpret *siyāsa* as meaning not politics but severe discretionary punishment, then the list of purposes which *siyāsa* is expected to achieve makes rather better sense.

Another example, again a simple word, is *'abd. 'Abd* in Arabic means slave; it comes from a root meaning to serve, and it occurs in the theophoric names through which it is generally familiar—'Abdallah, the slave of God, 'Abd followed by one of the other divine names—'Abd al-Karīm, 'Abd al-Hamīd, etc. But *'abd* went through certain changes of usage in classical Arabic. In the early centuries it simply meant a slave irrespective of origin. Then it was specialized to mean a black slave, other words being used to specify white slaves. Then it came simply to mean a black irrespective of status. This development of meaning is not reflected in the old dictionaries but is well established both in late classical texts and contemporary colloquial usage.[9]

One can adduce many examples of misunderstanding arising from the neglect of historical evolution and regional variation. Such words as *'askar, jaysh,* and *jund* are all translated "army" in the dictionaries—but they do not all mean the same thing and have different meanings in different times and places. A good historical dictionary would tell us how and why and where these words were used—but unfortunately no such dictionary exists.

Another common cause of misunderstanding is the blurred distinction. It is often said about Arabic, by those who do not know any, that it is vague and rhetorical and that Arabic texts are wordy, imprecise, and high-flown. This description of classical Arabic is quite untrue. Such a delusion may arise in part from the reader's inability to understand the text and may partly be due to a projection backward of the characteristics of some modern users of the language. But classical Arabic is a precise and accurate vehicle of thought. True, it is a language rich in poetry and eloquence, arts the practitioners of which may not always say exactly what they mean or mean exactly what they say. But that is only one aspect of Arabic. It is also a language of remarkable clarity and precision, and as an instrument of philosophical and scientific communication, its only peer until modern times was Greek. Individual writers may of course be vague and inaccurate, but it would be wise for the translator to assume that apparent vagueness may rather be due to his own ignorance or lack of understanding than to looseness or failure of expression on the part of the author.

Mistranslation may result from failure to recognize some technical or specialized meaning of a common Arabic word. Such mistakes often occur in translations of texts dealing with medieval Islamic administration, the technical vocabulary of which is still imperfectly known. An example may be seen in a pioneer French translation of a major Islamic legal work of the Middle Ages, in which the word *qānūn* in Arabic is translated "le maintien des lois."[10] The general meaning of *qānūn* in Arabic is undoubtedly law, as well as some specialized types of law or enactment. It was however used, especially in Iraq and the Islamic East, to designate a kind of cadastral and fiscal survey, and it is in this sense that the word is used in the text translated. The resulting misunderstanding is therefore considerable.

Similar problems may arise in virtually any classical Arabic text that one may care to look at. Any scholar who has mastered one branch of Arabic technical literature can fault any translator who is bold enough to venture into his corner. This is no doubt one reason why there are so few large-scale translations and indeed why most translations are prepared by beginners who have not yet learned the risks.

Sometimes misunderstandings may arise from failure to recognize the changing social context of the term and the concealed allusions which it may contain. A term often used by the Shīʿites to designate the Umayyads and their supporters is *al-muḥillūn*. This is an active participle from *aḥalla* meaning to permit or, more precisely, to allow as licit. This word, applied as a term of abuse by rebels to the government, has puzzled modern scholars who have translated it in various ways. One modern writer, for example, who has studied the early period in some detail renders it as heretics[11]—a translation which apart from the question of textual accuracy is open to criticism on other grounds. The expression is in fact an allusion to an earlier event—to the slaughter of the Prophet's descendants by Umayyad forces at the battle of Karbalā'. The *muḥillūn* are those who approve or condone this action—that is to say, who consider the shedding of the blood of the Prophet's kin licit. This description is applied to the Umayyad house and those who support it.

Sometimes, the meaning of a word is extended or modified by its use as a euphemism. Thus, several different words are used to address or denote eunuchs—a status too distasteful for direct description. Sometimes they are referred to as *ustādh*—a word also applied to master craftsmen, cab drivers, and professors; more often as *khādim,* which commonly means servant and also figures in the title *Khādim al-Haramayn,* the servant or servitor of the two holy places (Mecca and Medina), a title used by the sultans. There were times when almost every eunuch was a servant and when many male servants were eunuchs—but the two terms were never identical. This is obviously a rich field for misunderstanding.

The examples considered so far relate to sins of omission rather than of commission—that is to say, the failure to include in the translation some essential part of the meaning expressed in the original. Sometimes the error is the other way around. The translator has more or less understood what the text means but in passing it to his reader has added something of his own, not justified in the original.

The commonest form of addition to the text is the tacit false analogy, implied in translating a word by what is seen as an equivalent term in English. Thus some translators render *qāḍi'l-quḍāt* as lord chief justice and *ṣāḥib al-daftar* as chancellor of the exchequer. This kind of translation is a peculiar failing of Victorian British colonial translators, but it is also encountered elsewhere. A more recent and perhaps deliberately tendentious example is the translation of *Khalifa* (i.e., caliph) as President of the Republic.

These are self-evidently absurd. There can be other less obvious but equally misleading analogies in the use of such words as "state," "freedom," "democracy," "revolution," and the like to render superficially equivalent Arabic terms. Translations are often vitiated by anachronism and what we might call anatopism—rendering an Arabic word or term by an English word carrying with it the connotations and associations of another time and another place. The Arabic word *ḥurr,* for example, according to all dictionaries, corresponds to the English word "free." Free has had many different meanings in English and still varies greatly in content in the various countries where the English language is used. In Arabic until the beginning of Western impact, *ḥurr,* free, was primarily a legal, secondarily a social term. That is to say it meant free and not slave in the juridical sense and was sometimes also used with a social connotation of high status or privilege, raising the "free" man above the common mass of mankind. According to Westermarck, in Moroccan colloquial proverbs *ḥurr* means a white man in contrast to *'abd,* which means slave and hence a black man.[12] The first political use of the word *ḥurr* in Arabic, as far as I am aware, occurs in General Bonaparte's proclamations issued when he arrived in Egypt, describing the program of the French Republic. Later of course *ḥurr,* free, and *ḥurriyya,* freedom, became common political usage.[13]

Sometimes this form of mistranslation consists of introducing concepts which are not in the original. Thus in an early Arabic chronicle, the Conquests of the Provinces of al-Balādhurī, we find the full text of the *amān* (a technical term for the safe conduct or pledge of security granted by the Muslims to a non-Muslim person or group who surrendered to the protection of the Muslim state) which the Arabs gave to the people of Tiflis after capturing the city. This *amān* is set forth in the usual form; it is not a bilateral contract but a unilateral statement and indicates, in a letter addressed to the people of Tiflis, the conditions on which their surrender is accepted. It ends with this simple Arabic phrase, "Hadhā 'alay-kum wa-hādha lakum," which means literally, this is on or against you and this is to you, that is, this is what is due from you and this is what is due to you. This text was twice translated into a Western language. Once was in the United States in 1916, by a scholar who rendered the phrase "The above are your rights and obligations"; by an odd coincidence the second translation appeared almost simultaneously in Germany, by a very eminent Arabist whose rendering is practically the same.[14]

Both translators, by speaking of "rights," a word not present in the original, tacitly introduce a whole system of political and legal thought which may or not be relevant to the document in question. A similar form of words occurs in some other passages, for example, in the introduction to the so-called constitution of Medina cited in the Arabic biography of Muḥammad and purporting to be the document drawn up by the Prophet to regulate relations between the Muslims and the Jews and laying down "stipulations for them and stipulations from them." The earliest translator into a European language, Gustav Weil, is cautious and renders these words "unter gewissen Bedingungen." The English translator of the same books is similarly cautious: "stated the reciprocal obligations." Other scholars dealing with the same text however have spoken of "duties and rights"—a formulation which clearly introduces notions not in the original and probably alien to the society from which these documents emerged.[15]

Not all mistranslations are due to such sophisticated causes. Some arise quite simply from an inadequate command of the Arabic language. Thus Abū Shāma, an Arabic historian of the Crusades period, quotes a letter in which the ruler of Aleppo is accused of allowing the Assassins a mission house—*dār da'wa*—in which their heretical doctrines are taught. A translator, confusing the different meanings of the verb *da'ā,* to summon, to invite, etc., translates this as "bei einem Gastmahle in Ḥalab," at a banquet in Aleppo.[16] A more recent example occurs in a translation of an Arabic treatise on administrators and secretaries.[17] During the Umayyad period, the chronicler tells us, a new governor arrived in Iraq and went to seek counsel from a wise old man. The old man was more than willing to oblige, but before doing so he asked the new governor, "Why have you come here? Have you come here to please your God or to please him who sent you [i.e., the caliph] or to please yourself?" The governor's reply to this question is rendered by the translator as "I seek your advice only in order to please the people [*al-Jamī'*]." But *al-Jamī'* does not mean the people; it might be better translated as the lot—that is, all three—and what the governor was saying was "I seek your advice in order to please all three, that is God, the caliph and myself." By substituting the people—as the translator puts it, the governor's aim is "nur um dem Volke zu gefallen"—he has introduced a whole new world of populist and nationalist ideas, to confuse historians and others who rely on translated texts.

Finally there is the cultural difficulty—the fact that in classical Arabic we are dealing with a literature which was written for and by groups of relatively small interlocking coteries; a cultivated, sophisticated, highly literate, and indeed scholarly community; a number of in-groups, donnish, Bohemian, and literary, with a habit of discourse in rapid, multiple, and incomplete allusion, full of fleeting references to proverbs, to verses, to historical incidents long forgotten, to legendary persons and events—very often a private game between the long dead author and his long dead readers. To these we must add the normal difficulties of interpreting the social and cultural context of works from a society very remote from us in time and space and outlook, and with entirely different tastes and literary conventions.

A final question of some importance is the kind of English one should use in translating from Arabic. The cause of cultural communication has suffered some damage from a sort of Anglo-Arabese favored by many, particularly Victorian, translators—a pseudo-biblical, neo-gothic, mock-Elizabethan, bogus Oriental style which finds its ultimate form in Burton's translation of the *Thousand and One Nights* and still seems to contaminate some other translators, recent and even contemporary. There really is no need to create a special form of English in order to translate Arabic. The English language which we have is adequate to the purpose and should allow the translator to discharge his or her duty—to present the text in clear and accurate English, free from intrusive concepts and images, perceived within the context of the world from which it came.

4

The Ottoman Obsession

In 1603 an immense volume of more than six hundred leaves, *The Generalle Historie of the Turkes,* was published in London. By no means the first book printed in England on the subject of the Turks and the European efforts to halt their advance, it was, nevertheless, the first to attempt a general history

> from the first beginning of that nation to the rising of the Ottoman Familie, with all the notable expeditions of the Christian Princes against them, together with the lives and conquests of the Ottoman Kings and Emperours; faithfullie collected out of the best histories, both auntient and moderne, and digested into one continual historie until this present yeare 1603.

Its author was the English clergyman Richard Knolles, a former scholar of Lincoln College, Oxford, and headmaster of a school at Sandwich. Knolles did not know a word of Turkish—indeed very few Europeans of his day did—nor had he ever left his native island. He was, however, an educated Renaissance Englishman who could read Latin, Greek, French, Italian, and even German. Thanks to these attainments, he was able to make use of the writings of earlier authors whose linguistic skills and personal travels outstripped his own. "I collected so much of the History as possibly I could," he wrote, "out of the Writings of such as were themselves present, and as it were Eye-witnesses of the greatest part of that they writ."

Knolles's history, drawing extensively as it does on the literature of travel, mission, diplomacy, and scholarship, faithfully reflects the perceptions and concerns of Christian Europe as regards the Turks and their faith—the Ottoman Empire and the Islamic religion—during the preceding centuries.

The threat posed by the Turks had long been perceived as twofold: a challenge to Christendom from the rival Muslim faith, and a menace to Europe of conquest and incorporation into, in Knolles's words, "the glorious Empire of the Turks, the present terror of the world."

European Christendom seems to have had some initial difficulty in recognizing Islam as a rival world religion, preferring instead to designate the Muslim enemy by ethnic, rather than religious, terms. Some churchmen, however, were well aware that they were confronting not just an ethnic tide but a rival faith, similar in some ways to their own and with equal universal aspirations. They set to work to refute the Islamic faith and therefore, of necessity, to study it. But their efforts did not stop there: not only must Christians be safeguarded from the blandishments of Muslim emissaries, but the infidel must be converted to the true faith. In the sixteenth century, and even more so in the seventeenth, however, there occurred a decisive change of attitude. True, the theological arguments of the Reformation brought about a revival of interest in Islamic scripture and doctrines as certain warring Christian sects saw in Islam a possible ally for themselves or for their enemies. But in general, with the growing intellectual sophistication of Renaissance and post-Renaissance Europe, the Islamic religion was no longer feared as a serious rival threatening to convert large numbers of Christians.

Converts there still were, but mainly of two kinds. In the European lands conquered by Turks there were some—surprisingly few—who, for one reason or another, decided to adopt the religion of their new masters. There were others who came from Europe to seek their fortune in the lands of the Turks and at some stage embraced Islam, perhaps as a step in their careers, perhaps out of genuine religious conviction. But these converts in no way constituted a significant movement away from Christianity to Islam, and even Luther, though much concerned with the "Turkish peril," perceived it primarily in military and political, rather than in religious, terms. "Antichrist," he declared in his *Table Talk,* "is the Pope and the Turk together. A beast full of life must have a body and soul. The spirit or soul of Antichrist is the Pope, his flesh and body the Turk." And again, "The Turks are the people of the wrath of God."

Such indeed was now perceived as the main threat: Turkish military power menaced the very heart of Christendom. From the time the Turks first crossed the Straits of Gallipoli and set foot on the European mainland, they had achieved one brilliant victory after another, and advanced rapidly into southeastern Europe. In 1389 the Serbs and their Balkan allies were crushed at Kossovo; in 1396 a great crusade mounted by the chivalry of the West was defeated by Sultan Beyazid in a pitched battle at Nikopolis on the Danube. Many of the Frankish knights were taken prisoner, and the sultan paraded his resplendent captives as far east as Afghanistan to flaunt his triumph before the Muslim world. The fifteenth century brought further advances: the capture of Thessaloniki in 1430, the defeat of Christian forces at Varna in 1444 and at Kossovo in 1448, culminating in the conquest of Constantinople in 1453, henceforth the capital of the new empire of Europe and Asia, which the sultan and his forefathers had created.

they were threatening Italy at both ends. At the northern end of the Adriatic, the Turkish cavalry was skirmishing almost within sight of Venice; at the southern end, a Turkish expeditionary force seized and held the port of Otranto and prepared to embark on further campaigns in Italy. Only the death of Sultan Mehmed II in 1481 and an ensuing struggle for the succession between his sons led to the withdrawal of the garrison and the abandonment of plans for Italian conquest.

Under Mehmed's successors the Turks consolidated their eastern Mediterranean base by absorbing Syria, Palestine, and Egypt and then advanced into Europe, laying siege to Vienna in 1529. The siege ended in a stalemate, with the Turks in possession of half of Hungary, including Buda, which became the seat of a Turkish pasha. For the next 150 years the Ottoman and Hapsburg armies faced each other in central Europe in a struggle that would determine the fate of the entire continent. This stalemate was not resolved until 1683, when a second Turkish siege of Vienna failed, this one bringing unequivocal defeat and withdrawal.

For centuries, however, most of southeastern Europe remained under Turkish rule, while Turkish fleets dominated the eastern and menaced the western Mediterranean. All Europe was keenly aware of the threat that hung over it. As far away as Iceland the Lutheran prayer book included a prayer beseeching God to "save us from the evil designs of the Pope and the terror of the Turk." The latter, at least, was no idle fear. Iceland's historians and poets had much to say about a raid of Barbary corsairs, who descended upon their coasts in 1627 and carried off hundreds of captives to the slave markets of Algiers. One captive, a Lutheran pastor by the name of Oluf Eigilsson, who was subsequently ransomed and returned to his native land, wrote a book describing his adventures as a slave in North Africa; the discovery that his maidservant had fetched a much higher price than he had upset him as much as anything else.

But the vast and thriving empire of the Turk was not only a military threat to Europe; it was also an extensive and ramified market where European merchants could come in increasing numbers to profit from the open commercial policies of the Turks and the favorable treatment they accorded to foreign merchants. In earlier days, before the great technological and industrial advances gave Europe a decisive economic advantage over the rest of the world, there was little that the relatively backward and impoverished states of the West could offer. They came to the Turkish lands mostly as purchasers and were constrained to pay for their purchases in hard cash. The inflow of bullion from the newly discovered lands of the New World for a while provided them with the means to do this.

The one European product—apart from slaves—for which the Turks had a substantial and continuing demand was weaponry. Though such weaponry was needed principally to pursue the war against Christendom, there was never any dearth of Christian merchants willing to provide it and even, on occasion, to finance its purchase. By the sixteenth century,

European writings were full of accusations and recriminations by various Christian governments and communities, each accusing the other of supplying both weapons and military skill to the Turks. A papal bull issued by Clement VII in 1527 pronounced excommunication and anathema on

> all those who [took] to the Saracens. Turks and other enemies of the Christian name, horses, weapons, iron, iron wire, tin, copper, bandaraspata, brass, sulfur, saltpeter, and all else suitable for the making of artillery and instruments, arms and machines for offense, with which they fight against the Christians, as also ropes and timber and other nautical supplies and other prohibited wares.

A century later Pope Urban VIII issued a similar bull, this one with a slightly longer list of prohibited war materials, excommunicating and anathematizing those who, directly or indirectly, gave aid, comfort, or information to the Turks and other enemies of Christianity. Neither excommunication nor more immediate penalties in this world, however, were able to deter or even seriously limit the highly profitable traffic in weapons. Not surprisingly, the image of the Turk as trading partner, together with that of the Turk as invader and conqueror, figured prominently in European literature, easily overshadowing the image of the Turk as the standard-bearer of a rival religion.

By the time Richard Knolles set pen to paper to write his general history of the Turks, the educated European reader already had at his disposal, in print, a vast literature of books and pamphlets—a modern bibliographer has listed forty-nine in English alone—on the Turks and the countries over which they ruled, their history, manners, and customs, their armies, revenues, and system of government.

The stories and impressions recorded in this literature derived from a wide variety of sources, extending over several centuries. Some of the earliest information was provided by escaped or liberated slaves. The advance of the Turkish armies on the European mainland and of the Turkish and North African fleets in the Mediterranean and beyond brought about the capture and enslavement of many Christians. While the great majority of Christians who served as Turkish slaves, like the Turks who were enslaved in Europe, left no record of their experiences, some were men of letters who wrote accounts of their strange and wonderful adventures after their return. One of the first was the Bavarian Johann Schiltberger, who was captured by the Turks at the Battle of Nikopolis in 1396 and remained in captivity until 1427. A far more valuable account belongs to another liberated slave, a native of Transylvania known as Georgius de Hungaria, who was captured in 1438 at the age of sixteen by a Turkish raiding party. After eight attempts to escape, in 1458 he was finally rewarded with success. Some time thereafter he entered the Dominican order and wrote his memoirs, which, though composed when he was an old man, retained their freshness. His "Tractate on the customs, conditions and iniquities of the Turks," published in many editions and translations, became a major source of knowledge about Turkey for European readers.

Among the other returned slaves, two Italians are of particular importance. One of them, Giovan Maria Angiolello, was born in Vicenza about 1451 or 1452. As a young man he enrolled in the service of the Venetian republic and in 1470, at the fall of Negroponte, was taken prisoner by the Turks. More fortunate than most, he became the personal slave of Prince Mustafa, the son of Sultan Mehmed II. After the prince's death in 1474, Angiolello was sent to Istanbul, where he attracted the attention of the sultan himself and was appointed to a post in the palace treasury. After the death of Sultan Mehmed in 1481, Angiolello's position appears to have deteriorated, and he took steps to arrange his escape; in 1483 he returned to Italy, where he lived until his death, about 1524. Though his description of the Ottoman capital and imperial household long remained in manuscript, it was read and quoted extensively by contemporary and later European writers interested in the Ottoman establishment.

Another Italian slave who contributed greatly to Western knowledge of the Turk was Giovanantonio Menavino, a Genoese who was captured at the age of twelve when a cargo ship belonging to his father was seized by pirates. Sent to Turkey, Menavino was educated in the sultan's household and remained in the country for ten years, spending much of that time as a palace official. In 1513 he managed to escape to Italy via Trebizond and the Black Sea; back home, he published works on the life, law, and religion of the Turks, on the court of the sultan, and on some of the wars conducted by the Turkish armies.

After the first Turkish siege of Vienna in 1529, the situation in Europe more or less stabilized, and fewer captives remained in Turkey for any length of time. Of course Europeans were still captured at sea by the Barbary corsairs, but they were taken mostly to North Africa rather than to the Near East.

Returning slaves were not the only Christian travelers from the East. There were also Christian refugees from the lands conquered by the Turks: first Greeks from the former Byzantine territories and capital, and later Balkan Christians fleeing from the Turks and appealing to the West for shelter and help.

By the sixteenth century there was also a considerable movement of western Europeans to Turkey, where they had no great difficulty in entering, traveling around, and even establishing residence. This freedom was in marked contrast with the usually insuperable obstacles placed before such few Turks and other Muslims as tried to visit Europe.

European travelers to Turkey were of various sorts. Some were pilgrims, bound for the Christian holy places in Palestine. These became fewer—or at least less articulate—as the age of skepticism approached. Far more important were the merchants and traders who came in increasing numbers to profit from the rich commercial opportunities of the Turkish

Empire. At first they were mainly from Italy, from commercial cities such as Venice and Genoa; later merchants from France, Holland, England, and other European countries followed. Although most of these merchants confined themselves to their business dealings, a few recorded their impressions in books or in letters, thus adding their contributions to the Western image of the Turk.

Commerce was also a main concern of the diplomatic visitors, who from the sixteenth century onward wrote lengthy reports and sometimes books about Turkey. These envoys often had the advantage over casual visitors of long residence in the Turkish capital and time to form a circle of acquaintance—if not among Turks, at least among local non-Muslims—upon which to draw for deeper, and perhaps more accurate, knowledge of the country. Of particular importance were the Turkish letters of Ogier Ghiselin de Busbecq, a native of Flanders who was the ambassador of the Holy Roman Empire in Istanbul from 1554 to 1562. His letters, first published in Antwerp in 1581, were reprinted many times, both in the original Latin and, in translation, in most western European languages. Busbecq was a man of keen observation and penetrating judgment, and his letters exercised a profound influence on the European perception of the Turk. From the sixteenth century a series of envoys from Venice spent some time in Istanbul, and their reports are to this day a rich source of information on events and circumstances in the Turkish capital. Although these reports were not published at the time, their nonclassified contents seem to have been well known.

Slaves, refugees, pilgrims, merchants, and diplomats all contributed substantially to the growth of the Western image of the Turk. There were other travelers—soldiers, spies, and miscellaneous adventurers—whose writings were intended to throw light on the current situation and future prospects of relations between the Turks and Europe and thus to gratify a rapidly growing European curiosity. A good deal of the published literature consists of diplomatic, commercial, and intelligence reports, as well as writings to which it would not be inappropriate to apply the term "journalistic."

One category of visitor particularly well placed to satisfy the avid European curiosity concerning the domestic arrangements of the Turks were the physicians. By the sixteenth century Turks were becoming aware that European medicine was more advanced than their own, and the services of European doctors were in growing demand. The needs of their profession gave these men greater access to Turkish homes than was enjoyed by other visitors. Although even for doctors access was still severely limited, their accounts of the harems, of the sultans, and of lesser persons were eagerly studied.

Another group of European visitors who contributed substantially to the growth of the image of the Turk were artists. Some appear to have gone with personal commissions to paint portraits, as did the painter Gentile Bellini, sent by the Venetian republic to paint the portrait of

Sultan Mehmed the Conqueror. Others traveled on their own initiative. Most commonly they went in the suite of some great man. One of the first of these was the German artist Erhard Reuwich, who accompanied his noble and priestly patron Bernhard von Breydenbach on a pilgrimage in 1483–84 and joined with him in producing the first illustrated guidebook to the Holy Land, a work that depicted many Turkish figures and costumes. Two artists are particularly interesting: the Fleming Peter Coeck of Aelst, who was in Istanbul in 1533 and whose remarkable set of engravings was published in Antwerp in 1553; and Melchior Lorch, or Lorich, who stayed in Istanbul between 1556 and 1582, part of that time in Busbecq's entourage. These and many other European artists contributed the pictures that appeared time and time again as illustrations to the travel literature. Although some of these pictures are fantastic, many are drawn from life.

The artistic reflection of the image of the Turk in the West is not limited to those intrepid writers and artists who ventured into the Ottoman realms. Painters and illustrators, with or without the benefit of personal acquaintance, depicted Turkish figures and scenes in a tradition that often combined the exotic with the erotic. Western dramatists, for their part, peopled the stages of the blossoming European theater with thunderous and violent Turkish heroes and villains.

Mention should also be made of the role of the scholars in propagating the image of the Turk. The intellectual curiosity of the Renaissance extended even to what Europeans perceived as an alien and infidel empire. A number of historians, mainly in Italy, wrote books on the history of the Turks and their neighbors. Although most of these histories, like Knolles's, were based on Western sources and conceived in ignorance of the Turkish language and literature, an outstanding exception was the work of the German Johannes Löwenklau, known as Leunclavius. Leunclavius's Latin versions of Ottoman historical texts, published toward the end of the sixteenth century, were eagerly read and turned to account by European historians, who thereby contributed greatly to Europe's better understanding of its mighty and enigmatic Eastern neighbor.

European sources of information concerning the Turk were thus diverse. Even more diverse were the Europeans themselves. Italians and Frenchmen, Catholics and Protestants, merchants and missionaries, soldiers and diplomats, each had a different perception of the Turk, the result of widely differing experiences and concerns. There are, however, a few basic themes that recur and predominate, lending a certain consistency to the European perception of the Turk and response to the Turkish presence in Europe.

One of these themes concerns customs surrounding food and drink. In one of the earliest European references to coffee, the Venetian envoy Gianfrancesco Morosini, writing in 1585, noted that

> for entertainment it is their practice to drink publicly, both in shops and in the streets, not only men of low status but also among the greatest, a black liquid as boiling hot as they can stand, which is extracted from a seed which they call cavee, and which they say has the quality of keeping a man awake.

The Englishman George Sandys, who visited Turkey in 1610, noted the same habit:

> Although they be destitute of Taverns, yet have they their Coffa-Houses, which something resemble them. There they sit chatting most of the day; and sippe of a drinke called Coffa (of the berry that it is made of) in litle China dishes, as hot as they can suffer it: black as soote, and tasting not much unlike it . . . which helpith as they say, digestion, and procureth alacrity.

Even more remarkable than their habit of drinking this strange, hot, black drink was their rejection of alcohol, forbidden to them by their religion. Oluf Eigilsson, the captured Icelandic pastor, noted with astonishment that on the corsair ship that carried him and his fellows off to Algiers, the corsairs had casks of brandy, which they gave to their captives, while they themselves drank only water. Other travelers and prisoners made similar observations. Though it was well known that the Turks did not always strictly observe this ban, its very existence was strange to the European observer and formed a common theme in the European stereotype of the Turk. Thus, for example, in a play written in 1700 by the English playwright William Congreve we find this drinking song:

> To drink is a Christian diversion
> Unknown to the Turk and the Persian
> Let Mahometan fools
> Live by heathenish rules,
> And be damned over tea-cups and coffee.
> But let British lads sing,
> Crown a health to the king,
> And a fig for your sultan and sophy!
>
> (*The Way of the World,* act 4, scene 1)

Amid all the variety of literature about Turkey in the West, certain basic themes recur and indeed predominate. One of them is fear: the deep and ever present fear of the Turk as an intruder in Europe and a menace to Christendom. When Shakespeare's Othello spoke of "a malignant and a turbanned Turk," he was expressing the common idea of an evil and alien invader. Some Europeans saw themselves primarily as Christians threatened by a new assault from the old Islamic enemy. Others, more classically minded, saw themselves as the heirs of ancient Hellas defending civilization against the barbarous Asiatic heirs of the great kings of Persia. Others, again in a classical conceit, depicted the Turks as the descendants of the Trojans—Teucri—come to seek vengeance on their ancient Greek enemies.

For men of strong religious convictions, the Turk could be the embodiment of evil. "If an Englishman," says John Milton in his *Tenure of Kings and Magistrates,* "forgetting all laws, human, civil and religious, offend against life and liberty, he is no better than a Turk, a Saracen, a heathen." But such characterization was by no means unanimous, especially among those whose travels brought them into direct contact with the mysterious neighbors.

Indeed, there were some who openly protested against this hostile image. Thus the French traveler Jean Thevenot, who went to Turkey in 1652, observed:

> There are many in Christendom who believe that the Turks are great devils, barbarians, and people without faith, but those who have known them and who have talked with them have a quite different opinion; since it is certain that the Turks are good people who follow very well the commandment given to us by nature, only to do to others what we would have done to us.

Thevenot continued with the observation that these good qualities were to be found only among the native Turks and not among the converts "who are present in great numbers in Turkey, and who are surely capable of every kind of wickedness and vice." This observation was corroborated by other travelers. In contrast to what was commonly believed, "the native Turks are honorable people, and respect honorable people, whether Turks, Christians or Jews. They do not believe at all that it is permitted to deceive or to rob, no more a Christian than a Turk . . . they are very devout and very charitable."

The Scottish philosopher David Hume, speaking in his *Essays* of "the integrity, gravity and bravery of the Turk," echoed an old established tradition among European writers on Turkey, many of whom contrasted these qualities with the alleged defects of other peoples in the region. A feature of Turkish life that won the approval of many visitors was the administration of justice. In the traditional Islamic system there were no lawyers, that is to say, no advocates who, for a fee, would argue one side or another in a case. Litigants argued their own causes, and the justice dispensed by the Qadi was swift, expeditious, and inexpensive. European travelers, particularly those who had some experience of the costly and lengthy litigation procedures of most European countries, were not unimpressed, and the Turkish Qadi was often held up as a model. Another observation, made by a French traveler in the seventeenth century, was that the Turks "are not quarrelsome, do not fight duels, and do not carry swords in the city. Even the soldiers wear only daggers."

A virtue sometimes accorded the Turk—though by no means unanimously—was tolerance. Until the eighteenth century tolerance was a quality neither expected nor admired by many Europeans. They reproached the Turk, not because he imposed his doctrines by force—how else would one impose them?—but because his doctrines were false, that is, not Christian. In fact, however, the Turk did not impose his doctrines by force but instead allowed his subjects to follow their own religions, provided that they respected Muslim supremacy and paid their taxes. The result was that in the seventeenth century the Turkish capital was probably the only city in Europe where Christians of all creeds and persuasions could live in reasonable security and argue their various schisms and heresies. Nowhere in Christendom was this possible.

Some European writers had the grace to concede this point. Thus, the Englishman Thomas Fuller, in his *History of the Crusades* published in 1639, observed: "To give the Mahometans their due, they are generally good fellows in this point, and Christians among them may keep their consciences if their tongues be fettered not to oppose the doctrine of Mahomet."

Along with honesty, sobriety, and tolerance, hospitality was another quality singled out as a characteristic virtue of the Turks.

Among the faults and vices ascribed to the Turk, two themes dominated: arbitrary power and unbridled lust. So universal were these themes and so striking the terms in which they were presented, in both letters and arts, that one is impelled to seek their explanation in the European, rather than the Turkish, psyche. After all, on more than one occasion we of the West have projected our deepest hopes and fears onto strange peoples and distant realms.

Western writers have been virtually unanimous in depicting the Ottoman sultan—the *Gran Signor*—as a despotic and capricious autocrat, restrained by neither laws nor established interests, exercising the powers of life and death over all his subjects. Comparing absolute and limited monarchy, no less a connoisseur of political power than Niccolò Machiavelli took the sultan as the model of the former:

> The examples of these two different Governments now in our dayes, are the Turk and the King of France. The Turks whole Monarchy is govern'd by one Lord, and the rest are all his Vassalls; and deviding his whole kingdom into divers Sangiacques or Governments, he sends severall thither: and those hee chops and changes, as hee pleases. But the King of France is seated in the midst of a multitude of Lords, who of old have been acknowledg'd for such by their subjects, and being belov'd by them, injoy their preheminencies: nor can the King take their States from them without danger.
>
> (*The Prince,* translated by E. Dacres in 1640)

In the same spirit Shakespeare's Henry V, on succeeding to the throne, offered this reassurance to some courtiers who feared that they might suffer under the new monarch:

> This is the English not the Turkish court.
> Not Amurath an Amurath succeeds

But Harry, Harry.
(*Henry IV,* part 2, act 5, scene 2)

Although the sultan was certainly an autocrat with powers greater than most European monarchs were able to muster, he was no despot. Indeed, he was subject to the laws of Islam no less than the humblest of his slaves. In the course of time a whole series of groups and interests evolved within the empire, imposing effective limits on the sultan's power. Some Europeans who had the opportunity to observe more closely the Turkish system in its later phases were well aware of this development. Thus, in 1786, when the French ambassador Choiseul-Gouffier was trying to persuade the Ottoman government to adopt certain military reforms, he explained the reasons for his limited success in the following way: "Things here are not as in France, where the King is sole master; here it is necessary to persuade the ulema, the men of law, the holders of high offices, and those who no longer hold them."

But despite these developments and a growing European awareness of them, the older image of total and capricious power persisted. As late as the nineteenth century Sam Weller, in *The Pickwick Papers,* remarked, "It's over, and cannot be helped, and that's one consolation, as they always say in Turkey, ven they cuts the wrong man's head off."

Even more pervasive and persistent than the image of the capricious despot is that of the lustful and licentious Turk, whose alleged sexual prowess and practices have been described in what has sometimes amounted to pornographic literature and art. Rampant sexuality is an old accusation leveled by Europeans against their Eastern neighbors. Already in antiquity some Greek and Latin authors had made this point against the Saracens. The theme cropped up occasionally in Byzantine and Crusading times about the Muslims and deepened when Ottoman tolerance of foreigners brought greater numbers of Europeans to the lands of Islam. There was a curious convergence in this matter between Christian travelers to the East and the few Muslim travelers who ventured into Christian Europe. Almost all the Muslims were struck by the extraordinary license allowed to Western women: in the same spirit Western travelers displayed a prurient curiosity about the women's quarters of the Muslim household, especially the sultan's palace. Muslim travelers in Christendom were at once repelled and attracted by its forward and immoral women, while Westerners in the East spoke with barely veiled envy of its sensuous and lascivious men and the opportunities that Muslim usage afforded them. If the encounter between East and West was really a meeting between loose women and lustful men, it is remarkable that they did not get along better. In truth, of course, both images, like so many of the mutual perceptions of both sides, were stereotypes.

What chiefly aroused, in varying degree, the astonishment, reprobation, and envy of Western visitors were the institutions of polygamy and concubinage, and the processes by which the personnel of the harem were recruited and replenished. Western travelers dwelled in loving detail—much of it imaginary—on the staff of the seraglio, the odalisques, eunuchs, dwarfs, deaf mutes, and other exotic figures. It is revealing that in most European languages the word *saray*—which in Turkish and Persian simply means palace—came to connote only that part of the palace reserved for the women, presumably because that was the only part in which European travelers were interested. The more correct term is "harem," from the Arabic *ḥaram,* meaning forbidden in the sense of off limits or out of bounds. Although the law allowed a man four wives and as many slave concubines as he could afford, in fact such indulgence was limited to a small upper class. The possession of a large harem, from the days of King Solomon in all his glory to more recent times, was an important status symbol for a Middle Eastern monarch. It offered some other advantages, too.

Not surprisingly, the image of the Turk as an insatiable sensualist is the best known and most widespread of all the stereotypes. When Edgar in Shakespeare's *King Lear,* reciting his sins, wished to speak of his sexual excesses, he claimed that he had "in women, out-paramoured the Turk" (act 3, scene 4). By the nineteenth century, European travelers, fiction writers, and artists luxuriated in the sexuality of a largely mythical Orient and regaled Victorian drawing rooms with stories and pictures of the harem and its mysterious denizens.

One of the few European women to visit Turkey and to write about it was an Englishwoman, Lady Mary Wortley Montagu, born Pierrepoint, who in 1717 visited Istanbul, where her husband was ambassador. As a woman, she had access to the harem and could observe and describe the mysteries that had tantalized so many males; as the wife of an ambassador, she shared his social opportunities without his political constraints. In addition, she had the further advantage—by no means common among travelers—of being cultivated, intelligent, and perceptive.

What makes Lady Montagu's visit even more interesting is that it came at a time when the old myth of the Turk as a barbarous, despotic, and lustful infidel was just beginning to give way to the new myth, still in its embryonic form, of the non-European as the embodiment of mystery and romance and ultimately of wronged innocence. By the eighteenth century, Europe was looking at Turkey with somewhat different eyes. The religious certitude that for so long had made Christian Europeans look down on Islam was beginning to give way to a mood of self-questioning and, in time, self-doubt. Such a hint of the self-deprecation of a consumer society confronting another, more restful way of life is evident in one of Lady Montagu's letters:

> Thus you see, Sir, these people are not so unpolish'd as we represent them. Tis true their magnificence is of a different taste from ours, and perhaps of a better. I am allmost of opinion they have a right notion of Life, while they consume it in Music, Gardens, Wine, and delicate eating, while we are tormenting our brains with some Scheme of Politics or

> studying some Science to which we can never attain, or if we do, cannot perswade people to set that value upon it we do our selves ... I allow you to laugh at me for the sensual declaration that I had rather be a rich Effendi with all his ignorance, than Sir Isaac Newton with all his knowledge.

In the sixteenth century, when the Ottoman Empire was still at the pinnacle of power, it was, among statesmen at least, the Turkish menace that overshadowed all other aspects; two empires, two faiths, two different ways of life stood face to face, contending for the mastery of the known world. To some at the time it seemed that the centralized, disciplined power of the Ottoman must surely prevail over a weak, divided, and irresolute Christian Europe.

Yet how wrong they were. Though Ottoman power remained a factor on the European scene for years to come, it had already passed its peak. The Muslim faith no longer attracted Europeans; the Turkish menace was ceasing to frighten them. There was, in fact, no settlement between the Turks and the Persians, but continuous struggle and occasional wars until the eighteenth century, by which time neither Turkey nor Persia offered any threat to Europe. On the contrary, now they themselves were threatened. A new image of the Turk—weak and decadent, an invitation to foreign domination—was replacing the once prevalent images of power and menace, while a new image of the European—threatening, alien, and yet seductive—was looming on the Turkish horizon.

5

Gibbon on Muḥammad

Gibbon's interest in Islam seems to have begun at an early date:

> Mahomet and his Saracens soon fixed my attention, and some instinct of criticism directed me to the genuine sources. Simon Ockley, an original in every sense, first opened my eyes, and I was led from one book to another, till I had ranged around the circle of Oriental history. Before I was sixteen I had exhausted all that could be learned in English of the Arabs and Persians, the Tartars and Turks, and the same ardor urged me to guess at the French of De Herbelot and to construe the barbarous Latin of Pococke's Abulfaragius.[1]

The interest persisted. As an undergraduate at Oxford, Gibbon was impressed by the tradition of Oriental scholarship in the University: "Since the days of Pococke and Hyde, Oriental learning has always been the pride of Oxford, and I once expressed an inclination to study Arabic. His [Gibbon is here speaking of his tutor] prudence discouraged this childish fancy, but he neglected the fair occasion of directing the ardor of a curious mind."[2] Gibbon never did learn Arabic, but the "instinct of criticism" which he had displayed in his early reading served him well, perhaps the better because his ardor had not been directed by the teachings of early-eighteenth-century Oxford.

It was a time when interesting changes were taking place in the European Christian perception of Islam and its founder. Far from being prepared to recognize any merit or authenticity in Islam as a religion, Christendom had been unwilling even to take cognizance of the fact that it was a religion, as is shown by the persistence of European Christians in designating the Muslims by names which were ethnic rather than religious in connotation.

Medieval Christendom did, however, study Islam, for the double purpose of protecting Christians from Muslim blandishments and converting Muslims to Christianity, and Christian scholars, most of them priests or monks, created a body of literature concerning the faith, its Prophet, and his book, polemic in purpose and often scurrilous in tone, designed to protect and discourage rather than to inform. Despite the growth of a somewhat more detached scholarship, writing on this subject was still dominated by the prejudices and purposes of polemical writing at the time when Gibbon began to read about Islam.

But if the polemicists still dominated the subject, they no longer monopolized it—and more than one kind of polemic purpose was now represented. One important factor of change was the Reformation, which influenced the literature in several ways. Catholic authors frequently tried to discredit Protestant doctrine by likening it to Islam—Muhummad was an early Protestant, and the Protestants were latter-day Saracens. Protestant theologians in turn took up the challenge in several ways: sometimes by refuting it and showing that they were as fierce as the Catholics in their hostility to Islam; sometimes by turning it against their own protesters, such as Deists and Unitarians;[3] sometimes by accepting the accusation and turning it to their own advantage. This had some practical aspects in the occasional attempts by Protestant powers to seek a Turkish alliance against the Catholic empires,[4] and it reached its extreme in the Unitarian sympathy with Islam, at times even to the point of an espousal of the Islamic faith.

The Protestants, notably in Holland, England, and, later, Germany, made a major contribution to Arabic studies. Here again, there were several motives which impelled them in this direction. One was their concern with the Hebrew Bible and with the discovery that Arabic and Arabian lore could help in the better understanding of the Hebrew text of the Old Testament. Another was an interest in the Eastern Christians, who were seen as possible allies of the Protestants against the Church of Rome. A third was the growth of English and Dutch commerce in the Levant, which required a knowledge of local languages and customs and provided opportunities for Protestant scholars to spend some time in those parts.

One of the most important European Arabists of the seventeenth century, Edward Pococke (1604–1691), was the source of much of Gibbon's information, both directly through his own writings and indirectly through other later writers who relied very heavily on his work. Pococke began with Hebrew and Syriac and then went on to learn Arabic. In 1630 he was appointed by the Levant Company as chaplain in Aleppo and remained there until 1636, when he returned to Oxford to take up the newly created Laudian Chair of Arabic.

These practical and theological interests in Islam and its history were disciplined and directed by the new kind of philological and textual scholarship which, from the time of the Renaissance onward, was applied first to classical languages and then to Hebrew and Arabic.

Despite the practical interest in the Middle East—as the source of the Turkish danger and as a market for European goods—there was little material encouragement for scholars working in this field. The Cambridge scholar Simon Ockley (1678–1720), whose *History of the Saracens* first directed the young Gibbon's interest to this area, lived in penury. "I was forced," he says, "to take the advantage of the slumbers of my cares, that never slept when I was awake; and if they did not incessantly interrupt my studies, were sure to succeed them with no less constancy than night doth the day."[5] The second volume of his history was produced from Cambridge Castle, where Ockley was imprisoned for debt. The great German scholar Johann Jakob Reiske (1716–1774), whom Gibbon compares to Erasmus, Scaliger, and Bentley,[6] was unable to find a publisher for his Latin translation of the *Annales* of Abu'l-Fidā and had to print it at his own expense. When he had sold barely thirty copies of the first volume, he was compelled to stop the printing.

In a lengthy note on the sources for his chapter on the Prophet,[7] Gibbon names his main sources of information: three translations of the Qur'ān into Latin, French, and English by Marracci, Savary, and Sale; two biographies of Muḥammad by Humphrey Prideaux and the Count de Boulainvilliers; the relevant article in Herbelot's *Bibliothèque Orientale;* and "the best and most authentic of our guides," Jean Gagnier, "a Frenchman by birth and professor at Oxford of the Oriental tongue" and author of two "elaborate works," one of them an edition with Latin translation and notes of a biography of the Prophet by the Arabic author Ismā'īl Abu'l-Fidā (1273–1331), the other, Gagnier's own biography of Muḥammad in three volumes. In addition to these, Gibbon made extensive use of two other important works, a treatise on the Muhammadan religion by the Dutch scholar Adrian Reland, and Pococke's most important work, the *Specimen Historiae Arabum,*[8] an excerpt from an Arabic chronicle by the Syrian Christian author Bar Hebraeus (Abulfaragius), with a Latin translation and hundreds of pages of learned notes. The Arabic text itself occupies a mere fifteen pages and includes an account of the Arab tribes and a pre-Islamic Arabia, a brief biography of the Prophet, and a discussion of the biblical texts alleged by Muslims to prophesy his coming and of the miracles ascribed to him.

Each of the translations of the Qur'ān is introduced by a long "historical discourse" provided by the translator; all three of them, according to Gibbon, "had accurately studied by the language and character of their author." In fact, however, of the three translations, only that of Marracci is completely original and based exclusively on the Arabic text. Claude Savary (1758–1788) had some knowledge of colloquial Arabic acquired during a stay in Egypt but clearly had only a limited command of the written language. His translation is based on those of Marracci and Sale, with some reference to the Arabic text. His introductory biography of the Prophet, like those of most other European scholars of the time, rests in the main on a single Arabic source, the late medieval chronicle of Abu'l-Fidā. His chief difference from his predecessors lies in his approach. "Le philosophe y trouvera," he says, "les moyens qu'un homme appuyé sur son seul génie, a employés pour triompher de l'attachment des Arabes à l'idolatrie et pour leur donner un culte et des lois; il y verra, parmi beaucoup de fables et de répétitions des traits sublimes et un enthousiasme propres à subjuguer des peuples d'un naturel ardent."[9] This evaluation of Muḥammad is common to writers of the Enlightenment, and it is one of the determining influences in Gibbon's presentation.

Savary, both in his translation and in his preliminary discourse, relied very heavily on the English scholar George Sale (1697?–1736), the first English Arabist of any consequence who was not a clergyman, and one of the first in Europe. The son of a merchant and himself a practicing solicitor, he pursued the study of Arabic as a hobby and mastered it well enough to be commissioned by the Society for the Promotion of Christian Knowledge to correct an Arabic translation of the New Testament produced for them by a Syrian Christian. His Qur'ān translation, published in 1734,[10] is a major step in the progress of knowledge of Islam in Europe and was for a long time by far the most widely read and best known. It served as the basis for virtually all other translations into European languages until the nineteenth century. His translation is based on the Arabic text, and he made effective use of his predecessor, Marracci, as well as of one of the major Muslim commentators.

Sale's "preliminary discourse," dealing with pre-Islamic Arabia, the career of the Prophet, and the principles of the Muslim religion, greatly increased both the value and influence of this book. For his biography of the Prophet he relied in the main on Abu'l-Fidā and profited greatly from Pococke's *Specimen*. Sale, though not affected by the Enlightenment idealization of the Prophet, was commendably free from the religious prejudices shared by most of his predecessors and many of his successors, and did at least understand, in the words of a modern scholar, "that Arabic writers were the best sources of Arab history, and Muslim commentators the fittest to expound the Qur'ān."[11] Sale himself indicates his approach in the quotation from St. Augustine inscribed on the exergue of his book: "Nulla falsa doctrina est, quae non aliquid veri permisceat."

Sale, like all subsequent translators, relied very heavily on the pioneer work of the Italian priest Lodovico Marracci, published in Padua in 1698;[12] it consisted of a refutation of Islam, previously published in Rome in 1691, and the Arabic text of the Qur'ān with a Latin translation and a very full annotation. Marracci's purpose was frankly polemic, and he devoted forty years of his life to studying the Qur'ān and the Muslim commentators in order to destroy Islam with its own weapons. His refutation of Islam is aptly descried by Gibbon as "virulent, but learned."[13] Marracci knew Arabic well, and he consulted a wide range, impressive for that time, of Arabic sources. Many of those whom he cites, however, he knew only at second hand, chiefly from Pococke's *Specimen*. Apart from these, there were some earlier attempts at translating the Qur'ān, which Gibbon seems rightly to have disregarded.

The two biographies of Muḥammad by Dr. Humphry Prideaux[14] and by the Count de Boulainvilliers[15] were both polemical in purpose, and their weaknesses are well described by Gibbon: "The adverse wish of finding an impostor or an hero has too often corrupted the learning of the doctor and the ingenuity of the Count."[16] Prideaux's biography, first published in 1697, was enormously successful, being reprinted in numerous editions and translated into French. Its purpose is clear from the title: *The True Nature of Imposture fully Display'd in the Life of Mahomet. With a Discourse annex'd for the Vindication of Christianity from this Charge.* Prideaux is, of course, perfunctorily concerned to refute the claims of the Muslims—a somewhat unnecessary task in seventeenth-century England—but is more anxious to provide a terrible warning against the dangers of conflict within the church. It was the quarrels and arguments within the Eastern church, according to Prideaux, that "wearied the Patience and Long-Suffering of God," so that

> . . . he raised up the Saracens to be the Instruments of his Wrath . . . who taking Advantage of the Weakness of Power, and the Distractions of Counsels, which these Divisions had caused among them, soon overran with a terrible Devastation all the *Eastern* Provinces of the *Roman* Empire. . . . Have we not Reason to fear, that God may in the same Manner raise up some *Mahomet* against us for our utter Confusion. . . . And by what the *Socinian,* the *Quaker* and the *Deist* begin to advance in this Land, we may have Reason to fear, that Wrath hath some Time since gone forth from the Lord for the Punishment of these our Iniquities and Gainsayings, and that the Plague is already begun among us.[17]

Prideaux was principally alarmed by the Deists, and it is against them that he directs his main arguments. His book, though elaborately documented, is not a work of scholarship. He had no access to untranslated Arabic works and relied principally on three printed Latin translations—that of Pococke's *Specimen* and two others—while for the Qur'ān he used a twelfth-century Latin translation. His use of his sources is uncritical, and Gibbon is rightly suspicious of his treatment of them.

The French biography of the Prophet by Count Henri de Boulainvilliers (1658–1722), published posthumously in London in 1730, had quite a different purpose.[18] If Prideaux was concerned to refute Deists, Quakers, Socinians, and others who alarmed him, Boulainvilliers used the Prophet and the advent of Islam as a weapon against Christian dogma and the Catholic clergy. Though favorable, his tone is still more than a little patronizing. Muḥammad, for Boulainvilliers, was the Prophet of a nation of noble savages, among whom he appeared and for whom he knew how to temper nature with law. In its essentials, his religion was true and reasonable:

> En effect, tout ce qu'il a dit est *vrai,* par rapport aux Dogmes essentiels de la Religion; mais il n'a pas dit tout ce qui est *vrai:* et c'est en cela seul que notre Religion différe de la sienne, sans la grâce de la Révélation Chrétienne, qui nous éclaire bien au-delà de ce que Mahomed a voulu connoître et savoir, il n'y auroit système de Doctrine si plausible que le sien, si conforme aux lumières de la Raison, si consolant pour les Justes, et si terrible aux Pécheurs volontaires et inappliquez.[19]

Boulainvilliers's Islam was free from all the familiar and reprehensible excesses of religion: "On n'y connoit ni les Macerations, ni les Jeunes, ni les Fouets, ni les Disciplines. . . ."[20] As a further merit, it imposed no mysteries which could constrain reason. The Arabs asked him for miracles, but in this they were irrational, while Muḥammad himself was rational in denying the need for them. Muḥammad was "un Homme-d'État incomparable et un Législateur supérieur à tous ceux que l'ancienne Grèce avoit produits."[21]

This image of Muḥammad as a wise, tolerant, unmystical, and undogmatic ruler became widespread in the period of the Enlightenment, and it finds expression in writers as diverse as Goethe, Condorcet, and Voltaire—who, in some of his writings, condemns Muḥammad as the terrible example of fanaticism but in others praises him for his wisdom, rationality, moderation, and tolerance.[22]

Gibbon, while recognizing the polemic character and purpose of the Count de Boulainvilliers's biography, and occasionally commenting with some irony on his methods, was nevertheless himself deeply influenced by it.

The source whom Gibbon describes as "the best and most authentic of our guides" was Jean Gagnier, a French Protestant who settled in England and taught at Oxford. Of his two major works, one was an edition, translation, and commentary of the Arabic chronicle of Abu'l-Fidā, the other a biography of the Prophet in three volumes based in the main on Abu'l-Fidā and on another Arabic chronicle, that of Abū Muḥammad Muṣṭafā ibn al-Ḥasan al-Jannābī (d. 1590). Gagnier was the first to try to break away from the established habit of uninformed abuse and polemic. In 1723, through his edition and translation of Abu'l-Fidā, he made available to European readers for the first time an Arabic biography of the Prophet written by a Muslim. In his own biography published in 1732, he cautiously explained that his purpose was not to depict Muḥammad as he really was, but simply to acquaint the European reader with what orthodox Muslims tell and believe about him. This he did by translating long passages from the Muslim sources. His book was the basis of most other European writing on Muhammad until the publication of Gustav Weil's *Mohammed der Prophet* over a century later, the appearance of which in 1843 marked the beginning of an entirely new era in Islamic studies in Europe.

In addition to Gagnier's writings, two other books served as a major sources for Gibbon's discussion of Muḥammad. One was Pococke's *Specimen,* a work of epoch-making importance in the development of Arabic and Islamic studies in Europe and the basis of a good deal of subsequent scholarship. Prideaux, Marracci, Sale, and virtually all the other writers consulted by Gibbon relied very heavily on Pococke, who was the only scholar of his time to possess a mastery of the Arabic sources and literature sufficient to be able to read in bulk and cite with authority. The other was the biography by Boulainvilliers. Despite Gibbon's awareness of this work's defects, and occasional caustic comments about them, he nevertheless seems to have been much affected by Boulainvilliers's presentation of the Prophet and, still more, of the Prophet's time and place in the eighteenth-century mythic version which was first designed by the Count de Boulainvilliers and which become commonplace in the writings of the Enlightenment.

But beyond the work of these seventeenth- and eighteenth-century scholars, one must seek the original Arabic texts on which their presentations or misrepresentations of the Prophet are based. Virtually the only Arabic text known to European scholarship dealing with the subject was the history of Abu'l-Fidā. Jannābī was not then—and still has not been—published, and as Gibbon remarked, "I must observe that both Abu'l-Fidā and al-Jannābī are modern historians, and that they cannot appeal to any writers of the first century of the Hegira."[23]

This was precisely the problem. Abu'l-Fidā was a Syrian prince who lived seven centuries after the Prophet. His biography of Muḥammad, like other parts of his work, is little more than a transcript of the account given by an earlier Arabic historian, Ibn al-Athīr, who died in 1233, still a long time after the Prophet. He, in turn, relies almost entirely on a still earlier historian, Muḥammad ibn Jarīr al-Ṭabarī (d. 923), omitting the chains of authorities and arbitrarily harmonizing variant versions. Ṭabarī, in turn, cites or abridges several earlier authors: Ibn Sa'd (d. 843), who relies on his predecessor and master, al-Wāqidī (d. 823); Ibn Hishām (d. 834), who edited the work of his predecessor, Ibn Isḥāq (d. 768). These bring us, if not to the first century of the *hijra,* at least to a date reasonably near to it. But how reliable is the information which they provide?

In an essay first published in the *Revue des Deux Mondes* in 1851, Ernest Renan remarked that Islam was the last religious creation of mankind and also the best known. The faculty of originating religions, he said, like that of creating languages, has atrophied in our mature and reflective age, making it difficult, if not impossible, for us to understand that lost instinct of the childhood of our race. It is therefore fortunate that the origins of Islam are known to us so well and in such detail, while the origins of other earlier religions are lost in dreams and myths: "La vie de son fondateur nous est aussi bien connue que celle des réformateurs du XVIe siècle. Nous pouvons suivre année par année les fluctuations de sa pensée, ses contradictions, ses faiblesses."[24]

In making these remarks, Renan was referring to the *Sīra,* the great traditional biography of the Prophet which has been read and cherished by Muslims for over a thousand years. It was not until the nineteenth century that the *Sīra* became known to European scholarship, but the text of Abu'l-Fidā, though based on it at several removes, nevertheless retained enough of it to give the reader some idea of its content and character.

The idea of compiling a connected narrative of the life of the Prophet did not appear in the Muslim community until a comparatively late date; when it did, its appearance was caused by factors other than an interest in history. The oldest biographical data concerning the Prophet are to be found in two groups of sources. One of these is the great corpus of tradition—the record of the actions and utterances attributed to the

Prophet. In the years following his death, the Muslims came face to face with all kinds of problems and difficulties which had never arisen during his lifetime and for which the Qur'ān therefore offered no direct guidance. The principle was in time established that not only the Qur'ān, the word of God, was authoritative, but also the example and precept of the Prophet throughout his life. His opinions and sayings were therefore collected, sorted, and compiled in great corpora of traditions. While the collectors and students of tradition were primarily concerned with material on which to base rulings of law, doctrine, and ritual, the collections also included much that has a narrative or biographical content. In fact, every major collection of traditions contains sections on both the biography and the military campaigns of the Prophet.

This brings us to the second source—the Arabian saga. The peninsular Arabs of pre-Islamic and early Islamic times lived and sang in the heroic style—tribal, nomadic, warlike, obsessed with battle and vengeance, honor and shame, death and destiny, and personal, family, and tribal pride. Their poetry and legends mirror the conceptions and preoccupations of a heroic age. Muḥammad, the greatest of them all, was not only a prophet; he was also an Arab hero and a warrior of noble birth. Before long, writings appear celebrating the exploits and victories of the Prophet and his companions in their wars against the unbelievers. These works, though nearer to history in character and purpose than the tradition, are still very far from being historiography in the conventional sense. They are subjective and episodic, presenting a series of heroic figures and incidents without concern for chronology, sequence, or consistency—in a word, saga rather than history.

While a considerable mass of biographical data was accumulated in these various ways, the impulse for the collection and establishment of the biography of the Prophet came from another source—from the great transformation which had meanwhile been taking place in the personality of Muḥammad as conceived in the religious consciousness of the community established by his revelation. In a brilliant monograph,[25] the Swedish scholar Tor Andrae showed how, under the influence of the Christian and Jewish communities with which they came into contact, the Muslims began to see their Prophet in another light, as founder of their faith, to be compared with Jesus and Moses and, indeed, superior to them since his was the final revelation completing and supplanting those of his predecessors. Thus arose that cult of personal veneration—which Muḥammad himself had explicitly rejected—making him an examplar of ethical and religious virtues, the best and noblest of mankind. To meet and outdo the miracles of Jesus and Moses, Muḥammad, who had explicitly disclaimed any superhuman powers or attributes, was made the protagonist of a cycle of wonders and marvels stretching back to his early childhood and even to before his birth.

By the beginning of the second century of Islam, the main biographic pattern had been fixed. It was given its classic formulation by Muḥammad ibn Isḥāq, who was born in Medina about 719. A collector of traditions by training, he devoted himself to the study of the biography of the Prophet, collecting material from all available sources. In doing so he broke away from the formal rules laid down for the science of tradition and used by practitioners of that science to distinguish true from false tradition. He enlarged the scope of the source material and adopted a new and different attitude to it—that of a biographer rather than of a traditionist. This, not surprisingly, aroused the ire and resentment of the men of tradition, and it may have been because of this that Ibn Isḥāq was forced to leave his native Arabia and travel, first to Egypt and then to Iraq. He finally settled in Baghdad, where he died in 768. It was there, under the patronage of the Caliph al-Manṣūr, that he completed his biography of the Prophet.

The work in its original form is lost, but it survives in a later recension by Ibn Hishām, a scholar of Basra who died in 834. In the edition of Ibn Hishām, Ibn Isḥāq's biography of Muhammad has acquired almost the status of a sacred book all over the world of Islam. The information which it contains is supplemented by those other texts already mentioned above.

The primary question that will occur to the modern reader is: How far is all this authentic? Among Ibn Isḥāq's own contemporaries and coreligionists, the masters of the science of tradition regarded both his objectives and his methods with some suspicion, and there have been not a few since then who have echoed their doubts. The overwhelming majority of Muslims, however, have accepted this book as a true portrait of the life and work of their Prophet. The modern reader will get the impression that Ibn Isḥāq, unlike the compilers of some other religious texts, was at least concerned with historical accuracy. He is careful to distinguish between good authorities and poor ones, between those he cites with confidence and those he cites with reserve. He does not hesitate to tell stories which show the Prophet's enemies in a favorable light and—what is still more striking—stories that show the Prophet himself in what is to Western eyes an unfavorable light. One cannot, of course, build too much on this: the picture of the noble and courageous enemy is part of the heroic tradition on which Ibn Isḥāq drew, while, on the other hand, much that might seem discreditable to us would not have seemed so to Ibn Isḥāq. But we may be fairly sure that Ibn Isḥāq's failures are of judgment and not of historical integrity.

The first generation of Western scholars who worked on the biography of Ibn Isḥāq adopted, on the whole, a positive attitude. After discounting the obviously legendary and miraculous passages, they were ready to accept most of the remainder as an accurate record of the life and work of Muḥammad, whose career, in Renan's words, did indeed seem as well known and as well documented as those of the sixteenth-century Reformers. Since then, however, our knowledge of the life of Muḥammad has grown less and less as the progress of scholarly research has called one after another of the data of Muslim tradition into question.

The Jesuit Henri Lammens and the positivist Leone Caetani, from their different vantage points, subjected the tradition to minute historical and psychological analysis, while the meticulous scholarship of Tor Andrae was able to show the motives and influences which led the early Muslims to give a new shape and color to their image of the last and greatest of the Prophets. Lammens went so far as to reject the entire biography as no more than a conjectural and tendentious exegesis of a few passages of biographical content in the Qur'ān, devised and elaborated by later generations of believers.[26] Other Western scholars reacted against this extreme formulation and, while agreeing that there is much that is purely legendary in the biography, especially in the passages dealing with the Prophet's early life, were prepared to accept most of the remainder as substantially accurate. Gibbon, equally ignorant of past Muslim and future Western doubts about the authenticity of the *Sīra,* used his own critical judgment and was able to achieve a version which at least reflected an early Muslim view.

Eighteenth-century scholarship on Islam in Europe was still subject to many difficulties. Among the most important were the lack of adequate access to major Arabic sources and the lack of tools facilitating access to the Arabic language itself. Even now, Arabists have no historical dictionary or historical grammar of the Arabic language; the task of the seventeenth- or eighteenth-century Arabist, reading manuscript sources with virtually no research aids to assist him, was truly formidable. There were further problems: the remnants of theological prejudice, which still colored the views even of those who personally were free from them and which sometimes made the expression of a more objective opinion physically hazardous; the fables and absurdities inherited from the ignorant past; and—a new feature of the period—the various attempts to present Muḥammad and Islam in terms of current controversies in Christendom, between Catholics and Protestants, between Protestants of various persuasions, or between Christians and Deists or freethinkers.

Nevertheless, great progress was made. The more preposterous legends about Muḥammad—the trained dove who came to his ear, the coffin suspended in mid-air, and the like—were now abandoned even by the most bigoted of writers. New sources were made available in printed Arabic texts and in Latin translations, and the study of Islam was established as a serious subject worthy of attention and respect. The Muslims were no longer seen purely in ethnic terms as hostile tribes, but as the carriers of a distinctive religion and civilization; their Prophet was no longer a grotesque impostor or a Christian heretic but the founder of an independent and historically significant religious community.

Gibbon's "instinct of criticism" did not forsake him in dealing with the Arabic sources for the life of the Prophet. There was, indeed, little else to guide him. For Roman history, he could build on the work of Tillemont and a host of lesser historians. For Islam, his main guide was Simon Ockley's *History of the Saracens,* and this begins with the death of the Prophet. Gibbon recognized the late and legendary character of much of the Arabic material made available to him in Latin translations and attempted some critical analysis of its content. However, his own imperfect knowledge and the defective state of European scholarship at the time hampered his work and sometimes blunted the skepticism which he usually brought to the sources and subjects of his historical inquiries. The chapter on Muḥammad and on the beginnings of Islam is still much affected by myths, and in this, more visibly than in the chapters on Rome and on Byzantium, Gibbon gives expression to his own prejudices and purposes and those of the circles in which he moved.

There were several layers of myth and misunderstanding in the portrait of the Prophet as depicted in the literature available to him. Medieval Christian denigration of a rival product had little effect on him. Western scholarship was already in the process of demolishing the grosser errors, and Gibbon would have been the least likely of historians to be influenced by them. The Muslim religious myths enshrined in the traditional biographical literature on which all his sources ultimately rest were more difficult for him to detect, and there are failures of perception and analysis excusable in a historian of the time. Sometimes, indeed, he shows rather less than his usual acumen. Thus, his account of pre-Islamic Arabian religion—"liberty of choice . . . each Arab . . . free to elect or to compose his own private religion"[27]—would be difficult to sustain even in the light of the evidence available in the eighteenth century and is indeed self-evidently absurd. As Gibbon rightly remarked of his approach: "I am ignorant, and I am careless, of the blind mythology of the barbarians."[28]

Gibbon was, of course, well equipped to recognize the propaganda and counterpropaganda of Catholic, Protestant, Christian, and Deist, and he has some amusing comments to offer on this subject. Where he himself is very clearly affected is by the mythology of the Enlightenment—a vision of Islam which seems to have been initiated in the biography of the Prophet by Boulainvilliers and was widely accepted among the writers of the Enlightenment in various European countries. Europe, it seems, has always needed a myth for purposes of comparison and castigation: Prester John in the Middle Ages, the United States in the nineteenth century, the Soviet Union in the early twentieth. The eighteenth-century Enlightenment had two ideal prototypes, the noble savage and the wise and urbane Oriental. There was some competition for the latter role. For a while the Chinese, held up as a model of moral virtue by the Jesuits and of secular tolerance by the philosophers, filled it to perfection in the Western intellectual shadow play. Then disillusionment set in, and was worsened by the reports of returning travelers whose perceptions of China were shaped by neither Jesuitry nor philosophy, but by experience. By the time Gibbon began to write, there was a vacancy for an Oriental myth. Islam was in many ways suitable. While China was ceasing to impress, Islam no longer terrified, and it had the further advantage of being the intimate enemy of the church.

The mythopoeic process began with an attempt by historians to correct the negative stereotypes of the Middle Ages and to recognize the contributions of Islamic civilization to mankind. It developed into a portrait of Muḥammad as a wise and tolerant lawgiver, the founder of rational, undogmatic, priest-free religion and society.

The honor and reputation of Islam and its founder were protected in Europe neither by social pressure nor by legal sanction, and they thus served as an admirable vehicle for anti-religious and anti-Christian polemic. Gibbon occasionally accomplishes this purpose by attacking Islam while meaning Christianity, more frequently by praising Islam as an oblique criticism of Christian usage, belief, and practice. Much of his praise would not be acceptable in a Muslim country.

There are several lessons which he tries to draw from the biography of the Prophet and the subsequent history of Islam. One of these is that Islam is a religion with a purely human founder—a point also made by Boulainvilliers. This is, of course, an argument against the Christian doctrine of the divinity of Christ as the Son of God and all that is connected with it. In this, Gibbon and his predecessors in the Enlightenment did rely on something genuinely Islamic, and indeed showed some perspicacity in going back beyond the later and legendary accretions of the Muslim biographies of the Prophet to the authentic historical figure of Muḥammad and to the earliest Islamic tradition, which insists that Muḥammad, though a Prophet and a Messenger of God, was no more than a human being, mortal like others.

Another point which Gibbon is at some pains to impress upon his readers is the stability and permanence of the Islamic faith in the form in which it was founded by the Prophet—that is to say, it is free from subsequent and local accretions such as have overlaid the message of Christ, and retains its pristine content and character. In this, of course, he was greatly mistaken, as he could have ascertained by some attention to Islam as practiced in various parts of the Islamic world in his own day.

Linked with this is his insistence that Islam is a faith with few dogmas and without priesthood or church and, therefore, by implication much freer and better than Christianity, which is heavily burdened with all these. This is slightly better than a half truth. There is indeed no priesthood in the sacerdotal sense—no priestly ordination, office, or mediation; there is, however, a priesthood in the sociological sense, an order of professional men of religion, and these have played a part which, though entirely different from that of the Christian churches, is nevertheless of great importance in the history of Islam. His further argument that Islam has been free from schism and strife is exaggerated. Sectarian strife in Islam never reached the degree of ferocity which became normal in Christendom, but differences existed, and men were ready to kill and die, to suffer and persecute because of them. "The Metaphysical questions on the attributes of God and the liberty of man," says Gibbon,

> have been agitated in the schools of the Mahometans as well as in those of the Christians; but among the former they have never engaged the passions of the people or disturbed the tranquillity of the state. The cause of this important difference may be found in the separation or union of the regal and sacerdotal characters.[29]

This assessment is so manifestly wrong as to place its author almost on a par with the Persian letter-writers and Turkish spies who enlightened the West about its defects, rather than with serious historians of the East.

On the religious doctrines of Islam, Gibbon has little to say, since it was only in its public and social aspects that religion was of any interest to him. The Islamic creed, that there is no God but God and that Muḥammad is his Apostle, he describes as "compounded of an eternal truth and a necessary fiction"—a recognizable echo of Boulainvilliers's "mais il falloit être prophète, ou passer pour tel à quelque prix que ce pût être."[30] The same tolerant acceptance of the necessity of the fiction informs his other comments and asides on the sincerity of the Prophet:

> From his earliest youth Mahomet was addicted to religious contemplation; each year, during the month of Ramadan, he withdrew from the world and from the arms of Cadijah [his wife]; in the cave of Hera, three miles from Mecca, he consulted the spirit of fraud or enthusiasm, whose abode is not in the heavens, but in the mind of the prophet.[31]

A later passage is somewhat more severe:

> In the spirit of enthusiasm or vanity, the prophet rests the truth of his mission on the merit of his book, audaciously challenges both men and angels to imitate the beauties of a single page, and presumes to assert that God alone could dictate this incomparable performance.... The harmony and copiousness of style will not reach, in a version, the European infidel; he will peruse, with impatience, the endless incoherent rhapsody of fable, and precept, and declamation, which seldom excites a sentiment or an idea, which sometimes crawls in the dust and is sometimes lost in the clouds....[32]

On the other hand, "the Mohometan religion is destitute of priesthood or sacrifice; and the independent spirit of fanaticism looks down with contempt on the ministers and slaves of superstition."[33] The final version is moderately severe:

> It may perhaps be expected that I should balance his faults and virtues, that I should decide whether the title of enthusiast or impostor most properly belongs to that extraordinary man.... From enthusiasm to imposture the step is perilous and slippery; the daemon of Socrates affords a memorable instance, how a wise man may deceive himself, how a good man may deceive others, how the conscience may slumber in a mixed and middle state between self-illusion and voluntary fraud. Charity may believe that the original motives of Mahomet were those of pure and genuine benevolence; but a human missionary is incapable of cherishing the obstinate unbelievers who reject his claims....[34]

On the subject of tolerance, Gibbon seems undecided. At the beginning of his chapter on the rise of Islam, he describes how "Mahomet," "with the sword in one hand and the Koran in the other, erected his throne on the ruins of Christianity and of Rome."[35] "Mahomet," of course, is here used metonymically for the empire of the Caliphs. Even so, the statement is remarkably inaccurate. Both Christianity and Rome survived the advent of Islam; the Qur'ān did not become a book until some time after Muḥammad's death; only a left-handed swordsman could brandish both, since no Muslim would hold the sacred book in the hand reserved for unclean purposes—and most important of all, there was a third choice, the payment of tribute and acceptance of Muslim rule.[36]

Gibbon's influence on the Western perception of the Prophet, Islam, and their place in history was enormous. From recondite and learned books, most of them in Latin and little known outside the narrow world of clerics and scholars, he was able to present a picture of the Prophet and the rise of Islam that was clear, elegant, and above all convincing. Most important of all was that unlike previous writers, including the Arabists, he saw the rise of Islam not as something separate and isolated, nor as a regrettable aberration from the onward march of the Church, but as a part of human history, to be understood against the background of Rome and Persia, in the light of Judaism and Christianity, and in complex interplay with Byzantium, Asia, and Europe.

6

The Question of Orientalism

Imagine a situation in which a group of patriots and radicals from Greece decides that the profession of classical studies is insulting to the great heritage of Hellas and that those engaged in these studies, known as classicists, are the latest manifestation of a deep and evil conspiracy, incubated for centuries, hatched in Western Europe, fledged in America, the purpose of which is to denigrate the Greek achievement and subjugate the Greek lands and peoples. In this perspective, the entire European tradition of classical studies—largely the creation of French romantics, British colonial governors (of Cyprus, of course), and poets, professors, and proconsuls from both countries—is a long-standing insult to the honor and integrity of Hellas and a threat to its future. The poison has spread from Europe to the United States, where the teaching of Greek history, language, and literature in the universities is dominated by the evil race of classicists—men and women who are not of Greek origin, who have no sympathy for Greek causes, and who, under a false mask of dispassionate scholarship, strive to keep the Greek people in a state of permanent subordination.

The time has come to save Greece from the classicists and bring the whole pernicious tradition of classical scholarship to an end. Only Greeks are truly able to teach and write on Greek history and culture from remote antiquity to the present day; only Greeks are genuinely competent to direct and conduct programs of academic studies in these fields. Some non-Greeks may be permitted to join in this great endeavor provided that they give convincing evidence of their competence, as, for example, by campaigning for the Greek cause in Cyprus, by demonstrating their ill will to the Turks, by offering a pinch of incense to the currently reigning Greek gods, and by adopting whatever may be the latest fashionable ideology in Greek intellectual circles.

Non-Greeks who will not or cannot meet these requirements are obviously hostile and therefore not equipped to teach Greek studies in a fair and reasonable manner. They must not be permitted to hide behind the mask of classicism but must be revealed for what they are—Turk-lovers, enemies and exploiters of the Greek people, and opponents of the Greek cause. Those already established in academic circles must be discredited by abuse and thus neutralized; at the same time steps must be taken to ensure Greek or pro-Greek control of university centers and departments of Greek studies and thus, by a kind of academic prophylaxis, prevent the emergence of any further classical scholars or scholarship. In the meantime the very name of classicist must be transformed into a term of abuse.

Stated in terms of classics and Greek, the picture is absurd. But if for classicist we substitute "Orientalist," with the appropriate accompanying changes, this amusing fantasy becomes an alarming reality. For some years now a hue and cry has been raised against Orientalists in American and to a lesser extent European universities, and the term "Orientalism" has been emptied of its previous content and given an entirely new one—that of unsympathetic or hostile treatment of Oriental peoples. For that matter, even the terms "unsympathetic" and "hostile" have been redefined to mean not supportive of currently fashionable creeds or causes.

Take the case of V. S. Naipaul, author of a remarkable account of a tour of Muslim countries. Mr. Naipaul is not a professor but a novelist—one of the most gifted of our time. He is not a European, but a West Indian of East Indian origin. His book about modern Islam is not a work of scholarship and makes no pretense of being such. It is the result of close observation by a professional observer of the human predicament. It is occasionally mistaken, often devastatingly accurate, and above all compassionate. Mr. Naipaul has a keen eye for the absurdities of human behavior, in Muslim lands as elsewhere. At the same time he is moved by deep sympathy and understanding for both the anger and the suffering of the people whose absurdities he so faithfully depicts.

But such compassion is not a quality appreciated or even recognized by the grinders of political or ideological axes. Mr. Naipaul would not toe the line; he would not join in the praise of Islamic radical leaders and the abuse of those whom they oppose. Therefore, he is an Orientalist—a term applied to him even by brainwashed university students who ought to know better.

The ultimate absurdity was reached in a letter to the *New York Times,*[1] the writer of which is described as "a doctoral candidate in history and Near East studies" at a major university. Writing in protest against a favorable reference to Lord Curzon and his book on Iran, the letter writer describes him as "the very symbol of British Orientalist thinking" and observes that "even in his own time [he] was considered by Iranian and Western democrats alike to have played a principal part in the tragic fate of the people of that country." The writer of the letter then goes on to speak approvingly of E. G. Browne, whose *The Persian Revolution,* published in 1910, was "a very different book." In it "he spoke . . . of the accomplishments of the revolution" and revealed the sinister role of Lord Curzon.

There is no doubt about Lord Curzon's role as a doughty defender of British imperial interests or about Professor Browne's anti-imperialist and pro-Iranian stance. What is curious, to say the least, is that Lord Curzon, who in the course of a long and active political and imperial career rose to be viceroy of India and at a later date secretary of state for foreign affairs, is designated as "the very symbol of British Orientalist thinking," whereas E. G. Browne, professor of Arabic at Cambridge and one of the leading Orientalists of his day in England and indeed in Europe, is acclaimed for his presumed anti-Orientalism. Both the noble lord and the learned professor would surely have been surprised at these designations. To find a precedent for such high-handed treatment of language, one must go back to Humpty Dumpty, who, it will be recalled, when challenged on his use of "glory" to mean "a nice knock-down argument," replied: "When *I* use a word . . . it means just what I choose it to mean, neither more nor less." This use of the term Orientalism is clearly a perversion of language. It is, however, sadly accurate, since it reflects a by-now widespread perversion of truth.

What, then, is Orientalism? What did the word mean before it was poisoned by the kind of intellectual pollution that in our time has made so many previously useful words unfit for use in rational discourse? In the past, Orientalism was used mainly in two senses. One is a school of painting—that of a group of artists, mostly from western Europe, who visited the Middle East and North Africa and depicted what they saw or imagined, sometimes in a rather romantic and extravagant manner, sometimes even pornographic. The second, and more common, meaning, unconnected with the first, has hitherto been a branch of scholarship. The word, and the academic discipline which it denotes, dates from the great expansion of scholarship in western Europe from the time of the Renaissance onward. There were Hellenists who studied Greek, Latinists who studied Latin, Hebraists who studied Hebrew; the first two groups were sometimes called classicists, the third Orientalists. In due course they turned their attention to other languages.

Basically these early scholars were philologists concerned with the recovery, study, publication, and interpretation of texts. This was the first and most essential task that had to be undertaken before the serious study of such other matters as philosophy, theology, literature, and history became possible. The term "Orientalist" was not at that time as vague and imprecise as it appears now. Since theology was considered unsuited to non-Christian religions, the term applied to only one discipline, philology. In the early stages there was only one region, that which we now call the Middle East—the only part of the Orient with which Europeans could claim any real acquaintance.

Since its earliest recorded history, Europe has been looking at its neighbors in the East sometimes with fear, sometimes with greed, sometimes with curiosity, and sometimes with disquiet. For centuries, indeed for millennia, relations between the two have shown a pattern of conquest and reconquest, attack and counterattack. The great kings of Persia threatened and invaded the cities of Greece; they were in turn conquered by Alexander. The Arabs wrested Syria and Palestine, Egypt and North Africa, Sicily, Spain, and Portugal from Christendom; they lost their European acquisitions to the Reconquest, but Muslim arms were able to save the rest from the counterattack of the Crusaders. The Tatars conquered Russia, and the Ottoman Turks took Constantinople from the Byzantines and twice advanced as far as Vienna before beginning the long retreat that politicians and, later, historians called "the Eastern question." And as the Arabs departed from southwestern Europe and the Tatars and Turks from eastern and southeastern Europe, they were followed by their triumphant former subjects, who now embarked on their own still-vaster expansion into the Asian and African homelands of their former conquerors.

The problems presented by Ottoman weakness and withdrawal were called "the Eastern question" because for most Europeans the source of danger and invasion, from the first Persian vanguard to the last Ottoman rear guard, had been the area immediately to the east of Europe. This was *the* East, and no more specific definition was needed, since no other East was known. The Eastern question, in French *la question orientale,* was the question posed by Europe's immediate neighbor the Ottoman Empire, whether through the menace of its strength or, later, the temptation of its weakness. In French, as generally in European usage, the region to which the terms "Orient" and "Oriental" are applied begins in the eastern Mediterranean. In American usage the terms "Orient" and "Oriental" have come to be applied almost exclusively to far more distant regions, of which ancient and medieval Europe had very little knowledge or even awareness.

For the ancient Greeks, Asia meant the shore of the Aegean Sea opposite them. When they became aware of a more vast and remote Asia looming beyond, they named the immediate neighborhood Asia Minor. In the same way, when a greater, stranger, richer, and more distant East occupied the attention of Europeans, they began in time to speak of the old, familiar neighboring East by such terms as "Near" and "Middle," to distinguish it from what lay beyond. The Portuguese and the Dutch, the English and the French followed one another around the Cape of Good Hope to the fabulous lands of India and Southeast Asia; some penetrated even as far as China and Japan. European merchants brought back goods that transformed the economy and the social habits of the West. Scholars and missionaries brought back texts that philologists examined with the self-same methods that they had developed for Latin and Greek, Hebrew and Arabic.

With the progress of both exploration and scholarship, the term "Orientalist" became increasingly unsatisfactory. Students of the Orient were no longer engaged in a single discipline but were branching out into several others. At the same time the area that they were studying, the so-called

Orient, was seen to extend far beyond the Middle Eastern lands on which European attention had hitherto been concentrated and to include the vast and remote civilizations of India and China. There was a growing tendency among scholars and in university departments concerned with these studies to use more precise labels. Scholars took to calling themselves philologists, historians, etc., dealing with Oriental topics. And in relation to these topics they began to use such terms as "Sinologist" and "Indologist," "Iranist" and "Arabist," to give a closer and more specific definition to the area and topic of their study.

Incidentally, the last-named term, "Arabist," has also gone through a process of re-semanticization. In England, in the past, the word "Arabist" was normally used in the same way as "Iranist" or "Hispanist" or "Germanist"—to denote a scholar professionally concerned with the language, history, or culture of a particular land and people. In the United States, it has come to mean a specialist in dealings with Arabs, particularly in government and commerce. For some, though not all, it also means an advocate of Arab causes. This is another example of word pollution, which has deprived us of the use of a necessary term. The term "Hispanist" does not mean an apologist for Central American tyrants or terrorists, an admirer of bullfighters, an observer or practitioner of Spanish affairs, or a purveyor of bananas. It means a scholar with a good knowledge of Spanish, specializing in some field of Spanish or Latin American history or culture. The word "Arabist" ought to be used in the same way. This, however, is probably a lost cause, and some other term will have to be found. Some have even suggested the word "Arabologist," on the analogy of "Sinologist," "Indologist," and "Turcologist." This term might bring some gain in precision but also a considerable loss of elegance. A not unworthy group of scholars, engaged in the study of a truly great civilization, deserves a better label.

The term "Orientalist" is by now also polluted beyond salvation, but this is less important in that the word had already lost its value and had been in fact abandoned by those who previously bore it. This abandonment was given formal expression at the Twenty-ninth International Congress of Orientalists, which met in Paris in the summer of 1973. This was the hundredth anniversary of the First International Congress of Orientalists convened in the same city, and it seemed a good occasion to reconsider the nature and functions of the congress. It soon became clear that there was a consensus in favor of dropping this label—some indeed wanted to go further and bring the series of congresses to an end on the grounds that the profession as such had ceased to exist and the congress had therefore outlived its purpose. The normal will to survive of institutions was strong enough to prevent the dissolution of the congress. The movement to abolish the term "Orientalist" was, however, successful.

The attack came from two sides. On the one hand there were those who had hitherto been called Orientalists and who were increasingly dissatisfied with a term that indicated neither the discipline in which they were engaged nor the region with which they were concerned. They were reinforced by scholars from Asian countries who pointed to the absurdity of applying such a term as "Orientalist" to an Indian studying the history or culture of India. They made the further point that the term was somehow insulting to Orientals in that it made them appear as the objects of study rather than as participants.

The strongest case for the retention of the old term was made by the Soviet delegation, led by the late Babajan Ghafurov, director of the Institute of Orientalism in Moscow and himself a Soviet Oriental from the republic of Tajikistan. This term, said Ghafurov, had served us well for more than a century. Why should we now abandon a word that conveniently designates the work we do and that was borne with pride by our teachers and their teachers for many generations back? Ghafurov was not entirely pleased with the comment of a British delegate who praised him for his able statement of the conservative point of view. In the vote, despite the support of the East European Orientalists who unanimously agreed with the Soviet delegate, Ghafurov was defeated, and the term "Orientalist" was formally abolished. In its place the congress agreed to call itself the "International Congress of Human Sciences in Asia and North Africa."

The term "Orientalist" was thus abolished by the accredited Orientalists, and thrown on the garbage heap of history. But garbage heaps are not safe places. The words "Orientalist" and "Orientalism," discarded as useless by scholars, were retrieved and reconditioned for a different purpose, as terms of polemical abuse.

The attack on the Orientalists—more specifically on Western Arabists and Islamicists—was not in fact new in the Muslim world. It had gone through several earlier phases, in which different interests and motives were at work. One of the first outbreaks in the postwar period had a curious origin. It was connected with the initiation of the second edition of *The Encyclopedia of Islam,* a major project of Orientalism in the field of Islamic studies. The first edition had been published simultaneously in three languages—English, French, and German—with the participation of scholars drawn from these and many other countries. It took almost thirty years and was completed in 1938. The second edition, begun in 1950, was published in English and French only and without a German member on the international editorial board.

The Muslim attack was launched from Karachi, the capital of the newly created Islamic republic of Pakistan, and concentrated on two points, the lack of a German edition and editor and the presence on the editorial board of a French Jew, the late E. Lévi-Provençal. The priority, indeed the presence, of the first complaint seemed a little odd for Karachi, and was clarified when in due course it emerged that the organizer of this particular agitation was a gentleman described as "the *imam* of the congregation of German Muslims in West Pakistan," with some assistance from a still unreconstructed German diplomat who had just been posted there, and had taken this task upon himself.[2]

The episode was of brief duration and aroused no echo or very little echo elsewhere in the Islamic world. Some other campaigns against Orientalists followed, most of them rather more local in their origin. Two themes predominated, the Islamic and the Arab. For some, who defined themselves and their adversaries exclusively in religious terms, Orientalism was a challenge to the Islamic faith. In the early 1960s a professor at Al-Azhar University in Egypt wrote a little tract on Orientalists and the evil things they do.[3] They consist, he said, mainly of missionaries whose aim is to undermine and ultimately destroy Islam in order to establish the paramountcy of the Christian religion. This applies to most of them, except for those who are Jews and whose purpose is equally nefarious. The author lists the Orientalists who are working against Islam and whose baneful influence must be countered. He provides a separate list of really insidious and dangerous scholars against whom particular caution is needed—those who make a specious parade of good will.

These lists include among others the name of the late Philip Hitti of Princeton. The author of the booklet describes him as follows:

> A Christian from Lebanon. . . . One of the most disputatious of the enemies of Islam, who makes a pretense of defending Arab causes in America and is an unofficial adviser of the American State Department on Middle Eastern Affairs.
>
> He always tries to diminish the role of Islam in the creation of human civilization and is unwilling to ascribe any merit to the Muslims. . . . His *History of the Arabs* is full of attacks on Islam and sneers at the Prophet. All of it is spite and venom and hatred. . . .

The late Philip Hitti was a stalwart defender of Arab causes, and his *History* a hymn to Arab glory. This response to it must have come as a shock to him. Similar religious complaints about the Orientalist as missionary, as a sort of Christian fifth columnist, have also appeared in Pakistan and more recently in Iran.

Committed Muslim critics of Orientalism have an intelligible rationale when they view Christian and Jewish writers on Islam as engaged in religious polemic or conversion—indeed, granted their assumptions, their conclusions are virtually inescapable. In their view, the adherent of a religion is necessarily a defender of that religion, and an approach to another religion, by anyone but a prospective convert, can only be undertaken for defense or attack. Traditional Muslim scholars did not normally undertake the study of Christian or Jewish thought or history, and they could see no honorable reason why Christians or Jews should study Islam. Indeed, one of the prescriptions of the *dhimma,* the rules by which Christians and Jews were permitted to practice their religions under Muslim government, forbids them to teach the Qur'ān to their children. Medieval Christians had a similar view. When they began to study Islam and the Islamic scriptures, it was for the double purpose of dissuading Christians from conversion to Islam and persuading Muslims to adopt Christianity. This approach has long since been abandoned in the Christian world, except in a few outposts of religious zeal. It remained for much longer the prevailing perception of interdenominational relations in the Muslim world.

A different approach, expressed in a combination of nationalist and ideological terminology, is to be found among some Arab writers. Curiously, most of those involved are members of the Christian minorities in Arab countries and are themselves resident in Western Europe or the United States. A good example is an article by a Coptic sociologist living in Paris, Anouar Abdel-Malek, published in the UNESCO journal *Diogenes* in 1963, that is, a year or so after the publication of the Cairo pamphlet. In this article, entitled "Orientalism in Crisis," Dr. Abdel-Malek sets forth what became some of the major changes in the indictment of the Orientalists. They are "Europocentric," paying insufficient attention to the scholars, scholarship, methods, and achievements of the Afro-Asian world; they are obsessed with the past and do not show sufficient interest in the recent history of the "Oriental" peoples (more recent critics complain of the exact opposite); they pay insufficient attention to the insights afforded by social science and particularly Marxist methodology.

Dr. Abdel-Malek's article is written with obvious emotion and is the expression of passionately held convictions. It remains, however, within the limits of scholarly debate and is obviously based on a careful, even if not sympathetic, study of Orientalist writings. He is even prepared to concede that Orientalism may not be inherently evil and that some Orientalists may themselves be victims.

A new theme was adumbrated in an article published in a Beirut magazine in June 1974 and written by a professor teaching in an American university. One or two quotations may illustrate the line:

> The Zionist scholarly hegemony in Arabic studies [in the United States] had a clear effect in controlling the publication of studies, periodicals, as well as professional associations. These [Zionist scholars] published a great number of books and studies which impress the uninitiated as being strictly scientific but which in fact distort Arab history and realities and are detrimental to the Arab struggle for liberation. They masquerade in scientific guise in order to dispatch spies and agents of American and Israeli security apparatuses, whose duty is to conduct field studies all over the Arab states. . . . These are astonishing facts of which Arab officials should keep track if they are to distinguish between legitimate and honest research conducted by some American professors on the one hand, and that conducted by students and professors motivated by American security and hegemony on the other. These officials should not allow Arab wealth to support American and Israeli interests. They should carefully

> and honestly scrutinize every appeal for material or for moral support. They should never allow Arab money to be used for weakening, defaming, or compromising the Arabs.[4]

This is a key text, which may help us considerably to understand the politics of academic development in Middle Eastern studies in the period that followed.

Another attack against "the Orientalists" came from a group of Marxists. Their polemics reveal several oddities. One is the assumption that there is an Orientalist conception or line to which all Orientalists adhere—an illusion which even the most superficial acquaintance with the writings of Orientalists should suffice to dispel. Most of these critics are not themselves Orientalists. This does not mean that they reject the Orientalist doctrine or orthodoxy, which in fact does not exist; it means that they do not possess the Orientalist skills, which are exercised with little difference by both Marxist and non-Marxist Orientalists. Most serious Marxist writing on Middle Eastern history is the work either of Marxists who are themselves Orientalists, trained in the same methods and subject to the same disciplines as their non-Marxist colleagues, or of authors who rely on the writings of Orientalist scholars, both Marxist and non-Marxist, for the materials on which they base their analyses and conclusions.

A good example of this is Perry Anderson's perceptive book *The Lineages of the Absolutist State*. Though interesting and thoughtful, it bases its treatment of Middle Eastern and in general Islamic matters exclusively on secondary sources, on the works of the Orientalists. There is no other way—that is, unless of course the scholars are willing to take the trouble to acquire the necessary skills and read the primary sources in Arabic, Persian, Turkish, and other languages. But this, besides being difficult and time-consuming, would have the further disadvantage that the scholars themselves would then be exposed to the charge of Orientalism. Marxist scholars like Maxime Rodinson in France and I. P. Petrushevsky in Russia have made major contributions to Middle Eastern history which are recognized and accepted even by those who do not share their ideological commitments or political allegiances. They in turn, in their work, show far more respect for fellow Orientalists of other persuasions than for fellow Marxists with other conceptions of scholarship.

The main exponent of anti-Orientalism in the United States has for some time past been Edward Said, whose book *Orientalism*, first published in 1978, was heralded by a series of book reviews, articles, and public statements. This is a book with a thesis—that "Orientalism derives from a particular closeness experienced between Britain and France and the Orient, which until the early nineteenth century had really meant only India and the Bible lands" (p. 4). To prove this point, Mr. Said makes a number of very arbitrary decisions. His Orient is reduced to the Middle East, and his Middle East to a part of the Arab world. By eliminating Turkish and Persian studies on the one hand and Semitic studies on the other, he isolates Arabic studies from both their historical and philological contexts. The dimensions of Orientalism in time and space are similarly restricted.

To prove his thesis, Mr. Said rearranges both the geography and the history of Orientalism and, in particular, places the main development of Arabic studies in Britain and France and dates them after the British and French expansion in the Arab world. In fact, these studies were well established in Britain and France long before even the erroneously early date that he assigns to British and French expansion—and at no time before or after the imperial age did their contribution, in range, depth, or standard, match the achievement of the great centers of Oriental studies in Germany and neighboring countries. Indeed, any history or theory of Arabic studies in Europe without the Germans makes as much sense as would a history or theory of European music or philosophy with the same omission.

Mr. Said attempts to justify this procedure:

> I believe that the sheer quality, consistency, and mass of British, French, and American writing on the Orient lifts it above the doubtless crucial work done in Germany, Italy, Russia, and elsewhere. But I think it is also true that the major steps in Oriental scholarship were first taken in either Britain and France [sic], then elaborated upon by Germans. . . . What German Oriental scholarship did was to refine and elaborate techniques whose application was to texts, myths, ideas, and languages almost literally gathered from the Orient by imperial Britain and France. (pp. 17–18, 19)

It is difficult to see what the last sentence means. Texts, in the sense of manuscripts and other written materials, were certainly acquired in the Middle East by Western visitors. But the collections in Germany, Austria, and elsewhere are no less important than those of "imperial Britain and France." How precisely does one "gather" a language, literally or otherwise? The implication would seem to be that by learning Arabic, Englishmen and Frenchmen were committing some kind of offense. The Germans—accessories after the fact—could not begin to do their work of "refinement and elaboration" on these languages until the British and the French had first seized them; the Arabs, from whom these languages were misappropriated, along with myths and ideas (whatever that may mean), were correspondingly deprived.

The whole passage is not merely false but absurd. It reveals a disquieting lack of knowledge of what scholars do and what scholarship is about. The reader's anxiety is not allayed by the frequent occurrence of stronger synonyms such as "appropriate," "accumulate," "wrench," "ransack," and even "rape" to describe the growth of knowledge in the West about the East. For Mr. Said, it would seem, scholarship and science are commodities which exist in finite quantities; the West has grabbed an unfair share of these as well as other resources, leaving the East not only impoverished but also unscholarly and unscientific. Apart from embodying a hitherto unknown theory of knowledge, Mr. Said expresses a contempt for modern Arab scholarly achievement worse than anything that he attributes to his demonic Orientalists.

Anti-Orientalism is essentially an epistemology—concerned, in the words of the Oxford English Dictionary, with "the theory or science of the method or grounds of knowledge." In this sense it should deal with facts and not, so one would assume, with fantasy or invention. One of the most puzzling features of Mr. Said's *Orientalism* is precisely the idiosyncratic way, at once high-handed and inventive, in which he treats the facts on which it purports to be based. In his perception, the Orientalist was the agent and instrument of the imperialist, and his interest in knowledge was as a source of power. The Arabic scholar, along with the soldier, the trader, and the imperial civil servant, had a common purpose—to penetrate, subjugate, dominate, and exploit. To sustain this interpretation, Mr. Said presents a revisionist view of the growth of Arabic studies in Britain and France, the growth of British and French power in the Arab lands, and the connections between the two.

When I first read *Orientalism*, the narrative substratum—the numerous references and allusions to both sequences of events and the relationship among them—left me frankly mystified. Had Mr. Said devised one of those alternative universes beloved of science fiction writers? It seemed difficult at the time to find any other explanation of his maltreatment of several centuries of intellectual and general history. Some of the misstatements have no discernible polemic purpose and may be due to honest ignorance, as, for example, the belief that Muslim armies conquered Turkey before they conquered North Africa (p. 59). This would be rather like putting the English Civil War before the Norman Conquest. Although no doubt irrelevant to the main issue, this procedure would not inspire confidence in the writer's ability to evaluate work on English history. A similar approach, this time to comparative philology, is revealed in another passage in which the German philosopher Friedrich Schlegel is chided because even after "he had practically renounced his Orientalism, he still held that Sanskrit and Persian on the one hand and Greek and German on the other had more affinities with each other than with the Semitic, Chinese, American or African languages" (p. 98).

Even more remarkable is Mr. Said's transmutation of events to fit his thesis: "Britain and France dominated the Eastern Mediterranean from about the end of the seventeenth century on [*sic*]" (p. 17)—that is, when the Ottoman Turks who ruled the eastern Mediterranean were just leaving Austria and Hungary and when British and French merchants and travelers could visit the Arab lands only by permission of the sultan. The postdating of Arabic studies in England and France and the relegation of German scholarship to a secondary role are equally necessary to Mr. Said's thesis—and equally false.

The mystery of Mr. Said's alternative universe was not solved for me until some years later when for the first time I read a remarkable book by a French scholar, Raymond Schwab, entitled *La Renaissance orientale*.[5]

This book is not, as an unwary bibliographer might assume, a discussion of some revival of learning in the Far East. Schwab, a French poet and man of letters who died in 1956, uses the word "Renaissance" in its original sense as a revival of learning in Europe. The Orient of which he speaks is primarily India, with some extension both east and west. In the Middle East he has little to say about the European study of Islam, but he does pay some attention to the exploration of the ancient Middle East, the excavation of its buried monuments, the decipherment of its forgotten scripts, and the recovery of its lost languages by Western scholars.

From the Middle East and more especially from Iran, Schwab's trail of discovery led toward India and ultimately beyond. His book deals with two major and related themes. The first is the process of discovery itself, and Schwab tells the fascinating story of how successive scholars—first Englishmen and Frenchmen who had unique opportunities to study India firsthand and then others, above all Germans, who devoted their lives to building up a new corpus of knowledge concerning the languages, cultures, and religions of India. The second, and in the context of his work the more important of the two themes, is the way in which this new material from India became part of the European intellectual tradition. Many fascinating connections emerged, among them Hindu pantheism and the German philosophers, Sanskrit philology and the Aryan myth, the impact of Buddhism on Emerson and Thoreau, and the Indian component in the Romantic revival. Schwab's immense literary erudition and profound cultural insight enabled him to illustrate with many examples how the texts, translations, and studies published by European Orientalists reached and influenced writers as diverse as Goethe, Lamartine, Vigny, Wagner, Whitman, and Tolstoy. The same European Indologists also had some impact in India, but that is another story.

Orientalism and the ensuing wave of anti-Orientalism are obviously deeply influenced by a reading of Schwab's book, which is frequently and admiringly cited. The otherwise mystifying schema of Arabic studies in the West as seen by Mr. Said becomes intelligible, though not of course acceptable, when one compares it with Schwab, whose framework has been taken over and applied to another region and another purpose.

This change of purpose, like any other such argument, is debatable, but the change of region reduces the argument to absurdity. Between the development of Indic and Islamic studies in Europe, there is a world of difference. India had never invaded or even remotely threatened any part of Europe. The Western study of India came at a relatively late stage, when Europe was powerful and expanding and a weakened India was falling under foreign control. The recovery of texts was indeed made possible by Europe's commercial and ultimately military expansion into South and Southeast Asia.

The study of Islam in Europe, in contrast, began in the High Middle Ages and was concerned not with a conquered but a conquering world. Insofar as Islamic studies in medieval Europe had a practical purpose, it was defensive and not aggressive: the defense of a beleaguered Christendom against the Saracen, the Turk, and the Tatar. In the age of European expansion from the sixteenth century onward, a practical interest in the Middle East would have been better served by paying attention not to Arabic, least of all to classical Arabic, but to Turkish, at that time the language of government in all Arab countries east of Morocco. Those historians who work in archives know that the letters received in London and Paris from the rulers of Algiers, Tunis, and Tripoli, not to speak of the eastern Mediterranean countries, were written not in Arabic but in Ottoman Turkish.

Although the relationship between Europe and the Islamic world was later transformed and in some measure even reversed, it remained profoundly different from the European relationship with India. The processes of discovery were entirely different in their circumstances, their chronological sequence, their geographical distribution in Europe, the attitudes that inspired them, and the results that they achieved. Anglo-French domination in the Fertile Crescent lasted for only a few decades, from the end of the First World War to the aftermath of the Second. Their domination in Arabia, Egypt, and North Africa lasted somewhat longer, but only in Aden and Algeria did foreign rule reach and exceed one hundred years. Even during their period of domination, British and French rule in many of the Arab lands was indirect, mediated through such devices as the mandate and the protectorate. Nowhere in the Arab world was there anything remotely resembling British rule in India in its extent, depth, duration, and enduring effects. Mr. Said, who believes that Egypt was "annexed" by Britain (p. 35), presumes a similar process in the Arab world.[5]

The theme of violent seizure and possession, with sexual overtones, recurs at several points in the book. "What was important in the latter [*sic*] nineteenth century was not *whether* the West had penetrated and possessed the Orient, but rather *how* the British and French felt that they had done it" (p. 211). Or again: "the space of weaker or underdeveloped regions like the Orient was viewed as something inviting French interest, penetration, insemination—in short, colonization. . . . French scholars, administrators, geographers, and commercial agents poured out their exuberant activity onto the fairly supine, feminine Orient" (pp. 219–20). The climax (so to speak) of these projected sexual fantasies occurs in Mr. Said's bravura piece, where he reads an elaborate, hostile, and wholly absurd interpretation into a lexical definition of an Arabic root which I quoted from the classical Arab dictionaries.[6]

The limitations of time, space, and content which Mr. Said imposes on his subject, though they constitute a serious distortion, are no doubt convenient and indeed necessary to his purpose. They are not, however, sufficient to accomplish it. Among the British and French Arabists and Islamicists who are the ostensible subject of his study, many leading figures are either not mentioned at all (Claude Cahen, E. Lévi-Provençal, Henri

Corbin, Marius Canard, Charles Pellat, William and Georges Marçais, William Wright, all of whom made important contributions) or mentioned briefly in passing (R. A. Nicholson, Guy Le Strange, Sir Thomas Arnold, and E. G. Browne). Even for those whom he does cite, Mr. Said makes a remarkably arbitrary choice of works. His common practice indeed is to omit their major contributions to scholarship and instead fasten on minor or occasional writings.

All of this—the arbitrary rearrangement of the historical background and the capricious choice of countries, persons, and writings—still does not suffice for Mr. Said to prove his case, and he is obliged to resort to additional devices. One is the reinterpretation of the passages he cites to an extent out of all reasonable accord with their authors' manifest intentions. Another is to bring into the category of "Orientalist" a whole series of writers—litterateurs like Chateaubriand and Nerval, imperial administrators like Lord Cromer, and others—whose works were no doubt relevant to the formation of Western cultural attitudes but who had nothing to do with the academic tradition of Orientalism which is Mr. Said's main target.

Even that is still not enough, and to make his point Mr. Said finds it necessary to launch a series of startling accusations. Thus in speaking of the late-eighteenth early-nineteenth-century French Orientalist Silvestre de Sacy, Mr. Said remarks that "he ransacked the Oriental archives. . . . What texts he isolated, he then brought back; he doctored them . . ." (p. 127). If these words bear any meaning at all it is that Sacy was somehow at fault in his access to these documents and then committed the crime of tampering with them. This outrageous libel on a great scholar is without a shred of truth.

Another, more general accusation against Orientalists is that their "economic ideas never extended beyond asserting the Oriental's fundamental incapacity for trade, commerce, and economic rationality. In the Islamic field these clichés held good for literally hundreds of years—until Maxime Rodinson's important study *Islam and Capitalism* appeared in 1966" (p. 259). M. Rodinson himself would be the first to recognize the absurdity of this statement, the writer of which had obviously not taken the trouble to acquaint himself with the work of such earlier Orientalists as Adam Mez, J. H. Kramers, W. Björkman, V. Barthold, Thomas Arnold, and many others. All of them dealt with Muslim economic activities; Arnold was an Englishman. Rodinson, incidentally, makes the interesting observation that with some of Mr. Said's analyses and formulations carried to the limit, "one falls into a doctrine altogether similar to the Zhdanovist theory of the two sciences."[7]

The Germans are not the only scholars omitted from Mr. Said's survey. More remarkably, he has also omitted the Russians. Their contribution, though considerable, is less than that of the Germans or even of the British and the French. It could, however, have been very useful to him in another sense, in that Soviet scholarship, particularly in its treatment of the Islamic and other non-European regions of the Soviet Union, comes closest—far more so than any of the British or French scholars whom he condemns—to precisely the kind of tendentious, denigratory writing that Mr. Said so much dislikes in others. Curiously, however, the Russians, even in their most abusive and contemptuous statements about Islam, enjoy total exemption from Mr. Said's strictures.

This omission can hardly be due to ignorance of Russian; such disabilities have not inhibited Mr. Said's treatment of other topics, and in any case summaries of relevant Soviet scholarly works are available in English and French. The political purposes of Mr. Said's book may provide the explanation. Said, it may be recalled, believed that South Yemen was "the only genuinely radical people's democracy in the Middle East."[8] A writer who is capable of taking this self-description at face value is likely to be willing to let Academician S. P. Tolstov, who saw Muḥammad as a shamanistic myth, and Professor E. A. Belayev, who described the Qur'ān as the ideological expression of a slave-owning ruling class, full of slave-owning mentality, slip by without even a slap on the wrist.

One final point, perhaps the most astonishing. Mr. Said's attitude to the Orient, Arab and other, as revealed in his book, is far more negative than that of the most arrogant European imperialist writers whom he condemns. Mr. Said speaks of "books and journals in Arabic (and doubtless in Japanese, various Indian dialects and other Oriental languages) . . ." (p. 322). This contemptuous listing, and especially the assumption that what Indians speak and write are not languages but dialects, would be worthy of an early-nineteenth-century district commissioner.

Even more remarkable is Mr. Said's neglect—or perhaps ignorance—of Arab scholarship and other writings. "No Arab or Islamic scholar can afford to ignore what goes on in scholarly journals, institutes, and universities in the United States and Europe; the converse is not true. For example, there is no major journal of Arab studies published in the Arab world today" (p. 323). The first statement is hardly a reproach; the rest is simply untrue. Mr. Said is apparently unaware of the enormous output of journals, monographs, editions, and other studies being published by universities, academies, learned societies, and other scholarly bodies in many different Arab countries.[9] He is apparently equally unaware of the large and growing literature of self-criticism produced by Arab authors who try to examine some of the failings and weaknesses of Arab society and culture and in so doing make, in a much more acute form, many of the observations for which Mr. Said attacks the Orientalists and for which he accuses them of racism, hostility, and a desire to dominate. He does not even seem to know the considerable body of writing by Arab authors on the subject of Orientalism; at least, he does not mention it.[10]

Despite a predominantly unfavorable response among reviewers in learned journals (with the curious exception of *The Journal of the American Oriental Society,* the house organ of American Orientalists), Said's *Orientalism* has had a considerable impact.

The success of this book and the ideas or, to be more precise, the attitudes that it expresses, in spite of its science fiction history and its lexical Humpty-Dumptyism, requires some explanation. One reason is certainly its anti-Westernism—the profound hostility to the West but more particularly the liberal and democratic West, since Germany is accorded a partial and Russia a total exemption. This responds well to the sentiments of those in the West, and especially in the United States, who condemn their country as the source of all the evil in the world as arrogantly and absurdly as their forbears acclaimed it as the source of all good. Similarly, the book appeals by its use of the ideas and still more of the language of currently fashionable literary, philosophical, and political theories. It meets the world's growing need for simplification by reducing all the complex national, cultural, religious, social, and economic problems of the Arab world to a single grievance directed against a small group of easily identified and immediately recognizable malefactors. There is, as anyone who has browsed in a college bookshop knows, a broad market for simplified versions of complex problems. Precisely this kind of simplification, so attractive to Western readers, has evoked the most serious critique of anti-Orientalism among Arab writers and thinkers who feel that the best interests of their society and the solving of its genuine problems cannot be served by the blurring of issues and the naming of scapegoats.

Some of those who have adopted anti-Orientalist philosophies have themselves been competent professional Orientalists with a mastery of the skills of their trade. But there have been others for whom the new epistemology was a welcome relief from drudgery, and some part of the book's attraction may be attributed to its harsh strictures on textual and philological scholarship. These bring reassurance and even encouragement to some who wish to make a career of studying the Orient but have either failed or not attempted to master its languages.

There are several major languages in the Middle Eastern area, and all of them are difficult. All but one—modern Turkish—are written in scripts other than the Latin script. All are shaped by cultural traditions different from those of Europe and North America. The study of these languages is an arduous task. To learn Arabic even adequately, let alone well, can take as much time and effort as to learn several European languages. Inevitably, therefore, the study of Arabic and other Middle Eastern languages has become a specialized field in itself. In the past, those who engaged in this field of specialization usually lacked either the time or the inclination to equip themselves in the social science or, to a lesser extent, the historical disciplines. Historians, whose work is mostly based on written evidence, have been more ready to learn languages and acquire as much of the philological technique as is necessary for understanding their sources. But social scientists from outside the area have not always troubled to learn its languages.

Naturally both groups, sociologists and philologists, have tended to decry what they do not possess. The hard-core philologist is an almost extinct species; those who believe that social, economic, political, and even literary theory may not only inform but also replace the study of sources continue to flourish. One of them, in a recent review of a work on Middle Eastern history, spoke with contempt of Orientalists who try to understand the history of another civilization by "the minute examination of difficult texts." In addition to indicating a well-attested preference for the superficial examination of easy texts, the remark illustrates a profound need to which anti-Orientalism provides a welcome relief. According to a currently fashionable epistemological view, absolute truth is either nonexistent or unattainable. Therefore, truth doesn't matter; facts don't matter. All discourse is a manifestation of a power relationship, and all knowledge is slanted. Therefore, accuracy doesn't matter; evidence doesn't matter. All that matters is the attitude—the motives and purposes—of the user of knowledge, and this may be simply claimed for oneself or imputed to another. In imputing motives, the irrelevance of truth, facts, evidence, and even plausibility is a great help. The mere assertion suffices. The same rules apply to claiming a motive; goodwill can be established quickly and easily by appropriate political support. This is demonstrated in *Orientalism,* in which scholars whose methods and procedures are indistinguishable by any scholarly or methodological criterion are divided into sheep and goats according to their support or lack of support for Arab causes. Such support, especially when buttressed by approved literary or social theories, can more than compensate for any lack of linguistic or historical knowledge.

It does not seem to have occurred to those who hold such views that their attitudes are profoundly condescending to the Arabs and other non-Western peoples. Who, after all, would pretend that one could do serious scholarly work on France without French, on Germany without German, even on Sweden without Swedish? Or that the effort to learn these languages is commonly inspired by hostile motives?

The response to anti-Orientalism in the Arab world raises different and, in the last analysis, more interesting and more important questions.

Orientalists in Europe and America have dealt with all the cultures of Asia—China and Japan, India and Indonesia; and in the Middle East their studies are by no means limited to the Arabs but have included the Turks and Persians as well as the ancient cultures of the region. There is a radical, one might almost say a complete, difference in the attitudes of virtually all these other peoples toward the scholars who study them from outside. The Chinese, the Indians, and the rest are not always admiring of the Orientalists who deal with them, and are sometimes critical, on scholarly grounds, of their work. Sometimes they simply ignore them; sometimes they regard them with a kind of tolerant amusement; sometimes they accept them in the way that Greek scholars have accepted the Hellenists. The violent and vituperative attack on Orientalists is limited—apart from the Muslim reaction against the perceived threat from a rival faith—to one group and one group only among the peoples whom the Orientalists have studied, namely, the Arabs. This raises the interesting question of whether the Arabs differ significantly from other Asian and African peoples or whether the Arabic specialists differ in some significant way from other Orientalists.

Some help in answering this question may be found in another important fact—that this hostility to Orientalists is by no means universal or even dominant in Arab countries. Many of the Orientalists most violently attacked by the Saidian and related schools have taught generations of Arab students and have been translated and published in Arab countries.[11] Arab scholars working in the various fields with which the Orientalists have been concerned—history, literature, language, philosophy, and others—have made normal use of Orientalist publications. They have contributed extensively to Orientalist journals and have participated generally in Orientalist symposia, colloquia, and other international activities. Arab scholars have often differed from Orientalists in their findings and judgments, just as Arab scholars and Orientalist scholars have differed among themselves. These have, for the most part, been scholarly differences, not clashes of ethnic or ideological allegiances, and they have been discussed within the norms and courtesies of scholarly debate. The hue and cry against the Orientalists was raised not by scholarly colleagues interested in their work and competent to evaluate it but from quite other sources.

Significantly, the critique of the Orientalists has evoked a powerful and increasing countercritique from Arab writers. Although for the most part they share the disenchantment of the anti-Orientalists with Western civilization and their resentment at what the West has done in the Arab lands, these Arab writers are appalled by the smug, self-satisfied, and naively simplistic explanations that the critics offer of the disasters that the Arab world has suffered and the problems that it still faces. In a brilliant essay, the Egyptian philosopher Fu'ād Zakaria divides the anti-Orientalists into two main categories. The first school of criticism is religious and apologetic, a defense of the integrity and perfection of Islam against what they see as an attack by hostile forces, variously described as Christians, missionaries, Jews, Marxists, atheists, and the like, seeking to undermine and discredit Islam in order to impose their own beliefs. For the most part, these critics do not know the languages in which the Orientalists write and are therefore obliged to rely on quotations and a few translations. More important, they have no understanding whatever of the kind of modern critical scholarship of which Western Orientalism is a part and so are, for example, quite unaware that modern Western scholars are at least equally merciless in analyzing their own religious and cultural traditions.

The second group, according to Professor Zakaria, attack Orientalism from a political–cultural and not from a religious point of view. Indeed, the most vocal among them are not Muslims at all but are Christian or post-Christian expatriates living in Western Europe or the United States. They are perfectly familiar with modern Western secular civilization and its scholarly culture as well as its languages. Therefore, in this respect, they are able to wage war against the Orientalists with their own weapons. But they have a serious weakness—the poor knowledge that most of them possess of the classical Arab, Islamic civilization of which they claim to be the defenders. Here they are at a disadvantage not only as compared with the Muslim apologists but also as compared with the Orientalists themselves. If the defenders of Islam have a naive and essentialist view of the West about which they know so little, the Westernized defenders of the Arab political and cultural heritage have an equally naive and essentialist view of the realities of this heritage in the past and the predicament of its heirs at the present. The illusions offered by the anti-Orientalists can only worsen this predicament by delaying or impeding the cold, critical self-analysis that must precede any serious effort for improvement.

After examining the methods and modalities of anti-Orientalism in some detail, Professor Zakaria ends with a psychosocial analysis of the motives of both the Orientalists and their two types of opponent. In discussing those whom he calls the "westernizing expatriates," he suggests an interesting additional motive—the natural desire of the immigrant, in search of self-respect and the respect of his new compatriots, to maximize the achievements of his culture of origin and to minimize the differences that distinguish it from the culture of his new home.

This insight would appear to be confirmed by Mr. Said's assertion, in a PBS debate in 1977, that the fourteen-centuries-old Islamic tradition and civilization are no more meaningful for the Arab world today than are seventh-century events in Europe for an understanding of present-day America. Experts in Iraq and Iran thought otherwise. Only a few years later, in their war propaganda against each other, both countries daily evoked events and personalities of the seventh century, in the sure knowledge that they would be understood. One does not quite see American contenders for power making a point by a rapid allusion to the Anglo-Saxon heptarchy, the rise of the Carolingians, or the wars of the Lombards.

Professor Zakaria's concluding remarks are noteworthy:

> Orientalism is surely not without blemish, but the greater danger would be if we denied our faults merely because others speak of them for unobjective purposes. Our cultural task at this stage is to take the bull of backwardness by the horns and criticize ourselves before we criticize the image, even if it is deliberately distorted, that others make of us.[12]

The critique of Orientalism raises several genuine questions. A point made by several critics is that the guiding principle of these studies is expressed in the dictum "knowledge is power" and that Orientalists were seeking knowledge of Oriental peoples in order to dominate them, most of them being directly or, as Abdel-Malek allows, objectively (in the Marxist sense) in the service of imperialism. No doubt there were some Orientalists who, objectively or subjectively, served or profited from imperial domination. But as an explanation of the Orientalist enterprise as a whole, it is absurdly inadequate. If the pursuit of power through knowledge is the only or even the prime motive, why did the study of Arabic and Islam begin in Europe centuries before the Muslim conquerors were driven from eastern and western European soil and the Europeans embarked on their counterattack? Why did these studies flourish in European countries that never had any share in the domination of the Arab world and yet made a contribution as great as the English and French—most scholars would say greater? And why did Western scholars devote so much effort to the decipherment and recovery of the monuments of ancient Middle Eastern civilization, long since forgotten in their own countries?

Another charge leveled against the Orientalists is that of bias against the peoples they study, even of a built-in hostility to them. No one would deny that scholars, like other human beings, are liable to some kind of bias, more often for, rather than against, the subject of their study. The significant difference is between those who recognize their bias and try to correct it and those who give it free rein. (Accusations of cultural bias and political ulterior motives might also gain somewhat in credibility if the accusers did not assume for themselves and accord to Marxist-Leninist scholarship a plenary indulgence.)

Beyond the question of bias there lies the larger epistemological problem of how far it is possible for scholars of one society to study and interpret the creations of another. The accusers complain of stereotypes and facile generalizations. Stereotyped prejudices certainly exist—not only of other cultures, in the Orient or elsewhere, but of other nations, races, churches, classes, professions, generations, and almost any other group one cares to mention within our own society. The Orientalists are not immune to these dangers; nor are their accusers. The former at least have the advantage of some concern for intellectual precision and discipline.

The most important question—least mentioned by the current wave of critics—is that of the scholarly merits, indeed the scholarly validity, of Orientalist findings. Prudently, the anti-Orientalists hardly touch on this question and indeed give very little attention to the scholarly writings of the scholars whose putative attitudes, motives, and purposes form the theme of their campaign. Scholarly criticism of Orientalist scholarship is a legitimate and indeed a necessary, inherent part of the process. Fortunately, it is going on all the time—not a criticism of Orientalism, which would be meaningless, but a criticism of the research and results of individual scholars or schools of scholars. The most rigorous and penetrating critique of Orientalist, as of any other, scholarship has always been and will remain that of their fellow scholars, especially, though not exclusively, those working in the same field.

7

Other People's History

In his famous visionary poem "Locksley Hall," written in 1842, the English poet Tennyson expresses a view, fairly common at that time, of the relative importance of European and Oriental history: "Better fifty years of Europe than a cycle of Cathay." Cathay of course is China, and a cycle of Cathay implies that although the history of China is very long, it consists of meaningless repetition. Europe, in contrast, is a place where things happen, important things, and quickly.

Tennyson was by no means alone in this perception of Oriental history, which one finds widely, indeed, one might even say universally, expressed in European writings of the nineteenth century. Let me choose just one other example from the encyclical *Immortale Dei,* issued by Pope Leo XIII on 1 November 1885, in which he congratulates Christian Europe on having "tamed the barbarous nations and brought them from savagery to civility" and on being "the leader and teacher of peoples" in progress, liberty, and the alleviation of human misery by means of wise and beneficent institutions. In the encyclical, the reason for this achievement of Europe is of course that the Europeans adhere to the true faith, whereas the others lack this advantage. Tennyson, writing half a century earlier, had more practical reasons for the supremacy of Europe—"In the steamship, in the railway, in the thoughts that shake mankind," and, more remarkably, anticipated as its ultimate achievement "the Parliament of man, the Federation of mankind."

A similar perception of the relative importance of *our* history and *their* history can be seen in the apportionment of space and attention in some kinds of European historiography. If we look, for example, at one of the major historiographic achievements of the nineteenth century, the famous *Histoire générale,* edited by Ernest Lavisse and Alfred Rambaud, published in Paris between 1892 and 1901 in twelve volumes containing 291 chapters, we find that there is a fairly good coverage of the ancient Middle East, seen as our own background, in volume 1, after which there is one chapter on the medieval Arabs, three on the Ottoman Empire, two on India, six on the Far East—which does relatively well, getting almost as much space as Holland or Scandinavia—while the rest of Asia, including Iran and others, is merged into three general chapters on Asia. There is one chapter on North Africa and one on the rest of Africa, devoted mainly to the partition of that continent between the European powers. This is a representative example of how the nineteenth-century European historian saw history, saw the world. It is rather worse than the eighteenth century—less self-assured, more respectful of others—when the famous English *Universal History* devoted four volumes to biblical and ancient Middle Eastern history, eleven to Greece and Rome, twenty-seven to Europe and European settlements and activities abroad, and fifteen to the rest of the world.

Since then there has been some improvement in Western perspective, but the cycle of Cathay approach to Oriental history is by no means obsolete. A very distinguished English historian not so long ago spoke rather disparagingly of non-Western history as "the meaningless gyrations of picturesque barbarians." If I may be permitted a personal recollection, I remember the hard struggles that we had in my home university to persuade our colleagues to give a little more time and a little more attention to non-Western history. My colleague the professor of Anglo-Saxon history, that is, of the history of England before 1066, was particularly insistent that far too much attention was already being given to what he called "peripheral subjects." I asked him whether he thought that the history of Europe, Asia, and Africa was peripheral to the British Isles, to which he replied very firmly, "In terms of the interest and needs of our students, yes, I would say just that." This was of course also the prevailing attitude in non-Western civilizations, none of which made much attempt to study Western history until the West invaded them.

The question that opponents of the study of non-Western history usually put is: Why should *we* study *their* history? At first the question was usually asked with the implication that it wasn't worthwhile to do so, that there was simply nothing of value. Nowadays one doesn't hear that argument very often. It has been dropped either from conviction or more probably through fear of the quite severe penalties that the academic world can impose for offenses against the prevailing orthodoxies. The argument more frequently heard now is that it is not our business; it is not relevant—a word with new and sometimes menacing implications—to our needs or concerns or purposes.

However, despite some opposition and much indifference, there have always been some in the Western world, since the High Middle Ages, who did concern themselves with non-Western history. Even Tennyson, whom I quoted earlier, begins his poem "Locksley Hall" with these lines:

> Comrades, leave me here a little while, as yet 'tis early morn;
> Leave me here and when you want me sound upon the bugle-horn.

Any Arab or Arabist familiar with the ancient Arabian odes will at once recognize the source of this opening; indeed, Tennyson's son, in a memoir, said: "I remember my father saying that Sir William Jones' prose translation of the Moallakat . . . gave him the idea of the poem." Even Lavisse and Rambaud pay some attention to non-Western history, and although most of what they provide was written either by Lavisse or by Rambaud, some of it was indeed written by Western specialists on non-Western history, notably the chapters on the Far East, which are really quite professional.

There has been, from early times to the present day, a very vigorous tradition of the scholarly study of the East in Europe. Those specialists who, in spite of objections from within their own society, nevertheless thought it worthwhile to make an effort and devote themselves to the study of non-Western history and culture, are nowadays often confronted with a somewhat differently formulated question, which comes not from within but from outside, from the non-Western peoples themselves, or if not from them, then from others presuming to speak on their behalf. This time the question is not why should *we* bother with *their* history but, rather, what right have *you* to study *my* history? It is my property. If you concern yourself with it, you are an intruder. A nice example of this attitude, from a source that is non-Western in a different sense, was reported in the press in August 1989. On the anniversary of the intervention by the Soviet government and its Warsaw Pact allies in Czechoslovakia in 1968, statements were issued in both Poland and Hungary expressing disapproval of this action and contrition for their involvement in it. This brought an immediate rejoinder from Czechoslovakia, where the regime installed by the intervention still ruled, in the form of a resolution of the Czechoslovak parliament: "The assessment of Czechoslovak history is the exclusive right of the nations of Czechoslovakia, and Czechoslovak deputies insist on this right being respected to the full extent."

That is perhaps a reductio ad absurdum of this philosophy, but it is by no means a unique or untypical case. In that case the motivation was clearly political and ideological. It usually is. Sometimes there are other variants. Recently I came across an article in a Kuwaiti newspaper discussing a certain Western historian and saying that he is not competent to write the history of the Middle East for three reasons—he is not an Arab, he is not a Muslim, and he is a Jew. The writer then goes on to suggest that since the author in question is of English and Jewish background, he should confine himself to writing English and Jewish history.

This kind of criticism is often accompanied by very harsh, even coarse, language and has given rise to a new term of abuse, the word "Orientalist." This was a word originally coined, on the pattern of Hellenist or Latinist, to denote a certain type of predominantly philological and textual scholarship, concerned with texts emanating from the Orient. It now connotes a predatory, one might even say a larcenous, interest in other people's cultural possessions. According to this view, Orientalism is the intellectual arm of imperialism. Behind the necessarily false display of detached and objective scholarship, the real purpose of the scholarly study of the other is to subjugate, dominate, and exploit. Exponents of this view say in effect: "You have robbed us of our present. You have endangered and perhaps irretrievably compromised our future. Now you want to invade and pillage our past."

This perception has given rise to a kind of intellectual protectionism: control of access to resources and markets, limitation of imports, and of course, as with any protectionist policy, the payment of duty. Some conditions or requirements, relating not to why but to how the study is pursued, are eminently reasonable, even necessary: that the scholar should be competent (i.e., should possess the appropriate knowledge and skills); that he should be fair (i.e., that he should study and interpret other cultures by the same standards and criteria as his own, without prejudice or condescension or—one might add—idealization); that his scholarship should not be designed or even trimmed to serve some non-scholarly purpose, whether religious or national or ideological or other. Scholars, like the rest of humankind, are entitled to their beliefs and loyalties and purposes, but these should not distort—even if they inspire—their scholarship. Failures of scholarship in these respects are usually detected and criticized by other scholars, both from inside and outside the culture studied.

Stated in this form, such considerations are of no importance to those who believe that all scholarship or, rather, all scholarly discourse is ideological and that their ideology, and therefore their scholarly discourse, is better or stronger because it is openly avowed and, more especially, because it is theirs. For these critics, the same piece of Orientalist writing, informed by the same scholarly method, may be good or bad, depending on the identity—and for some, though not all, the origins—of the author and the motives rightly or wrongly attributed to him. Acceptance may be won by the payment of duty.

Often, the demand for payment of duty presented by or on behalf of the rightful owners of the history has little to do with scholarship, whether of the kind that claims to be objective or of the kind that proclaims itself to be committed, but might run something like this: "You want to study in my archives, read my literature, talk to my people, work on my history? Then you must pay your respects to my point of view, you must promote my national aspirations as I may from time to time define or redefine them." To comply with this requirement, the historian must choose for himself and demand of others a presentation of history that includes only what in the present climate of opinion is seen as positive and excludes, and if called upon denies, anything that in the present climate of opinion is seen as negative. And of course, since the climate of opinion changes from time to time, the requirements will change accordingly.

The two questions confronting the Westerner who looks at non-Western cultures—"Why should we bother?" and "Have we the right?"—are especially serious for those of us who have devoted our lives, or plan to devote them, to these studies. Have we really misspent our time and effort in the attempt to study, to understand, to interpret other cultures? Was it all just a useless digression, as some would tell us, or an unwarrantable intrusion, as others maintain? These questions become particularly acute at the present time when if we don't study and teach other cultures we are called arrogant and ethnocentric and if we do we are accused of spoliation and exploitation.

One answer to this dilemma, more often assumed than stated, is that while we may, indeed must, study our own heritage critically, we may do this only to our own and no one else's. As far as other cultures are concerned, the critical approach is forbidden to us, and we must be content to receive what the legitimate heirs of those other cultures select, prepare, process, and present for our instruction. Critical study, if and when it comes, will be their duty or, rather, prerogative.

To take a specific example: we may, indeed we must, study the history of Atlantic slavery and expose this great shame in the history of the Western world and of the Americas north and south, in all its horror. This is a task which falls upon us as Westerners and in which others may and should and do join us. In contrast, however, even to mention—let alone to discuss or explore—the existence of slavery in non-Western societies is denounced as evidence of racism and of imperialistic designs. The same applies to such other delicate topics as polygamy, autocracy, and the like. The range of taboos is very wide.

It is a curious fact that both these questions "Why should we . . . ?" and "Why do you . . . ?" have been put only to Western civilization and to no other. Why does a civilization study another civilization? Why do people adopt certain foreign, even dead, languages, from another civilization and teach them in their schools and universities? In the past, generally speaking, it has been that they saw the bearers of this other civilization as their masters in one or the other sense of that word—that is to say, either masters as teachers or masters as rulers. The Romans thought it instructive to learn Greek; the Greeks found it expedient to learn Latin. The Greeks were the teachers of the Romans, but the Romans were the rulers of the Greeks. In the same spirit, Japanese and Koreans learned Chinese; Persians and Turks learned Arabic; and in modern times vast numbers of people have learned English—but only English, not Anglo-Saxon. Interest in early European texts is, except in Japan, at best minimal, and we have yet to see any translations comparable in interest and impact with Sir William Jones's translation of the *Muʿallaqāt* of ancient Arabia from which Tennyson got the idea of "Locksley Hall."

Civilizations, in their educational systems, usually teach the languages of their classics, of their scriptures, and of government, later of business. In contrast to this general pattern, Europeans at one time or another have studied virtually all the languages and all the histories of Asia. Asians did not study Europe. They did not even study each other, unless the way for such study was prepared by either conquest or conversion or both. The kind of intellectual curiosity that leads to the study of a language, the decipherment of ancient texts, without any such preparation or motivation is still peculiar to western Europe, and to the inheritors and emulators of the European scholarly tradition in countries such as the United States and Japan. Those who do not share this curiosity are puzzled by it and naturally respond with incomprehension and suspicion. Since there is no intelligible motive, there has to be some ulterior motive. The crudest example was the response to the first archaeologists who went to dig up the remains of ancient pagans and who were generally assumed to be digging for buried treasure. Why else would one spend blood and treasure and effort in digging up ancient remains? Another charge often brought against archaeologists is that they were spies. Some of them did indeed serve their governments in intelligence, usually in wartime and against one another, but as an explanation of the Western archaeological enterprise, espionage hardly suffices. More recent explanations have gained in sophistication if not in accuracy.

Why, then, did we of the West engage in these studies, and why did those who grew up in non-Western societies not engage in these studies? Both sides adduce what one might not unfairly call obvious answers. An answer often given by Westerners is that higher civilizations study lower civilizations and not the other way around. A current non-Western answer is that knowledge is power and that the purpose of Western study was domination and exploitation.

Both answers meet a famous description by H. L. Mencken, who said that for every one of the great problems of life there is an answer—simple, plausible, and wrong—to which one may add, for these two explanations, a fourth common quality, self-serving. Both answers are false and fail on the simplest chronological tests. Even at a time like our own, when narrative history, *l'histoire évênementielle,* has been decried and discredited, it is still not generally acceptable to ascribe previous events to subsequent causes.

The first explanation, that the higher studies the lower, does not correspond to the facts. At the time when the European study of Islam began in the Middle Ages, Europe was manifestly lower and the Islamic world was manifestly higher. The civilization of Muslim Spain, North Africa, and the Middle East was in almost every significant field of human endeavor vastly more advanced than the relatively backward societies of Europe. Yet at that time, the West studied Islam. Islam did not study the West.

The second explanation, that the Orientalist studies the Orient as the predator studies his prey, is no better. For a thousand years of Muslim advance, it was not the Westerners but the Muslims who were the invaders and conquerors, first the Arabs, attacking Europe in the southwest; then the Turks, in the southeast. Both were equally innocent of scholarly designs on Europe. Even the advanced and sophisticated literature of the Arabs in Spain contains few references to the history and culture of their Spanish subjects or their Frankish neighbors. Such flickers of interest as we find are mainly among the Christian populations of Muslim Spain. Even the astute and highly competent makers and rulers of the Ottoman Empire showed only minimal interest in the history or languages of the peoples they had conquered or were planning to conquer.

The "knowledge is power" argument is no doubt emotionally satisfying, to some extent even intellectually satisfying, and it serves a double purpose: on the one hand, to condemn the Orientalism of the West; on the other, to make a virtue of the absence of any corresponding Occidentalism in the East. It also derives a certain plausibility from the fact that in modern times, in the nineteenth and twentieth centuries particularly, it has some relation to reality. But that relationship is narrower and more tenuous than has usually been realized. In England, for example, it was not usually the practice to recruit graduates in Oriental studies into the imperial service. The prevailing opinion seems to have been that they had already been spoiled by their teachers and would be unsuited for such work. The normal procedure was to recruit men with degrees in classics, at that time thought to be the best preparation for governing an empire, and then to send them to special centers to acquire such Oriental knowledge or languages as was required.

There was also a tradition of writing, particularly on history, the purpose of which was unmistakably imperial. One sees this in some early-nineteenth-century English writing on the history of India, which quite clearly has a double aim: on the one hand, to confirm English readers in the rightness of their rule in India and of the methods needed to maintain it, and on the other, to discourage Indians from developing dangerous ideas about their own past and consequently about their present and future. But all this was far removed from Orientalist scholarship in the universities. There was a similar literature in France, the purpose of which was to reinforce the French sense of mission and at the same time to discourage any sense of unity or any pride in the past among the North Africans, by presenting the different North African countries as a sort of pulverized ethnic dust inevitably attracted to *la mission civilisatrice de la France*. Again, that particular school of writing in France, though sometimes scholarly and often influential, was outside the Orientalist academic tradition. The only place where academic Orientalism was significantly affected by such purposes was in the Soviet Union under Stalin and some of his successors, in studies devoted to the history and culture of the Oriental republics in Trans-Caucasia, Central Asia, and beyond. These writings were clearly centrally controlled and directed to serve precisely these purposes—to justify Soviet power and to discourage national or religious movements among the peoples of those republics.

There is also another difficulty about the imperialist explanation, and that is the chronology. Arabic studies, we are told, were chiefly developed by the British and the French, and are closely linked with British and French penetration of Arab countries. Here I would utter a word of warning. English is extensively studied in the Netherlands, and the Dutch are now the second largest group of foreign investors in the United States, ahead of the much discussed Japanese, who come in third place. This is obviously a source of great danger. An American might say of the Dutch, "They master our language, they study our history, they even edit our texts, and sometimes they offer us the supreme insult of doing it better than we do. This, taken together with Dutch investment in North America, is clear evidence of imperialist designs linked with economic penetration."

Farfetched? As a portrayal of reality, no doubt—but as a comparison, surely not. Look again at the beginnings of Anglo-French Arabism in the sixteenth and seventeenth centuries. The first chair of Arabic in France was founded in the Collège de France by King Francis I in 1538. The first French incursion into an Arab country was in 1798. One must say that either the French Orientalists were extraordinarily prescient or the French imperialists were extraordinarily dilatory. In England, the first chair of Arabic was founded in Cambridge in 1633, the second in Oxford three years later in 1636. The first British incursion into the Arab world didn't come until the early nineteenth century, in the Gulf and in Aden. The British Orientalists were perhaps slightly less prescient or the British imperialists slightly less dilatory than their French colleagues, but this still leaves a remarkable gap.

In fact, to link the beginnings of English or French Orientalism with imperial expansion is to reverse history. When Francis I established the chair of Arabic at the Collège de France, the Moors had not long previously been expelled from Spain, and it was far from certain that they would not come back. The Turks were still threatening Vienna and had occupied the whole of southeastern Europe. Muslim fleets dominated the Mediterranean, and Francis himself was an eager suppliant for help at the court of Süleyman the Magnificent in Istanbul. Even a century later, when the two chairs of Arabic were founded at Cambridge and Oxford, all of the Balkans and half of Hungary were still under Turkish rule; there were still fifty years to go till the second Turkish siege of Vienna in 1683; and the south coasts of England and Ireland were still being raided by Barbary corsairs, carrying off captives for sale in the slave markets of Algiers.

Another difficulty about this explanation is that it leaves out the Italians and the Dutch and the Germans, whose role in the rise of European Orientalism on the whole is rather more important than that of the English or the French. It also fails to provide any explanation for the intensive development of the study of the ancient Orient. What imperial purpose was served by deciphering the ancient Egyptian language, for example, and then restoring to the Egyptians knowledge of and pride in their forgotten, ancient past?

This still leaves us with the question, why did we in the West do this in the past, and the more pressing question, why should we do it in the future? On the first question I can only offer some tentative suggestions. Christian Europe needed, from the beginnings of civilization on this continent, to look outward and to learn exotic and difficult languages in order to approach the mainsprings of its own faith and its own civilization. Its holy scriptures were written in Hebrew and Greek, with a few pages in Aramaic; three difficult languages, two of them non-Western, all written in strange and different scripts. The holy places of Christianity were in the Middle East; places of pilgrimage, the taking of which by Islam from Christendom inspired a deep sense of loss. Muslims had no such need and felt no such stimulus. Arabic was the language of scripture, government, commerce, and everyday life, over a vast area. Islam had no holy places in Europe.

A second element, which should not be underrated, was fear. We tend nowadays to forget that for approximately a thousand years, from the advent of Islam in the seventh century until the second siege of Vienna in 1683, Christian Europe was under constant threat from Islam, the double threat of conquest and conversion. Most of the early Muslim converts west of Iran and Arabia were converts from Christianity. Most of the new Muslim domains were wrested from Christendom. Syria, Palestine, Egypt, and North Africa were all Christian countries, no less, indeed rather more, than Spain and Sicily. All this left a deep sense of loss and a deep fear. The beginnings of the study of Arabic and Islam in Europe in the High Middle Ages were certainly linked with the fear of conquest by the Arabs and conversion to Islam. Muslims had no such fear and in consequence felt no such need during the early formative centuries when the character of their civilization was determined.

A third factor was the recognition of Arabic, along with Greek, as a language of science and philosophy. Europeans with a desire to learn could gratify that desire by learning these languages and studying in the schools where they were used. In the formative, early Middle Ages, there was no such attraction, for Muslims, in the languages or schools of Latin Europe.

A fourth factor is the intellectual development of Europe in the ages of the Renaissance, the Discoveries, the Reformation, the Enlightenment, and the scholarly revolution of the nineteenth century. These brought a new humanist curiosity, new scholarly methods and disciplines, new material, and also, through the religious conflicts within European Christendom, new links with the Arab Christians. At a time when Protestants and Catholics were struggling for control of Europe, Catholics and, to a lesser extent, Protestants looked toward the Eastern Christians as a possible source of support. A number of Arabic-speaking Uniate and other Christians, from Lebanon, Syria, and elsewhere, traveled to Europe, where they became the teachers of the West in Arabic studies, playing a role in the foundation of Arabic scholarship similar to that played by Jews in the foundation of Christian Hebrew scholarship. The Muslims of course had no such contacts in Europe. There were Christians in the Islamic lands; there were no Muslims in the Christian lands. They were expelled sooner or later after the Reconquest.

Another factor in the growth of Orientalist scholarship in the West is the expansion of trade and the development of the bourgeois urban society, which offered both encouragement and opportunity. One of the earliest professors of Arabic at Oxford, Edward Pococke, a very distinguished scholar and one of the major European Arabists of the seventeenth century, spent several years in Aleppo as chaplain to the Levant Company, an English merchant company with a trading post in Aleppo, courtesy of the sultan. Like most scholars in his day, Pococke was a clergyman, and his appointment as chaplain gave him the opportunity to spend a few years in an Arab city and to learn something of the culture as well as the language of the Arabs. In this respect also, there was no comparable opportunity for Muslims in Europe. The various Christian trading nations were permitted to establish trading centers in Middle Eastern cities from Crusading times onward, with some even before the Crusades. With few and minor exceptions, nothing of the kind was permitted by Europe to Muslims. When in Venice, which lived by the Levant trade, a proposal was put forward to establish an inn for traveling Turkish merchants, there were long and bitter struggles and arguments before the city finally agreed to allow a very small number of Turkish merchants to stay for short periods. And if Venice, the great trading city, was so reluctant to admit even a minimal Muslim presence, others were even less tolerant. Commerce and the opportunities afforded by commerce, and the kind of intellectual atmosphere that arises in a bourgeois society, were surely important elements in the rise of scholarship in Europe.

These are only tentative suggestions, on a subject still in need of further exploration. But let me turn now to my final topic: Why should we continue to do so? Why should we persist, in spite of criticism and sometimes even of abuse, in studying other people's civilizations?

There are a number of reasons for that, too. There is an obvious practical reason: the need for mutual understanding, whether for political or commercial or diplomatic or even simple human reasons. There is the by now generally accepted need of the social scientist for empirical data from other societies, without which he cannot make usable generalizations about his own. This is the more important at a time when the very vocabulary of discussion is structured to impede or obscure comparative analysis.

Beyond these practical and methodological considerations, there is also the inherent cultural, moral, and intellectual value of these cultures in themselves. Just as our students should know something about the major classics of Western literature, so they should know something about the major classics of non-Western literature, because even the understanding of our own Western civilization is distorted and incomplete unless it is seen in a global and not merely in a regional and parochial context. After all, Western civilization did not spring like Aphrodite from the sea foam. It has been enriched by contributions from many different sources, including the Islamic world and even the remoter regions of Asia and Africa. Without a recognition of that diversity of origin, our education and our self-perception are flawed and falsified. The interdependence of human existence at the present time, the unity of human culture, which is becoming more of a fact every day in spite of the political and other differences that divide us, require such mutual study. I stress the word "mutual." It is good that our students should study the *Muʿallaqāt;* it is also good that Arab students should study *Beowulf.*

In addition to what we might call these cultural and humanistic values, there is another, a more delicate issue, which must nevertheless be confronted. It is in a sense the scholar's duty to non-Western peoples to do something that some of them, for a variety of reasons, are prevented from doing for themselves. Some are practical reasons—lack of resources, lack of good libraries, lack of archival and other research facilities. During the early years of *The Encyclopedia of Islam*, the international editorial committee drew its contributors from all over the world, including, of course, Islamic countries. Time and time again the problem arose of a fine scholar in one or another Muslim city who couldn't do an article or had great difficulty in doing an article because there was no adequate library at his disposal. If one lives and works in Leiden or Princeton, or any major Western center, it is very easy to assemble the material one needs for a piece of research. There are very few places in the non-Western world where comparable facilities exist. This is one of the most acute problems for serious scholarship in these countries.

But that is not the only difficulty. There is also the political difficulty arising from the fact that many, not all, but many non-Western countries are governed by dictatorial regimes which quite rightly feel themselves to be threatened by independent historical research and which therefore take steps strictly to control the means of production, distribution, and exchange of historical knowledge. There was a time when scholars and other writers in communist eastern Europe relied on writers and publishers in the free West to speak the truth about their history, their culture, and their predicament. Today it is those who told the truth, not those who concealed or denied it, who are respected and welcomed in these countries.

There are also social and psychological pressures. A critical approach to the past is often seen as hostile—from outside as aggression, from inside as treason. There is a demand for recognition of the merits and achievements of the various cultures—a very reasonable request that has too often been denied in the past. But nowadays what is sometimes demanded is recognition not of merit, but of perfection, and that is not a reasonable demand.

Many generations of Indian and Egyptian graduate students went to England, both during and after the days of Empire, to do research on the iniquities of British imperialism in India and in Egypt. They had free access to libraries and archives, and they wrote what they wished to write. Much of what they wrote was in the form of doctoral theses, for which they received Ph.D.s from British universities, many of them with scholarships provided by the British government. Nobody saw anything amiss or raised any objection. It is one of the rules of a free society that there is such access to libraries and archives, and freedom, even for subsidized students, to present their view of the past as they see it. If their research and exposition met professional standards, they were entitled to their doctorates. One would hope that this view will spread to other parts, and indeed it has spread to some, but by no means to all. There are encouraging signs. At an international congress on the economic and social history of Turkey, hosted by the University of Marmara, of 135 papers presented, 80 were by non-Turks, many of them from former Ottoman possessions in southeastern Europe, Asia, and North Africa. The Turkish archives are now open to bona fide scholars, and numbers from these countries and elsewhere are already working there. One can only hope that others will follow the Turkish example.

Historians in free countries have a moral and professional obligation not to shirk the difficult issues and subjects that some people would place under a sort of taboo; not to submit to voluntary censorship, but to deal with these matters fairly, honestly, without apologetics, without polemic, and, of course, competently. Those who enjoy freedom have a moral obligation to use that freedom for those who do not possess it. We live in a time when great efforts have been made, and continue to be made, to falsify the record of the past and to make history a tool of propaganda; when governments, religious movements, political parties, and sectional groups of every kind are busy rewriting history as they would wish it to have been, as they would like their followers to believe that it was. All this is very dangerous indeed, to ourselves and to others, however we may define otherness—dangerous to our common humanity. Because, make no mistake, those who are unwilling to confront the past will be unable to understand the present and unfit to face the future.

ISLAMIC RESPONSE AND REACTION

8

The Return of Islam

In the great medieval French epic of the wars between Christians and Saracens in Spain, the *Chanson de Roland,* the Christian poet endeavors to give his readers or, rather, listeners some idea of the Saracen religion. According to this vision, the Saracens worshiped a trinity consisting of three persons: Muhammad, the founder of their religion, and two others, both of them devils, Apollin and Tervagant. To us this seems comic, and we are amused by medieval man unable to conceive of religion or indeed of anything else except in his own image. Since Christendom worshiped its founder in association with two other entities, the Saracens also had to worship their founder, and he too had to be one of a trinity, with two demons co-opted to make up the number. In the same spirit one finds special correspondents of European and American newspapers describing the civil war in Lebanon in terms of right-wing and left-wing factions. Just as medieval Christian man could conceive of religion only in terms of a trinity, so his modern descendant can conceive of politics only in terms of a theology or, as we say nowadays, ideology, of left-wing and right-wing forces and factions.

This recurring unwillingness to recognize the nature of Islam, or even the fact of Islam, as an independent, different, and autonomous religious phenomenon persists and recurs from medieval to modern times. We see it, for example, in the nomenclature adopted to designate the Muslims. It was a long time before Christendom was even willing to give them a name with a religious meaning. For many centuries, both Eastern and Western Christendom called the followers of the Prophet "Saracens," a word of uncertain etymology but clearly of ethnic and not religious connotation, since the term is both pre-Islamic and pre-Christian. In the Iberian Peninsula, where the Muslims whom they met came from Morocco, they called them Moors; in most of Europe, Muslims were called Turks, or, farther east, Tatars, another ethnic name loosely applied to the Islamized steppe peoples who for a while dominated Russia.

Even when Europe began to recognize that Islam was a religious and not an ethnic community, it expressed this realization in a sequence of false analogies, beginning with the names given to the religion and its followers, Muhammedanism and Muhammedans. The Muslims do not, and never have, called themselves Muhammedans or their religion Muhammedanism, since Muhammad does not occupy the same place in Islam as Christ does in Christianity. This misinterpretation of Islam as a sort of mirror image of Christendom found expression in a number of different ways—for example, in the false equation between the Muslim Friday and the Christian Sunday, in the reference to the Qur'ān as the Muslim Bible, in the misleading analogies between the mosque and the church, the ulema and the clergy, and, coming more directly to our present concern, in the imposition on Muslim history and institutions of Western notions of country and nation and of what goes on within them. Thus, for example, in Gibbon's fascinating account of the career of the Prophet, Muḥammad and his contemporaries were inspired by "patriotism and love of liberty," two concepts that somehow seem inappropriate to the circumstances of seventh-century Arabia. For many centuries, Europe called the lands of the Ottoman Empire Turkey, a name that the inhabitants of those lands did not apply to their own country until the final triumph among them of European political ideas, with the proclamation of the Turkish Republic in 1923.

Modern Western man, being unable for the most part to assign a dominant and central place to religion in his own affairs, found himself unable to conceive that any other people in any other place could have done so and was therefore impelled to devise other explanations of what seemed to him only superficially religious phenomena. We find, for example, a great deal of attention given by eighteenth-century European scholarship to the investigation of such meaningless questions as "Was Muḥammad sincere?" or "Was Muḥammad an Enthusiast or a Deceiver?" We find lengthy explanations by nineteenth- and early-twentieth-century historians of the "real underlying significance" of the great religious conflicts in Islam among different sects and schools in the past, and a similar determination to penetrate to the "real" meaning of sectarian and communal struggles at the present time. To the modern Western mind, it is not conceivable that men would fight and die in such numbers over mere differences of religion; there have to be other "genuine" reasons underneath the religious veil. We are prepared to allow religiously defined conflicts to accredited eccentrics like the Northern Irish, but to admit that an entire civilization can have religion as its primary loyalty is too much. Even to suggest such a thing is regarded as offensive by liberal opinion, always ready to take protective umbrage on behalf of those whom it regards as its wards. This is reflected in the recurring inability of political, journalistic, and academic commentators alike to recognize the importance of religion in the current affairs of the Muslim world and in their consequent recourse to the language of left-wing and right-wing, progressive and conservative, and the rest of the Western vocabulary of ideology and politics.

Until the revolution in Iran, there was a steadfast refusal on the part of the Western media to recognize that religion was still a force in the Muslim world. Since then, there has been a tendency to move to the opposite extreme, and some who previously could not see Islam at all now seem to have difficulty seeing anything else. The two are equally misleading. Islam is a living reality, and its importance as a political factor is immense. But having accepted Islam as a fact, we should remember that there still are other facts. Like other people, Muslims seek ways to protest and rebel against political oppression and economic privation; like other people, Muslims react and respond in ways that are familiar to them. Whatever the cause—political, social, economic—the form of expression to which most Muslims have hitherto had recourse to voice both their criticisms and their aspirations is Islamic. The slogans, the programs, and to a very large extent the leadership are Islamic. Through the centuries, Muslim opposition has expressed itself in terms of theology as naturally and spontaneously as its Western equivalent in terms of ideology. The one is no more a "mask" or a "disguise" than the other.

If, then, we are to understand anything at all about what is happening in the Muslim world at the present time and what has happened in the past, there are two essential points that need to be grasped. One is the universality of religion as a factor in the lives of the Muslim peoples, and the other is its centrality.[1]

The notion of church and state as distinct institutions, each with its own laws, hierarchy, and jurisdiction, is characteristically Christian, with its origins in Christian scripture and history. It is alien to Islam. The three major Middle Eastern religions are significantly different in their relations with the state and their attitudes toward political power. Judaism was associated with the state in antiquity and was then forcibly disentangled from it; its new encounter with the state at the present time, in Israel, has raised problems that are still unresolved. During the first formative centuries of its existence, Christianity was separated from and indeed antagonistic to the state, with which it only later became involved. From the lifetime of its founder, Islam *was* the state, and the identity of religion and government is indelibly stamped on the memories and awareness of the faithful from their own sacred writings, history, and experience.

For Muslims, Muḥammad's career as a soldier and statesman was not additional to his mission as a prophet. It was an essential part of it. In fulfillment of that mission, he became the head of a state and the founder of an empire, and his followers were sustained by a belief in the manifestation of divine approval through success and victory in this world. Islam was thus associated with the exercise of power from the very beginning, from the first formative years of the Prophet and his immediate successors. This association between religion and power, between community and polity, can already be seen in the Qur'ān itself and in the other early religious texts on which Muslims base their beliefs. One consequence is that in Islam religion is not, as it is in Christendom, one sector or segment of life regulating some matters and excluding others; it is concerned with the whole of life, not a limited but a total jurisdiction. In such a society, the very idea of separating church and state is meaningless, since there are no two entities to be separated. Church and state, religious and political authority, are one and the same. Different agencies, different individuals, may deal with the affairs of this world and those of the next, but in principle they derive their authority from the same source and administer the same law. In classical Arabic and in the other classical languages of Islam, there are no pairs of terms corresponding to "lay" and "ecclesiastical," "spiritual" and "temporal," "secular" and "religious," because these pairs of words express a Christian dichotomy that has no equivalent in the world of Islam. It is only in modern times under Christian influence that these concepts have begun to appear and that words have been coined to express them. Their meaning is still imperfectly understood, and their relevance to Muslim institutions dubious. Islamic fundamentalists, both conservative and radical, reject these notions as un-Islamic and therefore impious.

For the traditional Muslim, religion was not only universal but also central in the sense that it constituted the ultimate basis and focus of identity and loyalty. It was religion that distinguished and united those who belonged to the group and marked them off from those outside the group, even if they lived in the same country and spoke the same language. Muslims of different countries, speaking different languages, share the same memories of a sacred past, the same awareness of corporate identity, the same sense of a common predicament and destiny. It was not nation or country that, as in the West, formed the historic basis of identity, but the religio-political community. The subdivisions within that community were defined for the most part by dynastic allegiance, and the territorial and ethnic content of these dynastic states varied enormously in the course of the centuries. The imported Western idea of ethnic and territorial nationhood remains, like secularism, alien and incompletely assimilated. The point was made with remarkable force and clarity by a grand vizier of the Ottoman Empire who, in reply to the exponents of the new-style patriotism, remarked: "The Fatherland of a Muslim is wherever the Holy Law of Islam prevails." And that was in 1917.

In the eighteenth century, under the impact of Austrian and Russian victories against Turkey and British successes in India, Muslims were becoming aware that they were no longer the dominant power in the world but were, on the contrary, threatened in their heartlands by a Europe that was expanding at both ends. From the beginning of this awareness, there were two contrasting ways of responding to the threat. One was to learn from the enemy—first in the battlefield, then in politics, and finally in the whole range of what has come to be known as modernization. The other was religious revival. Since for Muslims Islam is, by definition, superior to all other faiths, the failures and defeats of Muslims in this world can only mean that they are not practicing authentic Islam and that their states are not true Islamic states. The remedy, therefore, is a return to the pure, authentic Islam of the Prophet and his Companions, a rejection and elimination of the accretions and innovations that had debased and corrupted the faith and enfeebled the Islamic society, making it incapable of resisting its external enemies. Both the Wahhābīs in Arabia and the Naqshbandī brotherhood that spread from India to the Middle East aimed in different ways at regenerating Islam and thus at restoring Muslim power. In the early nineteenth century, when the three major European empires (those of Britain, France, and Russia) ruling over Muslims were advancing in India, North Africa, and the Caucasus, the most significant movements of resistance in all three areas were offered by the Wahhābīs and the brotherhoods, inspired by charismatic religious leaders: Aḥmad Brelwī against the British in India, ʿAbd al-Qādir against the French in Algeria, and Shāmil against the Russians in Dagistan and the northern Caucasus. All three were defeated, and all three are remembered and revered.

For a while, Muslims were sufficiently overawed by the power, wealth, and success of Europe to desire to emulate European ways. But from the middle of the nineteenth century onward came a further wave of European imperial expansion—the suppression of the Indian mutiny followed by the disappearance of the last remnants of the Mogul monarchy in India, and the consolidation of the British Empire in that formerly Muslim realm; the rapid advance of the Russians in Central Asia; the expansion of the French into Tunisia and of the British into Egypt; and the growing threat to the Ottoman Empire itself. All these combined to bring a new kind of response, that of political pan-Islam.

The unification of Germany and of Italy was a source of inspiration in Muslim lands, particularly in Turkey, where some Turkish leaders thought that their country could play the role of Prussia or Sardinia and serve as the nucleus for a much larger, unified entity. But what would that entity be? Not a pan-Turkish entity. Such ideas were still far in the future and were not even discussed at that time. The basic political identity and allegiance were Islamic, and pan-Islamism was the first and natural response of Muslims to the examples of pan-Germanism and pan-Slavism. It was not until much later that pan-Turkism and pan-Arabism appeared on the political horizon, and even then there was some doubt as to what they really signified.

Political pan-Islamism, in the sense of an official policy of Islamic unity or at least cooperation, dates back to the 1870s, when the Ottoman government under Sultan Abdülaziz (1861–1876) and then, more actively, under Sultan Abdühamid II (1876–1909) tried to mobilize opinion all over the Muslim world in support of the faltering Ottoman state, and to provide it with much-needed help against its numerous and powerful enemies. Significantly, the pan-Islamic appeals of the Ottoman sultans evoked far more response in distant Muslim lands, especially those conquered or threatened by European imperialism, than among their own neighbors or subjects. Even after the Ottoman constitutional revolution of 1908, the policy of state pan-Islamism was continued by the modernizing Young Turk pashas. In November 1914, after the outbreak of war, the Ottoman authorities even proclaimed a *jihād,* or holy war, against the Allies and called on Muslims everywhere, including especially those under Allied rule, to do battle in the Islamic—that is, the Ottoman—cause. Understandably, the summons to a holy war for Islam under the aegis of the Young Turks and their German and Austrian comrades-in-arms had little appeal, and the response was minimal.

The end of the First World War, the breakup of the Ottoman Empire, the strains and stresses that followed, and the opportunities that seemed to be offered by the collapse of czarism in revolution and civil war also gave rise to a series of religiously inspired movements. The Young Turk leader, Enver Pasha, fleeing from a defeated Turkey, formed the ambitiously titled Army of Islam, whose purpose was to liberate the Muslim subject peoples of the fallen Russian Empire. Some of these movements were linked with the Communists or taken over by the Communists at a time when the fundamentally antireligious nature of communism was not yet understood. Almost all were expressed in religious rather than in national or even social terms.

By far the most significant among these movements, and the only one that was to achieve any real success, was what has since come to be known as the Turkish Nationalist or Kemalist movement, after its leader Mustafa Kemal, later surnamed Atatürk. The revolt of the Kemalists in Anatolia against the Allied occupation and the planned dismemberment of Turkey was in its early stages at least as much Islamic as nationalist, and Islamic men of religion formed an impressive proportion of its leaders and followers. The declarations and appeals of the rebels in Anatolia spoke of "Ottoman Muslims" rather than of Turks, and the movement evoked enthusiastic support all over the Muslim world. It was not until after their victory and the establishment of the republic in 1923 that the Kemalists began to lay the main stress on nationalist and secular aims.

They did so with spectacular success. Alone among the vanquished powers in the First World War, they defied and rejected the peace imposed by the victors; alone among the conquered and occupied Muslim nations, they defeated and ejected their conquerors and occupiers. Their achievement resounded all over the lands of Islam and inspired many to emulate their example.

During the interwar years, when the British and French empires ruled much of the Islamic and especially the Arab world, even anti-imperialism usually took a British or a French form, organized in political parties and expressed in the language of political, more or less secular, nationalism. But as later events made clear, neither the party organizations nor the nationalist ideologies really corresponded to the deeper instincts of the Muslim masses, which found an outlet in programs and organizations of a different kind, led by religious leaders and formulated in the language of religious faith and aspiration.

Already in the 1920s and 1930s, when nationalist leaders still dominated the political scene, and nationalist discourse alone was heard in public debate, there were gatherings where men spoke not of nation or country or their freedom, but of Islam and the community of believers, and of the need to revive their faith and restore the holy law. In the postwar years, when the imperialist rulers had gone and independence was no longer an issue, these gatherings heard a different and increasingly persuasive message, that national sovereignty alone was an empty sham, that the world of Islam still remained in bondage to its ancient enemy, whose dominance was expressed in so-called modern, non-Islamic laws and ways and morals, underpinned by foreign-style politics and economics and enforced, even when the infidel foreign rulers had gone, by their renegade Muslim agents and puppets. As one Muslim country after another gained independence, it was against their own Muslim rulers that the increasingly violent opposition of the religious movements was directed. At a time of political humiliation, economic privation, and social disruption, there was much to fuel their anger.

The first important movement of this type, known as the Muslim Brothers (al-Ikhwān al-Muslimūn), was founded in Egypt in 1928 by a religious teacher named Ḥasan al-Bannā'. The early history of the movement is not clearly known, but it appears to have been mainly concerned, for the first eight years, with religious and social activities. The founder, known as the "Supreme Guide," sent missionaries to preach in mosques and other public places all over Egypt. The Brothers undertook large-scale educational, social, charitable, and religious work in town and countryside and even engaged in some economic enterprises.

They began political action in 1936, after the signature of the Anglo-Egyptian Treaty in that year and, by taking up the cause of the Palestine Arabs against Zionism and British rule, were able to extend the range of the movement to other Arab countries and especially Syria. In 1941 Ḥasan al-Bannā' was imprisoned for a time because of his anti-British activities. The Brothers sent volunteers to fight with the Arab armies in the war of 1948 and thereafter seem to have maintained an armed militia. As a result, the Egyptian prime minister, Noqrāshī Pasha, dissolved the organization, confiscated its property, and ordered the arrest of many of its members. He was assassinated in 1948 by one of the Brothers, and shortly afterward the Supreme Guide himself was assassinated in circumstances that have never been clarified. Although illegal, the Brothers continued to function as a clandestine organization. In April 1951 they were again legalized in Egypt, though forbidden to engage in any secret or military activities. They took part in actions against British troops in the Suez Canal zone and seem to have played some role, of what nature is still unknown, in the burning of Cairo on 26 January 1952.

They had close links, dating back to the war years, with some members of the secret committee of the "Free Officers" who seized power in Egypt in 1952. Apart from some general similarities in ideology and aspiration, many of the officers who carried out the coup were either members or at least sympathizers of the Muslim Brothers.

At first, relations between the Brothers and the Free Officers were intimate and friendly, and even in January 1953 when the military regime dissolved all political parties, the Brothers were exempted on the grounds that they were a nonpolitical organization. Relations between the new Supreme Guide and the Free Officers deteriorated, however, and before long the Brothers were attacking the new regime for its alleged failure to live up to their Islamic ideals. A period of quiet but sharp conflict followed, during which the Brothers were very active, especially among workers and students and even among the security forces. In January 1954 the government again decreed the dissolution of the Brotherhood and the arrest of many of its leaders and followers. Later there was some reconciliation as a result of which the arrested Brothers were released and the organization was allowed to function on a nonpolitical basis.

A new phase of conflict began with the Anglo-Egyptian agreement of October 1954. This, like the treaty of 1936, was bitterly opposed by the Brothers, who insisted that only armed struggle could attain the desired objectives. On 26 October 1954, one of the Brothers just failed to assassinate President Nasser, who retaliated with severe repressive measures. More than a thousand were arrested and tried, and six, including some of the intellectual leaders of the movement, were sentenced to death and executed. The Brotherhood was now again illegal but nevertheless continued to function and seems to have engaged from time to time in conspiracies to overthrow the regime. Over the years there were many arrests, and in August 1966 three more executions took place. One of the victims was Sayyid Qutb, a leading ideologist. The Brotherhood continued to be active, albeit illegal, in some, and more openly in other, Arab countries. It remains a powerful force and has enjoyed the material support of conservative Muslim regimes, including, at different times, the Saudi, Jordanian, and Iranian monarchies. Partly for this reason, it has been overtaken in popular appeal by more radical and subversive Islamic groups, some of them sponsored by self-proclaimed Islamic revolutionary regimes and some of them expressing authentic grass-roots discontents. In Egypt, where the Brothers are permitted to operate as a religious organization but forbidden to act as a political party, they nevertheless took part in the 1987 general election as an ally of two secular parties, and won thirty-seven seats.

The Egyptian Free Officers Committee in 1952 was not the only political movement with which the Muslim Brothers were connected. Another is the Fataḥ, the largest and most important of the Palestinian guerrilla organizations. Here too, for obvious reasons, there are some uncertainties regarding the earlier history of the movement, but its past links with the Muslim Brothers seem to be clear. The imagery and symbolism of the Fataḥ are strikingly Islamic. Yāsir 'Arafāt's nom de guerre, Abū 'Ammār (the father of 'Ammār), is an allusion to the historic figure of 'Ammār ibn Yāsir ('Ammār the son of Yāsir), a Companion of the Prophet and a valiant fighter in all his battles. The name Fataḥ is a technical term meaning a conquest for Islam gained in the holy war.[2] It is in this sense that Sultan Mehmed II, who conquered Constantinople for Islam in 1453, is known as Fātiḥ, the Conqueror. The same imagery, incidentally, is carried over into the nomenclature of the Palestine Liberation Army, the brigades of which are named after the great victories won by Muslim arms in the battles of Qādisiyya, Ḥaṭṭīn, and 'Ayn Jālūt. To name military units after victorious battles is by no means unusual. What is remarkable here is that all three battles were won in holy wars for Islam against non-Muslims—Qādisiyya against the Zoroastrian Persians, Ḥaṭṭīn against the Crusaders, and 'Ayn Jālūt against the Mongols. In the second and third of these, the victorious armies were not even Arab; but they were Muslim, and that is obviously what counts. It is hardly surprising that the military communiqués of the Fataḥ begin with the Muslim invocation "In the name of God, the Merciful and the Compassionate."

The same Islamic identification could be seen in the very close links between the PLO and the Islamic revolution in Iran—links vividly illustrated in the embrace of Khomeini and Yāsir 'Arafāt when the latter visited Iran to congratulate the new rulers and in his promise to "plant the flag of Islam on the walls of Jerusalem." Later they parted company.

Since then, the Fataḥ, like other movements of its generation, has been overtaken in its bid for Islamic support by more radical and more consistent movements, of the kind that it has become customary to call "fundamentalist." Notable among these are the Palestinian Ḥamas, the Lebanese Shī'ite Ḥizb Allāh (Party of God), and the Algerian Islamic Salvation Front, which was suppressed after its electoral victory in early 1992.

The Muslim Brothers and their successors were in the main confined to the Arabic-speaking countries. But there were other parallel movements elsewhere. In Iran this trend was for a while represented by an organization called the Fidā'īyān-i Islām (Devotees of Islam). This group was active mainly in Tehran between 1943 and 1955 and carried out a number of political assassinations, the most important being that of the prime minister, General 'Alī Razmārā, in March 1951. The Devotees had some impact on Iranian politics, until another, this time unsuccessful, attempt on the life of a prime minister, Ḥossein 'Alā, in October 1955, led to their suppression and prosecution and the execution of some of their leaders. The Devotees had links with the Brothers and exercised considerable influence among the masses and, through terror, on politicians. They even seem to have enjoyed some limited support from the semiofficial religious leadership. After their suppression, the Islamic militants withdrew into clandestine opposition, from which they emerged in triumph in 1979, in the first successful Islamic revolution in modern times.

There have been other religiously inspired movements in many Islamic countries, as diverse as Indonesia, Pakistan, Bosnia, Sudan, and Senegal. One of the most interesting—and least known in the Western and even the Islamic world—is the Basmachi movement, active in Muslim Central Asia in the early period of Soviet rule. The word "Basmachi," which in Uzbek means brigand or marauder, was applied by the Soviet authorities to a succession of religiously inspired revolts against Russian or Soviet rule which began in January 1919 and continued until 1923, when the movement was decisively defeated. Activity by small groups of rebels continued for a number of years after that. The last Basmachi leader, Ibrāhīm Beg, withdrew to Afghanistan in 1926 and raided Soviet territory from there. He was captured by Soviet troops and executed in 1931. It is characteristic of Western attitudes that a search of a half-dozen major encyclopedias failed to disclose any article on the Basmachis—probably the most important movement of opposition to Soviet rule in Central Asia.[3]

It is not, however, only in radical and militant opposition movements that this kind of religious self-identification and alignment can be found. Governments, including avowedly secular and radical governments, have responded to the same instincts in times of crisis. After the Treaty of Lausanne of 1923, an exchange of population was agreed between Turkey and Greece, under the terms of which members of the Greek minority in Turkey were to be repatriated to Greece and members of the Turkish minority in Greece repatriated to Turkey. Between 1923 and 1930, 1.25 million "Greeks" were sent from Turkey to Greece and a somewhat smaller number of "Turks" from Greece to Turkey.

At first sight, this would seem to be a clear case of the acceptance, to the last degree, of the European principle of nationality: Greeks and Turks unwilling or unable to live as national minorities among aliens, returning to their own homelands and their own peoples. On closer examination, this exchange proves to have had a somewhat different character. The words used were indeed "Greeks" and "Turks," but what precisely did these words mean at that time and in that place? In the deserted Christian churches left by the Greeks of Karaman in southern Turkey, the inscriptions on tombstones are written in Greek characters but in Turkish; among the families of the so-called repatriates, the great majority had little or no knowledge of Greek but spoke Turkish among themselves, writing it in Greek characters, just as Jews and Christians in Arabic-speaking countries for long wrote the common Arabic language in Hebrew or in Syriac instead of in Arabic characters. Script all over the Middle East is closely associated with religion, with scripture. In the same way, many of the so-called Turks sent to Turkey from Crete and other places in Greece had little or no knowledge of Turkish but habitually spoke Greek among themselves, frequently writing their Greek vernacular in the Turco-Arabic script. By any Western definition of nationality, the Greeks of Turkey were not Greeks but Turks of the Christian faith, and the so-called Turks of Greece were for the most part Muslim Greeks. If we take the terms "Greek" and "Turk" in their Western and not in their Middle Eastern connotations, then the famous exchange of population between Greece and Turkey was not a repatriation of Greeks to Greece and of Turks to Turkey but a deportation of Christian Turks from Turkey to Greece and a deportation of Muslim Greeks from Greece to Turkey. It was only after their arrival in their putative homelands that most of them began to learn their presumptive mother tongues.

This occurred among two peoples, one of which is Christian though long subject to Muslim influence, and the other, though Muslim, is the most advanced in secularization of all the Muslim peoples. Even today, in the secular republic of Turkey, the word "Turk" is by common convention restricted to Muslims. Non-Muslim citizens of the republic are called Turkish citizens, but they do not call themselves Turks nor are they so called by their neighbors. The identification of Turk and Muslim remains virtually total. And here it may be noted that although the non-Muslim resident of the country is not a Turk, the non-Turkish Muslim immigrant, whether from the former provinces of the Ottoman Empire or from elsewhere, rapidly acquires a Turkish identity.

In Iran, the question hardly arose. Despite considerable ethnic diversity, the population is overwhelmingly Muslim, with only small minorities of Christians, Jews, and Zoroastrians. The Jews, Persian-speaking and established in the country for millennia, achieved a brief economic prosperity under the Pahlavi dynasty but remained outside the social, cultural, and political life of the country. The Christians, mostly Armenian or Assyrian, preserved separate national as well as religious identities and, like the Jews, remained, with few exceptions, outside the intellectual and political process. The Zoroastrians, seen by secular nationalists as the custodians of the true Iranian national identity, are viewed with corresponding suspicion by devout Muslims and are in any case too few to matter. The Bahā'īs, followers of a post-Muslim dispensation, are as such excluded from the tolerance prescribed by the *sharī'a*. Under the shah, they flourished and achieved a place of some consequence in Iran. Under the republic, those who persist in their faith are proscribed outlaws.

In Egypt and the Arab countries of the Fertile Crescent, the situation is somewhat more complex. In the Arabic-speaking countries there have for a long time been substantial minorities of Christians and Jews speaking the same Arabic language, though in the past writing it in a different script and in some regions speaking it with a slightly different dialect. When the idea of Arabism as a common nationality was first launched in the late nineteenth and early twentieth centuries, Arabic-speaking Christians were prominent in the movement. It was natural that they should be attracted by a national rather than a religious identity, since in the one they could claim the equal citizenship to which they could never aspire in the other. In the nationalist perspective, the Arabs were a nation divided into various religions, in which Christians and even at times Jews might hope to share a common Arabism with the Muslim majority.

From the beginning, Christians played a leading role among the exponents, ideologists, and leaders of secular nationalism. As members of non-Muslim communities in a Muslim state, they occupied a position of stable, sometimes even privileged, but nevertheless unmistakable inferiority. In an age of weakness and change, even the limited rights that this status gave them were endangered. In a state in which the basis of identity was not religion and community but language and culture, they could claim the full membership and equality denied to them under the old dispensation. As Christians, they were more open to Western ideas and identified themselves more readily in national terms. The Western or Westernized education to which they had access gave them a significant advantage in both intellectual and commercial life. Christians, especially Lebanese Christians, contributed disproportionately to the foundation and development of the newspaper and magazine press in Egypt and in other Arab countries, and Christian names figure prominently among the outstanding novelists, poets, and publicists in the earlier stages of modern Arabic literature. Many even of the leaders and theoreticians of the nationalist movements were members of Christian minorities. This prominence in cultural and political life was paralleled by a rapid advance of the Christian minorities in material wealth. For a brief moment in the history of the Middle East, mission-educated Christian Arabs, principally from the greater Syrian area, were the pioneers and spokesmen of a new Arab world, and American and French missionaries were the mentors and patrons of the Christian Arabs, who looked to them with appropriate piety and deference. That interval inevitably ended when the vast Muslim majority awoke from its torpor and reacted, sometimes rather sharply, against minority leadership and foreign sponsorship. Such is the way of majorities, everywhere.[4]

In recent decades and for many Muslims this Christian prominence has ceased to be tolerable. Partly through measures of nationalization adopted by socialist governments and partly through other more direct means, the economic power of the Christian communities has been reduced in one country after another and finally even in its last stronghold, Lebanon. Christian predominance in intellectual life has long since ended, and a new generation of writers has arisen, the overwhelming majority of whom are Muslims. There are still Christian politicians and ideologists, but their role is much circumscribed in a society increasingly conscious of its Muslim identity, background, and aspirations. Among the various organizations making up the Palestine Liberation Organization, the Fataḥ is overwhelmingly though not exclusively Muslim. On the other hand, many of the extremist organizations tend to be Christian, for in the radical extremism that they profess, Christians still hope to find the acceptance and equality that eluded them in nationalism. A parallel may be seen in the motivations, and probably also in the ultimate fate, of the Jewish revolutionaries in czarist Russia. As the nationalist movement has become genuinely popular, so it has become less national and more religious—in other words, less Arab and more Islamic. In moments of crisis—and there have been many in recent decades—it is often the instinctive communal loyalty that outweighs all others.

In the traditional view (still the instinctive response) the world is divided basically into two groups. One is the community of the Muslims, the other that of the unbelievers, and subdivisions among the latter are of secondary importance.

The response to an apparently secular struggle in Iraq between nationalists and communists is instructive. On 17 March 1959, a prayer was recited in Egyptian mosques and published on the front pages of the Egyptian papers for those who had been killed fighting the Communists in Mosul:

> God is great! God is great!... May He strengthen the martyrs with His grace and ordain them everlasting life in His mercy and abase their enemies in shame and ignominy!... Whoever offends, God will crush him; whoever exalts himself by wrongdoing, God will humble him! Consider not those who are killed in the cause of God as dead, but as living, with their Lord who sustains them....
>
> O God, Almighty, All-powerful, strengthen the community of Thy Prophet with Thy favor, and ordain defeat for their enemies.... In faith we worship Thee, in sincerity we call upon Thee, the blood of our martyrs we entrust to Thee.... For the glory of Thy religion they shed their blood and died as martyrs: Believing in Thee, they greeted the day of sacrifice blissfully. Therefore place them, O God, as companions with the upright and the martyrs and the righteous. (cf. Qur'ān 4:69)

The religious passion and fervor were unmistakable and did not fail to alarm Christian minorities at the time in Lebanon and elsewhere as indicating a resurgence of Islamic feeling.

Since then, regimes in many Muslim countries have become more, not less, avowedly Islamic. This affects the self-styled radical and revolutionary states as well as, and sometimes even more than, the politically conservative states. The most authentically popular revolution in the Islamic world, that of Iran, has gone the furthest in restoring traditional Islamic norms in such matters as penal law, enforced religious observance, the position of women in the home and in society, and the status of non-Muslim minorities. For Jews and Christians, followers of religions recognized by Islamic law, this status is one of protected subordination, with some but not all of the rights of their Muslim compatriots. For those who practice nonrecognized religions, like the Bahā'īs in Iran, the Aḥmadīs in Pakistan, and the followers of African religions in the southern Sudan, the strict application of *sharī'a* law would give them the choice between conversion and death, with the latter possibly commuted to enslavement.

The concerns of non-Muslim minorities in the Middle East were increased by the Iranian revolution and the rise of Islamic fundamentalism—sometimes popular, sometimes preemptive—in other countries. Part of their concern arose from the generally heightened feeling of communal loyalty and religious passion, which inevitably places those who do not share the dominant faith in a position of some delicacy. After a long period of secular, liberal, and nationalist ideologies and programs, the non-Muslim minorities of the Middle East are no longer conditioned to revert to their former position of inferiority. Some have sought a solution to their problem in emigration; some have resorted to radical politics; and some look anxiously, with decreasing confidence, for saviors from outside.

The formal abolition of the Ottoman caliphate by the Turkish republic and the abandonment of all its pan-Islamic policies and activities left a void. Ottoman pan-Islamism was of recent origin and had achieved meager results, but it had responded to a psychological need of a Muslim world under attack. The feeling of endangerment and the desire for unity remained, and a succession of claimants to the abandoned leadership tried to respond to that desire. Four of them were Arab kings, the fifth a remarkable religio-political leader, and all of them failed. Twice in Arabia—King Ḥusayn of the Hijāz in 1924 and King 'Abd al-'Azīz ibn Sa'ūd in 1926—and twice in Egypt—King Fu'ād in 1926 and King Fārūq at various times—a reigning monarch tried to prepare the ground for his acceptance as universal Islamic caliph. They won little support and aroused much opposition. A more sustained attempt was made by the Grand Mufti of Jerusalem, Ḥājj Amīn al-Ḥusaynī, who tried to mobilize world Muslim opinion in support of the Palestine Arabs and who, after his flight to Germany in 1941, tried to create an Axis–Islamic alliance. But the Muslim world, already disillusioned with an Ottoman *jihād* "made in Germany" and an Arab revolt "made in England," disappointed his hopes, and even the Germans, who had other plans and commitments, were extremely cautious. They found a use for the Grand Mufti in trying to win Muslim support for the Axis in occupied Balkan countries and among Red Army prisoners of war and of course as an exponent of the cause (at that time far more active) of Arab nationalism. But forewarned by the experience of the Western powers whose place they intended to inherit, the Germans were very sparing even with promises.

In retrospect, it is clear that political pan-Islamism in the interwar period was a hopeless cause. Only two Muslim countries, Turkey and Iran, were genuinely independent, and both of them were led by Westernizing, modernizing rulers, who quite deliberately renounced all adventures beyond their own frontiers. The model they offered, the example they gave, was of a self-reliant modern nation-state committed to joining, not opposing, the modern civilization of the West.

This remained the policy of the Turkish republic and, until the revolution of 1979, of Iran. But in the postwar reorganization of the Middle East new states appeared, some of them with ambitions extending far beyond their own frontiers. In the pursuit of these often conflicting ambitions, they had recourse to religious as well as nationalist appeals.

Attempts to create an inter-Islamic congress and organization date back to the late nineteenth century and had led nowhere. The first major postwar initiative was the Islamic Congress convened in Mecca in 1954. From the first, the most important initiative in the Mecca congress was Egyptian. President Nasser's intentions could already be seen in his booklet, *The Philosophy of the Revolution:*

> There remains the Third Circle [the first two were the Arab and African circles]—the circle encompassing continents and oceans which, as I have said, is the circle of our Brethren-in-Islam who, wherever their place under the sun, turn with us toward the same Qibla, their lips solemnly saying the same prayers.
>
> My faith in the magnitude of the positive effectiveness that could result from strengthening the Islamic tie that binds all Muslims grew stronger when I accompanied the Egyptian mission to Saudi Arabia to offer condolences on the death of its great king.
>
> As I stood before the Kaaba, with my thoughts wandering round every part of the world which Islam has reached, I fully realized the need for a radical change of our conception of the Pilgrimage.
>
> I said to myself: The journey to the Kaaba should no longer be construed as an admission card to Paradise, or as a crude attempt to buy forgiveness of sins after leading a dissipated life.
>
> The Pilgrimage should have a potential political power. The world press should hasten to follow and feature its news not by drawing attractive pen pictures of its rites and rituals for the delectation of readers, but by its representation as a periodical political conference at which the heads of all the Islamic states, leaders of opinion, scientists, eminent industrialists, and prominent businessmen assemble to draw up at this world Islamic Parliament the broad lines of the policies to be adopted by their respective countries and lay down the principles ensuring their close cooperation until they have again gathered together in the following session.
>
> They assemble demure and devout, but mighty and strong; unambitious of power, but active and full of energy; submissive to Divine Will, but immutable in difficulties and implacable with their enemies.
>
> They assemble confirmed believers in the Life to Come, but equally convinced that they have a place under the sun which they should occupy in this life.
>
> I remember I expressed some of these views to His Majesty King Saud.
>
> His Majesty assented, saying, "Truly this is the real purpose of the Pilgrimage."
>
> Truth to tell, I personally cannot think of any other conception.
>
> As I contemplate the eighty million Muslims in Indonesia, the fifty million in China, the few millions in Malaya, Thailand, and Burma; the hundred million in Pakistan, the well-nigh over a hundred million in the Middle East, the forty million in the Soviet Union, and the millions of others in other remote and far-flung corners of the earth—as I ponder over these hundreds of millions of Muslims, all welded into a homogeneous whole by the same Faith, I come out increasingly conscious of the potential achievements cooperation among all these millions can accom-

> plish—cooperation naturally not going beyond their loyalty to their original countries, but which will ensure for them and their Brethren-in-Islam unlimited power.[5]

Under the skillful and energetic leadership of Anwar Sadat, who was appointed secretary general, the Islamic Congress thus conceived served as a useful adjunct to Egyptian policy, along with such parallel organizations as the Afro-Asian Solidarity Conference and the Arab League. But it was no doubt this kind of use that also led to its failure. Like the previous attempts by other Muslim governments, this new Egyptian-sponsored pan-Islamism was too obviously related to state purposes and failed to arouse the necessary response from elsewhere.

Since then, an informal association of Muslim governments has developed, acting jointly on matters of common concern at the United Nations (where for some purposes, but not others, they form a Muslim bloc) and in other international bodies.

In 1969 the first steps were taken toward the formation of a permanent, inter-Islamic body. After several meetings of Muslim foreign ministers and of Muslim heads of state, the "Organization of the Islamic Conference," first mooted in 1971, was finally constituted at a summit conference in Lahore in February 1974. The original membership of thirty-six has since increased, notably by the adherence of several former Soviet republics. With a permanent headquarters, a secretariat, and a number of subsidiary bodies, the OIC has concerned itself principally with religious, cultural, and economic matters but has had remarkably little impact in politics or even diplomacy.

There are obvious political and diplomatic reasons for this lack of common purpose among Muslim governments. But there is perhaps a deeper reason for the persistent weakness of official pan-Islamism. In the first century and a half of the caliphate, Islam was indeed one single world state. But at that early date, it ceased to be so and was never reunited again. Thus although the political experience and shared historical memories of Muslims give them a sense of common social and cultural identity, they do not bring them any tradition of a single Islamic state but, rather, one of political pluralism and, more often than not, rivalry and conflict.

Attempts at international pan-Islamism have produced limited results. They have, however, already gone much further than anything comparable within the Christian world and have occasionally had diplomatic consequences, as, for example, when the Arab states as a bloc voted for Pakistan against India's candidacy for the Security Council, and this despite India's devoted and selfless service to the Arab cause. Similar choices could be discerned in the support given to Muslims in the Philippines, Eritrea, and some African countries when they found themselves in collision with non-Muslim majorities or governments.

But these were relatively safe enemies. Policy, even comment, was far more circumspect with regard to the position of Muslims in the Soviet Union, in Eastern European states, and in China.[6] The cautious approach to Soviet–Islamic relations became more and not less noticeable after the invasion of Afghanistan. At the end of 1979, the Soviet Union, which had already by a series of sponsored subversions obtained a dominant position in Afghanistan, decided that armed force was necessary to maintain it. The Soviet army and air force, therefore, embarked on a full-scale invasion of the country, in the course of which they violated an international boundary, arrested and executed the government of the country—which incidentally they themselves had had no small share in installing—and resorted, in order to maintain themselves, to the most brutal repression of the Afghan civil population. One would have thought that this was a clear-enough case of aggression. The aggression was certainly clear, but the menace was clearer and the response accordingly subdued. At the United Nations General Assembly, at gatherings of Third World or nonaligned states, even at Islamic summit conferences, it proved impossible to muster general support for an explicit condemnation of Soviet aggression and occupation. Instead, the most that could be accomplished was mildly worded reproaches, avoiding such offensive terms as "aggression" and "occupation" and for the most part even avoiding the mention of the Soviet Union by name, but merely "requesting" or "urging" the removal of "foreign troops" from Afghanistan. Notable in the discussions leading to these resolutions was the active lobbying of Syria, South Yemen, the PLO, and sometimes also Algeria and Libya on behalf of the Soviet Union. Pan-Islam, with its mini-*jihād* against a mini-enemy and its extreme caution elsewhere, did not carry conviction as a genuine force in international politics.

But the power and vitality of Islam should not be judged by the failures of old-style pan-Islamic diplomacy. Islam has shown its strength much more clearly in the internal politics of Muslim countries. Two examples, both of them in countries under autocratic rule, may serve. The first case was in Tunisia, where in February 1960 President Habib Bourguiba put forward the interesting idea that the month-long fast of Ramaḍān, with the resultant loss of work and production, was a luxury that a poor and developing country could not afford. For a Muslim ruler simply to abolish or disallow a major prescription of the holy law is unthinkable. What President Bourguiba did was to try to justify its abolition in terms of the holy law itself. This law allows a Muslim to break the fast if he is on campaign in a holy war, or *jihād*. Bourguiba argued that a developing country was in a state of *jihād* and that the struggle to obtain economic independence by development was comparable with a defensive war for national independence. In pursuit of this argument he proposed to abolish the rules whereby restaurants, cafés, and other public places were closed by day and by night during the month of Ramaḍān and to oblige them to keep normal hours. In support of this new interpretation of the law, he tried to obtain a *fatwā*, a ruling, from the mufti of Tunis and other religious authorities. The religious authorities refused to give him what he wanted. The great mass of the people observed the fast despite the president's dispensation, and Bourguiba was finally compelled to beat a more or less graceful retreat. Even an autocratic socialist head of state, in pursuit of so worthy an end as economic development, could not set aside a clear ruling of the holy law.

A more striking illustration of the religious limits on autocracy occurred in Syria in the spring of 1967. On 25 April of that year, the Syrian official army weekly, *Jaysh al-Sha'b* (Army of the People), published an article by a young officer named Ibrāhīm Khalas on how to form the character of "the new Arab Socialist Man." The only way, according to this article, to build Arab society and civilization was to create a new Arab socialist man who believes that God, religions, feudalism, capitalism, and all the values that prevailed in the old society are no more than "mummies in the museums of history" and that there is only one authentic value: faith in the new self-reliant man of destiny who works for mankind and knows that death is the inescapable end and that beyond death there is nothing—"no heaven and no hell. . . . "

In present-day Christendom, such sentiments would hardly raise an eyebrow, even in a theological journal. Among Muslims, even in a radical and revolutionary state, they raised considerably more than that. An apparently submissive population had acquiesced without serious demur in a whole series of radical political and economic changes: the suppression of free speech, the confiscation of private property, and the abrogation of almost all constitutional rights. But the denial of God and the rejection of religion in a government-sponsored journal revealed the limits of acquiescence, the point at which a Muslim people would rise in protest and defy even a ruthless dictatorship.

For several consecutive days there were strikes, protests, and public demonstrations in many cities. On 5 May, after a Friday sermon by a leading sheikh denouncing the atheism of the regime and the Ba'th party, tens of thousands of protesters demonstrated in the streets of Damascus.

The government, by now thoroughly alarmed, responded with several kinds of action. One was to arrest a number of religious leaders; another was to confiscate copies of the journal containing the offending article and to take action against its author and the members of the editorial board. They were imprisoned, and on the following day the semiofficial newspaper, *Al-Thawra* (The Revolution), proclaimed the reverence of the Syrian regime for God and religion. On 7 May, Radio Damascus announced that

> the sinful and insidious article published in the magazine *Jaysh al-Sha'b* came as a link in the chain of an American–Israeli reactionary conspiracy. . . . Investigation by the authorities has proved that the article and its author were merely tools of the CIA, which has been able to infiltrate most basely and squalidly and to attain its sinful aims of creating confusion among the ranks of the citizens.

The religious demonstrations, it was later announced, had been organized in concert with "the Americans, the British, the Jordanians, the Sa'udis, the Zionists, and Selīm Ḥāṭūm" (a Druse opponent of the regime). On 11 May, the author and editors were sentenced by a military court to life imprisonment. The author confessed to the court that he had been induced "by foreigners" to write the offending article.

Even in Nasserist Egypt, Islam continued to provide a main focus of loyalty and morale. Thus in the manual of orientation of the supreme command of the Egyptian forces, issued in 1965, the wars in the Yemen and against Israel are presented in terms of a *jihād* for God against the unbelievers. In reply to questions from the troops as to whether the classical Islamic obligation of *jihād* has lapsed or is still in force, orientation officers are instructed to reply that the *jihād* for God is still in force at the present time and is to be interpreted in our own day in terms of a striving for social justice and human betterment. The enemies against whom the *jihād* is to be waged are those who oppose or resist the achievement of these aims—that is, imperialism, Zionism, and the Arab reactionaries.

> In accordance with this interpretation of the mission of Islam and in accordance with this understanding of the *jihād*, we must always maintain that our military duty in the Yemen is a *jihād* for God and our military duty against Israel is a *jihād* for God, and for those who fight in this war there is the reward of fighters in the holy war for God. . . . Our duty is the holy war for God. "Kill them wherever you come upon them and drive them from the places from which they drove you."
>
> (Qur'ān 2:191)

That is, the war is a holy war, and the rewards of martyrdom as specified in scripture await those who are killed in it. Similar ideas are found in the manual of orientation issued to Egyptian troops in June 1973, and it is noteworthy that the operational code name for crossing the Suez Canal was Badr, the name of one of the battles fought by the Prophet against his infidel opponents. Incidentally, the enemy named in the manual is not Zionism or even Israel but simply "the Jews." One of the major contrasts between Syrian and Egyptian orientation literature is the far greater stress laid by the Egyptians on religion, as contrasted with the more ideological approach of the Syrians.

The war between Iraq and Iran revealed interesting similarities as well as differences between the declared war aims and war propaganda of the two protagonists. The Iranians, as one would expect, preferred to present the struggle in religious terms. The adversary was never described as Arab and rarely even as Iraqi, and their own cause in the early stages at least was only rarely named as Iran. Rather, they preferred to see themselves as defenders of Islam or of the Islamic revolution and republic, against a regime of apostates, atheists, backsliders, and renegades. Their war was against the Ba'th, not against the Iraqis or the Arabs, whom they sought to liberate from this anti-Islamic regime. The Iraqi regime, though not admitting that it was in any sense anti-Islamic, was at that time committed to a secular, nationalist ideology. Iraqis, therefore, spoke of a struggle against "the Persians," using the term *Furs*, which in classical Arabic was applied by the conquering Arabs to the conquered people of Iran. Sometimes they went even further and referred to the Persians as *Majūs*, Magians, a name used by the early Muslims to designate Zoroastrians, whom they regarded as idolaters. As well as the triumphs of Nebuchadnezzar, adopted as an Iraqi national hero, the Iraqis celebrate the great victory of Qādisiyya, in which an Arab Muslim army destroyed the might of the ancient empire of Iran. Both religious and patriotic themes appeared on both sides, the Iraqis invoking the memory of the first great Islamic *jihād* against imperial and pagan Iran, the Iranians—as so often before—reasserting the religious purity and revolutionary dynamism of authentic Islam against those who have corrupted it. As the war progressed, the Iraqis, without renouncing their nationalist and radical ideology, began to make more use of religious themes; the Iranians, without any visible slackening of their religious commitments, rediscovered something of the territorial patriotism that they had condemned in the shah.

There have been two recent wars in which Muslims fought against non-Muslims—the Turkish landing in Cyprus and the subsequent fighting, and the Syrian and Egyptian war against Israel in October 1973. In both Egypt and Turkey, the language and the rhetoric accompanying the offensives were strikingly religious. Popular legend of the kind that flourishes in wartime in all societies also assumed an overwhelmingly religious character, with stories of intervention by the Prophet and the angels of Allah on the side of the Muslims—that is, the Egyptians against their enemies. A writer who complained of this in the press, pointing out that it devalued the achievement of the Egyptian armed forces, was bitterly denounced. Not all Egyptians are, of course, Muslim. An important minority is Christian, and they too fought in the army and, indeed, number several senior officers among them. This fact is recognized in the guidance manual of the army, which invokes Christian as well as Muslim religious beliefs. Yet at the moment when news broke of the Israeli crossing to the west bank of the canal, a rumor immediately appeared ascribing this penetration to the treachery of a Coptic officer. There was of course no truth whatsoever in this story, and the Egyptian government took immediate steps to discount and deny it. It was probably not entirely coincidental that a Coptic general was promoted to an army command at that moment. Even more striking is the appearance of religious language among the secular Turks, who in the fighting in Cyprus used numerous Islamic terms to describe themselves, their adversaries, and the struggle between them.

If such is the reaction of Turks at a time of tension and conflict, the revival of Islamic feelings among other Muslim peoples, who have neither enjoyed a successful national liberation nor experienced a secular revolution, is incomparably more powerful and more passionate. The return to religious loyalties and the response to religious appeals have become stronger as the exponents of one secular ideology after another—liberalism, nationalism, capitalism, socialism, communism—have failed utterly to resolve the rapidly mounting problems of the Islamic world. Humiliation and privation, frustration and failure have so far discredited all the imported solutions and made increasing numbers of Muslims ready to believe those who tell them that only in a return to their own true faith and divinely ordained way of life can they find salvation in this world and the next.

In one Muslim country after another radical, popular movements of the kind commonly if inaccurately called fundamentalist have won mass support. In some, as in Egypt and Jordan, they are kept under uneasy restraint. In others, as in Algeria, they have been ruthlessly repressed. In two, Iran and Sudan, they have won power. Like their royal and national predecessors, they will be judged by what they do and fail to do.

It is not easy to assess the relative strengths of the Islamic fundamentalists and their moderate or modernist rivals. Only one Muslim country, Turkey, holds regular elections in which different parties compete and campaign freely and in which governments can fall and be replaced by democratic processes, not just once, as has happened elsewhere, but normally. In the Israeli-occupied territories, elections are from time to time held for civic, professional, and academic bodies, in which nationalist, leftist, and fundamentalist candidates compete against one another. These, exceptionally, provide a gauge of opinion and change. In most other countries, elections are avoided, controlled, or disregarded.

In recognizing the extent to which communal loyalty remains a significant force in the life of Muslim countries, one should not fall into the opposite error of discounting the degree of effective secularization. Particularly in the more developed countries, changes that are probably irreversible have already taken place, especially in the realms of social and economic life and in the organization of the law and the judiciary. In some countries, such as Turkey, Iran, and Egypt, geography and history have combined to give the inhabitants a special sense of separate identity and destiny and have advanced them on the path toward secular nationhood. But even in these, Islam remains a significant, elsewhere a major, force. In general, the extent of secularization is less than would at first appear. In education, for example, ostensibly secular schools and universities have to an increasing extent been subject to religious influences. Even in radical states like Syria, the net effect of secularization seems to be directed against minority religions much more than against Islam. A Syrian government report published in October 1967 states that private schools—meaning for the most part foreign-based Christian schools—would be obliged to use Ministry of Education textbooks on Christianity and Islam in which the teaching of the two religions was unified "in a manner that would not leave room for confessionalism . . . incompatible with the line of thought in our age."

From the foregoing, certain general conclusions emerge. Islam is still the most effective form of consensus in Muslim countries, the basic group identity among the masses. This will be increasingly effective as the regimes become more genuinely popular. One can already see the contrast between the present regimes and those of the small, alienated, Western-educated elite that governed until a few decades ago. As regimes come closer to the populace, even if their verbiage is leftist and ideological, they will become more Islamic. Under the Ba'thist regime in Syria, more mosques were built in the three years after the *Jaysh al-Sha'b* incident than in the previous thirty. And even Saddam Hussein, who ostensibly fought his own war against Iran as a defender of secular, modern values against religious fanaticism, himself resorted to passionate religious language during the Gulf War.

Islam is a powerful but still an undirected force in politics. As a possible factor in international politics, the present prognosis is not favorable. There have been many attempts at a pan-Islamic policy, none of which has made much progress. One reason for their lack of success is that those who have made the attempt have been so unconvincing. This still leaves the possibility of a more convincing leadership, and there is ample evidence in virtually all Muslim countries of the deep yearning for such a leadership and a readiness to respond to it. The lack of an educated modern leadership has so far restricted the scope of Islam and inhibited religious movements from being serious contenders for power. But it is already effective as a limiting factor and may yet become a powerful domestic political force if the right kind of leadership emerges. In Iran, clearly the right kind of leadership did emerge—right, that is, in that it was able to evoke and direct a remarkable outpouring of popular, revolutionary enthusiasm to overthrow and utterly destroy the old regime and to establish a new Islamic order in its place. How this new religious leadership will fare in exercising and retaining political power remains to be seen.

9

The Shīʿa in Islamic History

Shīʿa is an Arabic word, meaning party or faction. It was originally used of the Shīʿatu ʿAlī, the party of faction of ʿAlī, of those who thought he should be caliph—that is, in modern language, the supporters of a candidate for political office. As described in the earliest Arabic historical narratives, they formed a group with a political and, in the initial stage, largely a personal choice, as the basis for their group actions. In time, the word came to denote one of the major divisions of the Islamic religious community.

In accordance with a common but nevertheless misleading practice, outside observers often use words like "sect" and "schism" to describe these Islamic differences. Some go even further and use such words as "orthodox" and "heterodox" or "heretical" to describe Islamic religious disagreements. This is, for two reasons, inappropriate. For one thing, it is surely presumptuous for those who are not Muslims to say what is orthodox and what is heretical in Islam. That is neither our business nor within our competence. But perhaps rather more important, it is also inappropriate in that the very notion of orthodoxy and heterodoxy is specifically Christian. It has little or no relevance to the history of Islam, which has no synods, churches, or councils to define orthodoxy, and therefore none to define and condemn departures from orthodoxy, which we normally designate by such terms as "heterodoxy" and "heresy." Even such words as "sect" and "schism" are not appropriate to Islamic religious divisions, as regards neither the basis on which they are defined nor the forms of organization and action that they adopt and follow.

In trying to explain the difference between Sunnis and Shīʿa to Western audiences, some have described them as the equivalents of Protestants and Catholics. Except in the sense that it connotes a major division with large numbers of people on each side of a dividing line, this description is not very helpful. The absurdity of the comparison is shown by a simple test. If the Sunnis and the Shīʿa are Protestants and Catholics, which, then, are the Protestants and which the Catholics? The impossibility of answering this question immediately demonstrates the falsity of the comparison.

Western scholarship has at various times offered other explanations. In the nineteenth century, in a Europe fascinated by race, some saw the division as one between Semites and Aryans, the Sunnis representing the Semitism of Arabian Islam and the Shī'a representing the upsurge of Aryan Iran, in a racial revolt against Semitic domination. Later, in an age when Europe was riven by class war and obsessed with class-war ideologies, the Shī'a were seen as "representing" the dispossessed masses, while the Sunnis became the establishment, and a whole series of interpretations along these lines received currency. None of these is wholly false; none of them is wholly true. They have clarified some things that were obscure. They have also obscured some things that were reasonably clear.

In earlier times, the divisions between Sunni and Shī'a and between the many groups among the Shī'a were not as rigid as they later became; they were never, even later, as rigid as the differences between Protestants and Catholics or even between the different Protestant churches in Christendom. To the present day, the difference is strongly felt only in countries like Iraq, Lebanon, and Pakistan, where Sunni and Shī'a communities live side by side. Among Muslims in both Arab and black Africa and in Southeast Asia, where Shī'ites are little known, the difference is of far less importance, and Shī'ite leaders can win Sunni followers. In the earlier period especially, movement was easy from one to the other. And when seen from a Sunni point of view, even Shī'ism is not necessarily a religious aberration, a theological deviation. Sunni jurists and theologians have sometimes been willing to consider moderate Shī'a views as falling within the permitted limits of difference of opinion.

The principle that believers may agree on essentials and differ on particulars is deep rooted in Islam. It is frequently cited to justify the accepted disagreements among the four major schools of Sunni jurisprudence, and there have always been some who were willing to recognize a form of Shī'ism as constituting a difference or departure no greater, or not much greater, than that separating, say, Mālikīs from Ḥanafīs. This kind of permissible Shī'ite inclination or sympathy is called *tashayyu' ḥasan,* a lawful partisanship, of which there are many examples in Islamic history. Indeed, a mild *tashayyu'* seems to have affected the intellectual life of medieval Islam in much the same way that liberal and leftist notions have affected the intellectuals of the modern West, with the same range of gradations from mild sympathy through intellectual dissent to violent opposition.

The split between Sunni and Shī'a began as a political quarrel, a difference between two groups of Muslims over who should be their leader; who, that is, should be the successor of the Prophet as head of the community and head of the state. In the earlier stages, there seems to have been no more to it than that, no more than disagreements about what one might nowadays call nominations and candidatures. And these, as happens in other contexts and other societies, were usually settled by political or military means.

But what began as a political disagreement acquired in the course of time a much wider and deeper character. There were legal differences, which are of minor importance, for the most part no greater than those that divide the Sunni juristic schools. There were doctrinal differences, which perhaps in the larger perspective are also of minor importance. What are probably much more important than either are the psychological and emotional differences, the differences of mood and attitude resulting from the contrasting experience of those who were Sunnis and those who adhered to the Shīʿa.

The Ayatollah Khomeini has been quoted as defining the distinction between Sunnis and Shīʿa in this way: that the Sunnis have on the whole been quietist, teaching and practicing submission to authority however evil and however repressive, while the Shīʿa have represented the principle of resistance and opposition, of seeking the overthrow of illegitimate or tyrannical rule. This is very much an oversimplification. We find quietist and activist groups and individuals and doctrines among both Sunnis and Shīʿa; the Shīʿa indeed give us what is probably the extreme form of quietism in the doctrine of *taqiyya,* that one may not only submit to illegitimate power, but also feign acceptance and conceal one's true beliefs if this is necessary for survival. There is, however, an important element of truth in the Ayatollah's dictum. It may be an oversimplification; it is not a falsehood. And it may be useful to consider at greater length these two aspects of Islamic tradition, the radical and the conformist.

From the first, there were some who felt that Abū Bakr, the first caliph, was not the best candidate; others went further and condemned him as a usurper. Many of these saw in ʿAlī ibn Abī Ṭālib—the kinsman of the Prophet, husband of his daughter Fātima, and father of his grandchildren—the true and only rightful successor. As the polity and community of Islam grew rapidly through conquest and conversion, its people were subjected to increasing strains, and growing numbers of them began to feel that Islam had been deflected from its true path and that the Muslims were being led back into the paganism and injustice from which the Prophet had been sent to save them. For those who held such views, the reigning caliphs appeared more and more as tyrants and usurpers, while for many, the claims of the Prophet's kin, embodied first in ʿAlī and then in his descendants, came to express their hopes and aspirations for the overthrow of the corrupt existing order and a return to pure, authentic, and original Islam.

In their own perception, the Shīʿa were the opposition in Islam, the defenders of the oppressed, the critics and opponents of privilege and power. The Sunni Muslims, broadly speaking, stood for the status quo—the maintenance of the existing political, social, and above all religious order. There was a doctrinal basis for this claim. After the death of the Prophet and the completion of the revelation vouchsafed to him, God's guidance, in Sunni belief, passed from the Prophet to the Muslim community as a whole. According to a much-quoted saying of the Prophet, "God will not allow my people to agree on an error."[1] The notion of consensus embodied in this dictum was the guiding principle of Sunni theology and jurisprudence, including the political and constitutional provisions of the holy law. History for the Sunni, therefore, is of profound importance, since the experience of the Sunni community reveals the working out of God's purpose for mankind. In another much-quoted saying, the Prophet urges the believer "not to separate himself from the community."[2] This gives a special, even a theological, value to precedent and tradition and makes conformism and obedience basic religious obligations.

In principle, the Shīʿite philosophy is the exact opposite. After the death of the Prophet and still more after the murder of ʿAlī thirty years later, history, in the Shīʿite view, took a wrong turning, and the Muslim community has, so to speak, been living in sin ever since. For the Sunni, obedience to authority is a divine commandment that lapses only in rare and extreme cases. For the Shīʿite, obedience to the existing authority is a political necessity owed as long as it can be exacted and no longer.

Any inquiry into early Islamic history, any study based on the Islamic sources that purport to preserve the record of the early formative years, must now take account of two major developments in recent scholarship devoted to this period. One of them is the growing skepticism among modern scholars as to the authenticity, even the historicity, of many of the early Arabic narrative sources. There has been great controversy in recent years about whether early Islamic historiography is really historiography and whether the events recorded in these writings ever happened. The other major development is the tendency to see the advent of Islam not so much as a discontinuity, an abrupt change and a new beginning as contrasted with pre-Islam, but, rather, in many respects at least, as a continuation, admittedly in new forms and to some extent even in new directions, of processes that can be traced back to a more remote past.

Obviously, any consideration of the early history of Shīʿism must take account of these developments in scholarship. But neither of these views need necessarily invalidate conclusions based on the examination of early and, for that matter, later Islamic material. Scholars have argued, with varying degrees of plausibility, that the earliest Arabic historical sources are neither historical nor sources, but are later creations designed and assembled, according to some, to furnish a background of case law for subsequent jurisprudence; according to others, to provide retroactive legitimization for later political structures and doctrines.

But for the history of ideas and attitudes, which is our present concern, the factual accuracy of the historical narrative is of secondary importance. The narrative as preserved, transmitted, and studied contains what Muslims believed to be their past. And it was this perceived past, handed down in sometimes contrasting versions, that shaped their ideas and that they used to justify their actions. With a religion as political as Islam, in a polity as religious as the Islamic caliphate, such questions as the source and nature of authority, the duty and limits of obedience, the definitions of legitimacy, justice, and tyranny, and the manner of dealing with a tyrant or a usurper acquired a central importance. And in formulating and answering these questions, the record of early Islamic times as transmitted to later Islamic times furnished ample if somewhat contradictory guidance, much of which—as the war propaganda of both Iran and Iraq between 1980 and 1988 demonstrated—is still relevant. The names of ʿAlī, Muʿāwiya, and Yazīd are as contemporary as this morning's newspaper, more so than yesterday's. Even the fading memories of a more distant past—a pre-Islamic past that survived in a disguised or attenuated form after the Islamic dispensation—are still important.

Some of these vestiges are relevant to the evolution of Shīʿism. From the Judaeo-Christian scriptures and traditions came the notion of a prophet who arises to rebuke an unjust ruler, and the belief in a Messiah who comes to establish God's order on earth. Both are rather political notions; both are obviously religious. From the Greco-Roman world, which also bequeathed a considerable heritage to Islam, came some rather interesting arguments and stories about the theory and practice of tyrannicide. From pre-Islamic Persia came distant but still dangerous memories of religiously formulated defiance of authority, of revolutionary movements that challenged simultaneously the political, moral, and social basis of the existing order, with a religious doctrine as ideology and a religious sect as instrument. We may recall the words attributed to a medieval extremist leader who tried to win support by evoking the memory of Mazdak, the great revolutionary of Zoroastrian times. "Mazdak has become a Shīʿī."[3]

In a sense, the advent of Islam itself was a revolution. It began during the early career of the Prophet as a challenge to the old leadership and the old order of Mecca. Its success overthrew and supplanted them both, one by the Prophet and his Companions and the other by Islam, not as a religion in the limited modern sense of that word, but in the wider Islamic sense—that is, a new social and political order differing in many significant ways from the old.

According to the traditional biography, the Prophet Muḥammad began his career in Mecca as an opposition leader, and was for some time engaged in a struggle against authority as established among his people and in his birthplace. When his position as an opponent of the regime became untenable, he moved to another place, to Medina, a move that marks the beginning of the Muslim era. There he formed a government and raised an army, and from this external base he finally returned and accomplished the forcible overthrow and supersession of the old order. In this, as in all else, the Prophet is seen as the model and pattern of behavior.

In the Qur'ān (23:21; cf. 60:4, 6) the Prophet is described as *uswa ḥasana,* which might be translated into the language of modern sociology as role model. His sequence of resistance, migration, and return became a paradigm for Islamic movements that sought to challenge the existing order and to establish a new one in its place. Such were the 'Abbasids who went east to Khorāsān and then returned to the center to establish their caliphate in Baghdad; the Fatimids who went west to Ifrīqiya, North Africa, and thence returned to the center to found their caliphate in Cairo; and, of course, the Ayatollah Khomeini, who found his Khorāsān or his Ifrīqiya in Neauphle-le-Château and returned to Qom. There were many others, during the Islamic centuries, who tried the same gambit. Few succeeded; many failed.

The radical tradition inaugurated by the Prophet in Mecca was continued under his successors, the caliphs, with the Islamic conquests known to Islamic historiography as *futūḥ,* literally openings. In early Islamic historiography, these are not seen as conquests in the vulgar sense of territorial acquisition, but as the overthrow of regimes and hierarchies that had forfeited their legitimacy. They were seen as the "opening" of these people to the new revelation and the new dispensation. This use of the verb *fataḥa,* to open, is obviously parallel to the mid-twentieth-century use of the verb "to liberate," by which indeed it is often replaced in twentieth-century Arabic writing. The notion of an old order superseded by the new is vividly expressed in the invocation of the ultimatum said to have been sent by the Arab Muslim commander Khālid ibn al-Walīd to the princes of Persia: "Praise be to God who has dissolved your order, frustrated your evil designs, and sundered your unity."[4]

In Islam, as in other societies, the victors faced the eternal problem of all successful revolutionaries: how to defend their own accession, to justify their own actions in overthrowing and replacing their predecessors, without at the same time giving anticipatory justification to others who might want to do the same thing to them. They found answers. For the Prophet and his contemporaries, their position was clear: the test was God's authorization by revelation. This justified the Prophet in attacking and overthrowing the pagan oligarchs of Mecca; and also his remaining in power against anyone else who might try to resist or end his authority. For the generation of the *futūḥ,* the position was almost equally clear: the test was the possession of God's faith and God's law. The objective was the replacement of unbelief, which as such cannot be legitimate, by Islam, through which alone God conferred legitimate authority. The idea is incidentally linked with the doctrine of *fiṭra,* according to which all human beings are born Muslims but some are turned into Jews, Christians, or pagans by their parents.

The basic problem of legitimacy assumed a different and much more difficult form when the regime or the ruler subject to challenge was not Christian, not pagan, but Muslim, and when successful revolutionary action would mean the removal of a Muslim ruler or the overthrow of a Muslim regime. With the establishment of the caliphate and the creation of a vast Muslim oecumene extending from the Atlantic to India and to China, it was in this form that the problem commonly arose. In addressing it, Islamic doctrine and sacred history embodied two distinct and in part conflicting traditions: the one quietist, the other activist.[5] Both are part of pristine Islam, both based in the Qur'ān and buttressed by *ḥadīth,* and both reinforced by traditions inherited and by principles learned from the older civilizations and religions of the Middle East, in what had by now become the heartlands of the Islamic state, society, and culture.

The quietist tradition is classically grounded in the Qur'ānic text (4:59): "Obey God, obey his Prophet and obey those among you who hold authority" and is amply documented in tradition and in jurisprudence. According to this doctrine, obedience even to the most improbable authority is a religious duty as well as a political necessity, and disobedience is therefore a sin as well as a crime to be punished in both worlds, this and the next. The same idea is expressed in a *ḥadīth:* "Obey him who holds authority over you, even if he be a mutilated Ethiopian slave"[6]—thus expressing the ultimate improbability at once in physical, racial, and social terms.

But the activist tradition also rests on Qur'ān and *ḥadīth.* There are Qur'ānic texts in which the believers are commanded not to obey a variety of ancient and pagan tyrants, notably Pharaoh, the archetype for Muslims as well as for Jews and Christians of the pagan oppressor of God's people. These passages are confirmed and clarified in *ḥadīth* and in the commentaries. The most commonly cited *ḥadīth* to this effect quotes the Prophet as saying: "There is no obedience in sin." That is, when the ruler commands something that is sinful, the duty of obedience lapses. Some go even further and say that the duty of obedience is replaced by a duty of disobedience.

According to traditional historiography, the question was first posed in an acute form on 17 June 656, when ʿUthmān ibn ʿAffān was murdered. ʿUthmān was not the first caliph to be murdered. But whereas his predecessor ʿUmar was murdered by a foreign infidel, ʿUthmān was killed by Muslim Arab mutineers. This act of armed rebellion inaugurated the first of a series of civil wars that brought deep divisions to the Islamic polity and community.

In the course of these civil wars, two basic positions emerged. For one side, ʿUthmān was a rightful and a just ruler. His killing was therefore a crime and a sin, and ʿAlī, who gave shelter to those who had killed him and refused to hand them over to the justice of Muʿāwiya, was condoning a sin. For the other side, 'Uthmān was a wrongful and unjust ruler. His killing was therefore an execution, a lawful, indeed a necessary, act, and 'Alī was acting properly in sheltering the executioners and refusing to hand them over to the vengeance of ʿUthmān's kinsman and fellow malefactor. In time, one of these two views of the death of ʿUthmān became identified with the Sunnis, the other with the Shīʿa. But this was a long and complex evolution and went through a number of stages before it was crystallized in this form.

In the course of Shīʿa history, certain themes recur that seem to be characteristic of the Shīʿa role among Muslims. One has already been mentioned, the theme of usurpation and tyranny, the belief that the rulers of Islam are usurping places that rightfully belong to others and sometimes, in addition, that they are ruling in evil ways. The difference between usurper and tyrant was clearly understood, but in time the two notions came to coalesce. There is a pervasive feeling among the Shīʿa that the established authority, the established ruler, is illegitimate, lacking the legitimacy that alone can come from God. This perception is associated with a strong sense of injustice, of oppression. A resonant word that is frequently used to denote the victim of injustice is *ḍaʿīf,* also familiar in the derived verbal form *mustaḍʿaf,* meaning humbled, oppressed, downtrodden. *Ḍaʿīf* literally means weak, but it has a number of additional technical meanings. Sometimes, for example, it seems to mean *ḍaʿīf al-nasab,* weak of pedigree, opposed to those who are noble—that is, something like plebeian, as opposed to patrician. Often it is used to denote those who do not have the right to bear arms, an important disability in a society in which one of the major social distinctions is between those who bear arms and those who do not. The latter, of course, included women, non-Muslims, and nonmilitary slaves but also important groups of free male Muslims. Of the five occurrences of the word *mustaḍʿaf* in the Qurʿān, three (4:75, 98, 127) appear in a context of woman and children; two (4:97 and 8:26) refer to the Muslims when they were a persecuted minority. In Shīʿa propaganda, especially in revolutionary Iran, it is in the latter sense that the cause of the *mustaḍʿaf* is commonly championed.

A second characteristic feature of Shīʿa action is armed insurrection, of which we find innumerable examples throughout the length and breath of the Islamic world and through the centuries of Islamic history. Often this action was linked with the notion of tyrannicide, the personal removal of the ruler seen as a tyrant, of which the murder of ʿUthmān is the earliest paradigm and of which there are many later examples. And since small groups of opponents of the regime are rarely able to accomplish much by armed insurrection, this leads over time to the evolution of what we nowadays call terrorism and what its perpetrators see as the ultimate act of devotion. The more autocratic and personal the regime, the more hopeful the prospect of changing it by killing the ruler. Often this kind of terrorism is associated with an almost sacramental cult of weapons and sometimes also with the notion that the terrorist, the assassin, must not survive the act of terror but must himself perish as a final sacrifice. The same spirit seems to inspire the suicide bombers of the present day. In this they differ from the state-sponsored and private-enterprise hijackers, kidnappers, and wholesale murderers whose activities have brought terrorism into disrepute.

Most Shīʿa attempts to gain power ended in failure: the suppression of the rebellion, the extirpation of the terrorists, the death or disappearance of their leaders. This in turn led to another distinctive feature of Shīʿism, a Shīʿa conception of martyrdom significantly different from that of Sunni Muslims.

The notion of martyrdom is common to Christendom and Islam. Indeed, the same word is used—"martyr" is from a Greek word meaning witness, and the Arabic *shahīd* has the same meaning. But in Sunni Islam, the *shahīd* is one who is killed in battle; he achieves martyrdom by dying in the holy war. This is very different from the Jewish and later also Christian notion of martyrs as those who voluntarily endure torture and death rather than renounce their beliefs. The Shīʿa share the Sunni idea of martyrdom by death in battle, but they also use the word for those who suffer personally, through imprisonment, torture, and execution, for their beliefs or their actions—a notion much closer to the Judaeo-Christian conception of martyrdom. And with this sense of martyrdom came a whole cluster of other feelings, of suffering and passion, betrayal and penitence, and self-immolation.

The suppression of many risings and the disappearance of their leaders gave rise to another characteristic feature of Shīʿa doctrine, the related themes of *ghayba* and *rajʿa,* concealment or occultation, and return. The leader, the *mahdī,* the *imām* (he is known by various names), disappears. His followers say that he is not dead; he has gone into concealment, from which—and this is an essential part of the belief—he will in time return. And each leader who disappeared and did not return enriched the growing eschatological myth with some new detail. This messianism became an essential feature of Shīʿa Islam.

Not all the uprisings were suppressed. Some were, so to speak, taken over. There was the successful rebellion of the ʿAbbasids, who used Shīʿa and pro-ʿAlī slogans to overthrow the Umayyads and then set aside the ʿAlids and installed themselves in their place. There was the civil war between al-Amīn and al-Maʾmūn after the death of Hārūn al-Rashīd, in which again the pro-ʿAlī faction was victorious, but the ʿAlids were again outmaneuvered by the victorious ʿAbbasid claimant. There was the revolution of the Ismāʿīlīs, which reached its high point with the victory of the Fatimids, a Shīʿa though not a Twelver Shīʿa group. Theirs was the other kind of failure: success. They overthrew their predecessors. They gained power. And they carried on without any great or significant changes until, in the course of time, their power waned and their regime was overthrown and replaced, this time by Sunnis.

It was these revolts and especially their almost invariable failure that gave a distinctive quality to Shīʿite Islam. Certain recurring features may be seen in the participants, the tactics, the leadership, and the doctrines of these revolts. As challengers of the existing order, the Shīʿa naturally found their main support among those who saw themselves as oppressed by it, and Shīʿite writings lay great stress on their appeal to the wronged, the downtrodden, the deprived. Although the Shīʿa certainly had their own noble, wealthy, and learned families, their main following seems to have been among the artisans and workers in the cities and among peasants in the countryside. At certain periods, Shīʿite ideas had a considerable appeal for intellectuals. In most Muslim lands, however, the Shīʿa were a minority. Even where they became a majority, with the exception of Iran, they remained in a subordinate position. A striking case is that of Iraq, where a Shīʿite majority has remained subject to a Sunni ascendancy—to borrow a word from Anglo-Irish history—that can be traced back from the present regime to the monarchy, the British Mandate, the Ottoman Empire, and beyond into the Middle Ages.

The one major political success gained by the Shīʿa since the Middle Ages was the accession to power of the Shīʿite Safavid dynasty in Iran at the beginning of the sixteenth century. Until then, Iran, like most other Muslim countries, appears to have been predominantly Sunni. The Safavids and their supporters were fervent Shīʿites, and succeeded not only in imposing Shīʿism as the state doctrine of Iran, but also in winning the adherence of the majority of the population. In its initial phase, the Safavid movement arose from a radical, extremist branch of the Shīʿa, with millenarian overtones and far-reaching aspirations and ambitions. These were contained by the surrounding Sunni powers in Turkey, Central Asia, and India and in due course were abandoned even in Iran. Even before the Safavids, there were other Shīʿite leaders who succeeded in gaining power. But without exception, they failed to fulfill their promise. Most were ousted after a longer or shorter interval; the remainder, once established in power, forgot their earlier programs and conducted their affairs in ways not significantly different from those of the Sunnis whom they had overthrown.

What, then, is the basic difference between Sunni and Shīʿa Islam? From the Sunni point of view, what is, is right, in a very important sense. The community is God's community, obeying and exemplifying God's law and ruled and led by a caliph whose office is established by God but whose person is chosen by the community. In principle—and according to Sunni belief, in early times also in practice—the caliph was the sole lawful head of that community. His office was both required and regulated by divine law, and his main task was to uphold and enforce that law and to extend its jurisdiction.

But the caliphate deteriorated. The caliphs abused or lost their authority and in time were replaced by a succession and a variety of dynastic and other rulers, who seized, retained, and exercised sovereignty by military power. The Sunni jurists, well aware of the brute facts of usurpation and tyranny, could not, according to the logic of their own principles, simply denounce the usurpers and tyrants and demand their overthrow, since to do so would violate the rule of law and thus endanger the unity of the Muslims and the coherence and stability of Muslim society. This in turn could frustrate the ultimate purpose of all government and law—to enable the Muslims to live the good Muslim life in this world and thus prepare themselves for eternal life in the next.

"Whose power prevails must be obeyed" and "The world can live with tyranny but not with anarchy," two commonly cited sayings, express the sad resignation of the Sunni jurists and theologians to political realities. As long as a ruler maintains order and upholds the basic principles of the Muslim faith and law, he must be obeyed as a religious obligation. In Sunni doctrine, the caliphate is a contract, imposing obligations on both ruler and subject, and dissoluble if either party fails in his obligations. But under many if not most regimes, the performance required of the ruler was ever more minimally defined, and the duties of the subject were ever more strictly enforced.

Like the Shīʿa, the Sunnis have their radical, activist movements, but their requirements for action are far more stringent than those of the Shīʿa, and in the Sunni view, far greater evil must be endured before the duty of obedience lapses and an evildoing ruler may lawfully be overthrown.

Sunni Muslims never renounced, and sometimes strongly asserted, the principle that the subject need not, indeed must not, obey when the commands of the ruler are themselves unlawful. This principle underlies the teaching and actions of the radical Sunni fundamentalist groups at the present time. But the jurists never discussed, let alone prescribed, any procedure for testing the lawfulness of the rulers' actions, and the decision was usually left to the arbitrament of force. In whatever circumstances, when a ruler was ousted and a new ruler took his place, the same duty of obedience, for the same reasons, was due to him as to his ousted predecessor. There is therefore a sense in which the acceptance of existing facts is a religious obligation, because to deny them would be to admit that the whole Islamic community is, so to speak, living in sin, an unacceptable position from a Sunni viewpoint.

For the Shīʿa, this is not so. For them, virtually all Islamic government since the murder of ʿAlī ibn Ṭālib has been illegitimate or, at best, provisional. There is no legitimacy in the existing order. Sometimes the response to this is passive acquiescence—separation and withdrawal rather than involvement; at other times, the Shīʿa embark on great projects and actions whose purpose is to restore history to the right path.

So far they have always been defeated: sometimes because they were crushed by those who already held power; sometimes, in the more tragic case, because they themselves, after gaining power, were transformed and corrupted. The tragedy is deepened when, however transformed and corrupted, they remain in power.

10

Country and Freedom

In the twelfth book of the *Iliad,* the Trojan hero Hector, dismissing the fears of Polydamas that inauspicious omens may presage a bad result in the impending battle, robustly assures him: "One omen is best, to fight for one's country."[1] Hector was mistaken about the omen, since he himself was killed and Troy was doomed, but the duty to fight was not affected. Centuries later, the Roman poet Horace, in his *Odes,* goes a step further and asserts that "it is sweet and becoming to die for one's country."[2] The Greek *patris* and the Latin *patria,* translated as country in the foregoing citations, are obviously related, and both derive from words meaning father. Both convey the meaning of paternal and ancestral home. In ancient Greek and Roman civilization, this usually meant a city—the normal unit of political identity, loyalty, and authority. A Greek or Roman was not merely a city-dweller; he was a citizen, in Greek *politēs,* in Latin *civis,* with the right to share in the formation and conduct of the government of his city and a corresponding duty to fight and, if necessary, to die in its cause.

In the Roman Empire, the unit of identity became larger and could extend from a city to a whole province or even to what we would nowadays call a country. The level of civic responsibility and political participation was sharply reduced, but the duty to fight for one's *patria,* however redefined, remained.[3]

It continued into medieval and early modern Europe, where despite the definition of identity by the churches and the claims to allegiance of feudal kings and lords, the sense of country, as the ultimate identity and loyalty, remained strong and became stronger. The Byzantine *Autokratōr* and the Holy Roman *Kaiser* put forward their competing claims to be head of all of Christendom, but in most Christian lands, rule was exercised by kings who defined their sovereignty in terms of territory—kings of England and of Scotland, of Denmark and of Sweden, of Poland, Hungary, and Bohemia, and later, because of an Arab hiatus, of Portugal and Spain. The same process may be seen in the work of the historians of medieval Europe, who proceeded, fairly rapidly, from the history of kings and tribes and peoples to the history of kingdoms and countries. By the sixteenth century, Joachim du Bellay celebrates his country as "France, mère des arts, des armes et des lois," and Shakespeare, in one of several passages, expresses his love for

> This blessed plot, this earth, this realm, this England,
> This nurse, this teeming womb of royal kings.

The Greek *patriōtēs* and the late Latin *patriota,* which were used in the sense of compatriot or fellow countryman, in their later European versions acquire a new meaning, of one devoted to the service and cause of his country, and a new word, "patriotism," denotes the sentiments and beliefs of the patriot.

The Arabic word *waṭan,* which, with slight changes of pronunciation, is also used in Persian, Turkish, and other Islamic languages which draw on Arabic for their conceptual vocabulary, had a somewhat different evolution. The Arabic verb *waṭana* means to reside or sojourn in a place; it also means to choose a place of residence or to settle in it. The noun *waṭan* has none of the paternal or ancestral connotations of *patris* or *patria,* but simply means one's place of residence, which may be adopted or temporary. Normally a *waṭan* is a town, but it may also be a village or, more extensively, the province in which one's town or village of *waṭan* is situated. The plural form *awṭan* appears commonly in the sense of provinces. The fourteenth-century author Juzjānī distinguishes between the *waṭan* proper, "a man's birthplace and the place where he lives," and the *waṭan* of sojourn, where a man spends at least fifteen days but does not establish permanent residence.[4] This is obviously very far from the classical and modern connotations of *patris, patria,* and their equivalents in European languages.

Despite this lack of political content, the word *waṭan*—in the simple meaning of home or homeland—could have many sentimental associations, and there are many allusions in classical Arabic and other Islamic literatures, in both prose and verse, to the love and devotion which people felt for their birthplace or homeland.[5] Even the nomadic bedouin felt a kind of association, an emotional involvement, with the pasturages through which they roved at different times of the year. One of the basic themes of ancient Arabian poetry is the nostalgic sentiment evoked in the poet by the traces of an abandoned camp, where he and his tribe had halted at some time in the past. The great ninth-century essayist Jāḥiẓ even devoted a whole essay to the subject of love of one's *waṭan,*[6] and a late and therefore certainly spurious *ḥadīth* even attributes to the Prophet the dictum that "love of one's *waṭan* is part of the faith." The thirteenth-century Syrian geographer Ibn Shaddād begins his geographical work with his native city of Aleppo and defends his choice with a series of quotations from poetry and tradition, exalting the love of *waṭan.*[7] A fifteenth-century central Asian Turkish poet, 'Alī Shīr Navā' ī, even speaks of fighting for one's *waṭan* but significantly links it with family:

For family and *watan,* as long as he has life
A man will fight as long as he can.[8]

Another central Asian text of the same period tells how a pious Sufi sheikh was asked: "How can love of *waṭan* be part of the faith, since the infidels also love their *waṭan*? What therefore is the meaning of this *ḥadīth?*" To this the sheikh replied that when someone passes from the world of contemplation to the world of darkness, he then loves the previous world, and such loving is part of the faith.[9]

The *waṭan* was thus a focus of sentiment, of affection, of nostalgia, but not of loyalty, and only to a limited extent of identity. The great Arab historian Ibn Khaldūn relates that on a certain occasion the caliph 'Umar said to the Arabs: "Learn your genealogies, and don't be like the Nabataeans of Mesopotamia who, if asked about their origin, reply: 'I come from such and such a village'."[10] There may be some question about the authenticity of the quotation and its attribution, but there can be no doubt about the authenticity of the sentiment, which is echoed and re-echoed throughout the centuries. It is attested in the titulature of Muslim monarchs, who in inscriptions, documents, and coins usually defined their sovereignty in religious terms, rarely in ethnic terms, never in territorial terms. European monarchs might call themselves the king of England, the king of France, or the king of Spain, but in the lands of Islam, territorial titles were used to belittle a rival, not to aggrandize oneself. In the conflicts and also in the correspondence between competing Muslim great powers in the sixteenth and seventeenth centuries, the sultan of Turkey and the shah of Persia called each other by these titles, but never themselves.[11] Each was concerned to reduce his rival to the level of a local potentate. Each in his own titulature was the Supreme Lord of the Muslims. This same perception of identity and authority may be seen in the work of premodern Muslim historians, who write the history of Islam, of caliphs and sultans and dynasties, and sometimes also local history, but not the history of countries or nations.

The use of the word *waṭan* (Turkish *vatan*) in a political sense, equivalent to the French *patrie,* the English "country," or the German *Vaterland,* dates from the late eighteenth century and is clearly due to European influence and example.[12] The earliest occurrence that I have been able to trace of the use of the word *waṭan* in this sense is in a Turkish document—a report by Morali Esseyyid Ali Efendi, who served as Ottoman ambassador in Paris under the *Directoire.* In a description of the hospitals and homes provided by the French authorities for pensioned and disabled soldiers, he speaks of these soldiers as having striven "in the cause of the republic and out of zeal for the *waṭan* [*Cümhur uğurunda ve vatan gayretinde*]."[13] Both words, *cümhur* and *vatan,* were old, with roots in classical Arabic. *Cümhur* had already acquired a political connotation at an earlier date, throughout Ottoman acquaintance with Venice and other European republics.[14] Patriotism was a new discovery, from the French Revolution.

The phrase was almost certainly translated by Ali Efendi's interpreter from a document made available to him in French, and one may wonder how much meaning it conveyed to him. Later in the same report he speaks frequently of the French Republic, and occasionally of the French state (*devlet*) and nation (*millet*), terms which would have been more familiar, rather than of *vatan*.

Nevertheless, the new meaning of the word gradually became increasingly familiar. The earliest references in the nineteenth century are mostly in translated texts or descriptions of European events, but by the 1830s the word had entered Ottoman official usage. A report published by the Board of Public Works in 1838,[15] speaking of the need for better and more extensive education, observes that "without science, the people cannot know the meaning of love for the state and *vatan*." In the following year, *vatan* even appears in an Ottoman official document, no less than the great reform decree of 1839, known as the Edict of the Rosebower, *Gülhane*. In this the Sultan, speaking of military matters, observes that "it is the inescapable duty of all the people to provide soldiers for the defense of the fatherland [*vatan*]."[16] In 1840, a Turkish diplomat called Mustafa Sami lists the praiseworthy qualities of the people of Paris as modesty, composure, love of country (*vatan*) and nation (*millet*), and the safeguarding of the law.[17] By the mid-century, the association of country (*vatan*) with state (*devlet*) and nation (*millet*) as something not only to be loved but also to be served and if necessary fought for has become commonplace. A striking example of this association of ideas occurs in a letter which the Turkish poet and journalist Şinasi wrote to his mother from Paris in 1851: "I want to devote (or sacrifice) myself to the cause of my religion, state, country [*vatan*] and nation [*millet*]."[18]

The events of the Crimean War (1854–56) in many ways favored the development of the new patriotic sense of identity, loyalty, and duty. Since the beginning of the sixteenth century, almost all the many wars of the Ottoman Empire, apart from a few with its Shīʿite rivals in Persia, were against Christian powers, and the Ottomans had become accustomed to seeing each of these wars as a *jihād*. In their perception, even in their language of warfare, their cause was Islam, their enemy the infidels; their fighters were Gazis, their dead were martyrs. In their early wars in the Balkan peninsula, the Ottomans sometimes made use of local Christian auxiliaries and mercenaries. In their later wars, notably in the Napoleonic period, they found themselves involved in larger European struggles, with Christian powers supporting as well as opposing them. But these had little effect on Ottoman perceptions, and as late as the early nineteenth century, those Christian powers that joined them against their Christian enemies were not allies but rather loosely associated cobelligerents. The Crimean War was a new and unprecedented experience. For the first time, the Ottoman Empire fought against its old enemy, Russia, with two major West European powers as allies—this time not as remote and barely visible associates but as comrades in arms, with armies on Ottoman soil and fleets in Ottoman waters, fighting side by side against the common enemy. The rapid and forced development resulting from involvement in a major war brought many changes to Turkey, among them the telegraph, the daily newspaper, and a wide range of new ideas. The patriotism of the British and the French and their lack of concern at fighting with Muslim allies against a Christian enemy can hardly have escaped Turkish notice. The term *vatan* begins to appear frequently in Turkish newspapers, and a poet of the time, Halis Efendi, published what was probably the first patriotic poem.[19] Before long, there were many others, and some of them sounded a different note.

The adoption of this new patriotic ideology was by no means unresisted. No less a person than the great jurist and historian Cevdet Paşa made a powerful protest against it. During the Grand Vizirate of Fuad Paşa, a special commission was appointed to consider the incorporation of non-Muslim subjects of the Ottoman state into the armed forces, from which hitherto they had with few exceptions been excluded. Cevdet Paşa was consulted on this proposal and objected in the strongest terms. The non-Muslim subjects of the Ottoman state, he said, were of many different varieties—"Orthodox, Catholic, Armenian, Jacobite, Protestant . . . Melkite, Maronite, Syriac, Chaldee, and many others. . . . " They would all need their different priests, as the Jews would need their rabbis, and while Muslims fasted during Ramadan, the others would also observe their various fasts. Such a mixed body would be unmanageable. In times of strain and stress, military commanders use their eloquence to call on their men for greater endurance and sacrifice. For Muslims, the most effective call is to holy war or martyrdom in the cause of the true faith. These are words familiar to them from childhood, inculcated in them at school. The vigor and endurance of Muslim soldiers in battle, greater than that of other religions, are due to such religious sentiments.

> But in time of need, how could the colonel of a mixed battalion stir the zeal of his soldiers? In Europe, indeed, zeal for country has taken the place of zeal for religion, but this arose after the decline of their feudal age. Their children hear the word *vatan* when they are still small, and so, years later, the call of patriotism is effective with their soldiers. But among us, if we say the word "*vatan*," all that will come to the minds of our soldiers is their village squares. If we were to adopt the term *vatan* now, and if in the course of time, it were to establish itself in men's minds and acquire the power that it has in Europe, even then it would not be as potent as religious zeal, nor could it take its place. But even that would take a long time, and until that time our armies would be left without spirit. In a tight spot, would Private Hasan obey the order of Captain Christo, who sends him to his death? In India the English may promote non-Christian soldiers to the level of sergeant but no higher, and no one interferes or objects. But among us, if we accept Christians as soldiers, it will be necessary to give them the ranks to which they are legally entitled in the same way as Muslims. If they are not given these ranks, the so-called friendly states will offer friendly advice by way of

protecting them, and our military organization, hitherto exempt from interference by foreigners, will be exposed to foreign interventions.

And that is not all.

During military operations, Muslim soldiers have an extraordinary capacity to endure the fatigues of battle. As soon as they smell powder, they want no more than ammunition and dry biscuit. But Christians cannot endure such hardships. It will be necessary to give them regular pay at the beginning of every month and to secure and provide food and drink regularly every day. And if we don't, we shall again be the target of foreign objections.[20]

Cevdet Paşa's dire forebodings were by no means groundless, and a far more serious problem arose when first the Christian and later even some of the non-Turkish Muslim subjects of the empire began to see their *waṭan* not as the Ottoman realm but as their own ethnic homeland.

Among Ottoman Turkish Muslims, their *vatan* was the Ottoman Turkish Empire, embracing most of the heartlands of Islam in the Middle East. Its former rulers included Arab caliphs as well as Turkish sultans; among its great men, in whom they took pride, there were also Arab poets and Persian philosophers, who lived and died long before the Ottoman state was founded. Its present sovereignty was embodied in the Ottoman sultanate, the last and legitimate successor of the great Islamic realms of the past. Patriotic loyalty was owed to the *vatan* and payable to the Ottoman sultan.

But other ideas were current, and some of them made their first appearance in the Arabic-speaking provinces of the Empire. One of the first writers to express patriotic sentiments in Arabic was the Egyptian sheikh Rifā'a Rāfi' al-Tahtāwī. Between 1826 and 1831 he had lived in Paris, as religious preceptor to an Egyptian student mission, and his writings make clear how deeply he was affected by what he saw. In 1855 he published an Egyptian patriotic ode, *Qaṣīda waṭaniyya Miṣriyya,* in praise of the new ruler of Egypt, Sa'īd Pasha. The Pasha, in fulfillment of his duty to his suzerain the Ottoman Sultan, sent a contingent of Egyptian troops to join the Turks in the Crimean War, and Sheikh Rifā'a published a collection of "Egyptian Patriotic Verses" in their praise. He later produced further patriotic poems, to celebrate the accession of Ismā'īl Pasha in 1863 and another group of poems to honor the return of the battalion of black troops whom the Pasha had sent to Mexico, as part of Napoleon III's expeditionary force.[21]

Sheikh Rifā'a's poems and the various prose works in which he tried to inculcate patriotic sentiments in his readers enjoyed the support of the dynastic rulers of Egypt and were part of their campaign to establish that country as a separate entity, with its own ruling dynasty and a large measure of autonomy under the loosest of Ottoman suzerainty. Sheikh Rifā'a's patriotism is not Ottoman, since it shows little interest in the larger Ottoman *waṭan*. It is not Muslim, since it takes pride in the glories of both pagan and Christian Egypt before the advent of Islam. It is not Arab, since it is not concerned with other Arabic-speaking countries—the idea of a greater Arab political fatherland did not arise until sometime later. Sheikh Rifā'a wrote extensively on ancient Egypt—something of a novelty in Arabic historiography. Until his time, histories of Egypt began with the Arab conquest. His was the first to end with that event. This idea of a country and its people, maintaining a living, continuing identity through several changes of language, religion, and civilization, was new and unknown in the Muslim world. Some time was to pass before Sheikh Rifā'a's Egyptian patriotism found imitators in other Muslim countries.

Sheikh Rifā'a's patriotism, as we saw, was encouraged and indeed sponsored by the rulers of Egypt, who appreciated the help it could give to the realization of their dynastic and separatist purposes. In the neighboring Syrian lands, still under more direct Ottoman rule, the first patriots adopted another and more radical component of European patriotism—the idea of freedom. The great Lebanese Christian scholar and writer Buṭrus al-Bustānī made the point explicitly in 1860: "It is for the sons of the *waṭan* to claim their *waṭan*'s protection of their most precious rights, namely, their life, honor, and property, including freedom of their civic, cultural and religious rights."[22] Significantly, it is not, according to al-Bustānī, to the ruler that the patriot devotes himself in return but, rather, to his country's welfare.

Such ideas became commonplace in the writings of the Young Ottomans, the first important Ottoman opposition group, and particularly in the journals published by them in exile. An article published in 1873 by the leader and most distinguished writer of the group, Namık Kemal, explains what *vatan* means for them:

> The *vatan* does not consist of imaginary lines drawn on a map by the sword of a conqueror or the pen of a scribe. It is a sacred idea, sprung from the union of many lofty sentiments, such as nation, freedom, welfare, brotherhood, property, sovereignty, respect for ancestors, love of family, memory of youth . . .[23]

During the century and a half that have passed since the first patriotic writings of Namik Kemal in Turkey and Sheikh Rifā'a in Egypt, the idea of country—of the national territory as the basis of identity and the focus of loyalty—has had a checkered history in the Middle East. It has in particular had to compete with two very powerful rivals. One was the old, deep-rooted and now renascent religious and communal loyalty to Islam; the second was another importation from Europe, the idea of the ethnic nation, defined by language, culture, and real or imagined descent. The one retained, the other rapidly acquired a powerful hold on the sentiments and loyalties of Middle Easterners, many of whom found it difficult to accept the idea of kinship and common identity with their pagan forbears and their infidel neighbors. In many countries, nationalism, which corresponded more accurately to the ethnic confusion of the Middle East, was both more intelligible and more appealing than territorial patriotism, and even where the language of patriotism is used in public discourse, it often masks a deeper commitment to communal and ethnic loyalties. In Egypt there has been intermittent tension—sometimes conflict, sometimes interaction—between Egyptianism, Arabism, and Islam.

In Turkey, the patriotic idea has by now virtually supplanted all others. Despite a continuing commitment to Islam and even a return to inter-Islamic organizations and notwithstanding a growing interest in the affairs of their Turkic kinsfolk in the former Soviet Union, the people of Turkey remain, first and foremost, Turkish patriots, defining their primary identity and loyalty on the basis of the country called Turkey, which was created by the Turkish Republic from the ruins of the multinational, dynastic Ottoman Empire. In Iran, the idea of country, assiduously fostered by the late shah, has had a setback with the establishment of an Islamic republic that explicitly rejects the shah's notion of a common identity between Islamic and pre-Islamic Iran. But even in Iran, the rejection of patriotic notions may not be as complete as would at first appear. When, after the fall of the monarchy, the sultan of Oman requested the return of three small Arabian islands which had been seized by the shah, the republic refused. More strikingly, the constitution of the Islamic republic lays down that the president must be an Iranian by birth and origin—rather more than is required in the American system, where birth is sufficient. The long war with Iraq gave encouragement and provided expression for patriotic loyalties.

In the Arab lands, the situation is more complex. Of these, only Egypt, a country sharply defined by both geography and history, can claim and demonstrate a continuing national identity, in the same country, from remote antiquity to the present day. The other Arab countries vary widely, from venerable monarchies like Morocco, through old-established Ottoman autonomies like Kuwait and Lebanon, to artificial imperial creations like Libya and Jordan. And yet even the most artificial of these have shown a remarkable persistence—a determination to survive as separate entities, despite all the appeals and occasional actions of the pan-Arabists. By now it is becoming increasingly clear that pan-Arabism, for the time being at least, has ceased to be a realistic political objective and survives only as a noble ideal. Its enactment in so many constitutions of Arab states, along with other noble ideals, is an indication of this change. In the Arab world, as in most other regions, a citizen owes his first loyalty to his country. The question that remains to be determined is whether the primary claim on that loyalty will be obedience to the country's rulers or service to its people.

11

Religious Coexistence and Secularism

The term "coexistence," as it is used at the present time, implies a willingness to live at peace, and perhaps even in mutual respect, with others. It might therefore be useful to begin with a glance at the notion of "otherness," which, no doubt as a result of the conspicuous failures of coexistence—religious, national, racial, social, ideological—in our century, has received a good deal of attention of late.

The two most articulate peoples of eastern Mediterranean antiquity, the only ones who have retained both their voices and their memories, have left us two by now classical definitions of the other—the barbarian and the gentile, "barbarian" meaning not Greek, "gentile" meaning not Jewish. Both of these terms, in classical usage, contain at least an element of hostility, in which the notion of the other easily changes into the somewhat different but closely related concept of the enemy. Yet both of these notions—barbarian and gentile—represent a considerable advance on what had gone before.

The urge to define and reject the other goes back to our remotest human ancestors, and indeed beyond them to our animal predecessors. Both the Jewish and Greek definitions represent an immense change in that the barriers which they raise are permeable. They are not impenetrable barriers, and in this they are different from the more primitive and universal definitions of identity and otherness based on birth and blood. They can be crossed or even removed by the adoption, in the one case of a language and culture, in the other of a religious belief and law. It was not easy, but it was possible, and already in classical antiquity we confront the phenomenon of Hellenized barbarians and Judaized gentiles, even indeed of Hellenized Jews and—albeit rarely—of Judaized Hellenes. The Romans carried the principle of inclusiveness a major step further, with the gradual extension of Roman citizenship to all the provinces of the empire. This identity, that of a Roman citizen, was political and legal—allegiance to Roman authority and obedience to Roman law, both symbolized by a pinch of incense for the Roman gods.

The Jewish definition of identity and otherness, by religious belief and practice, was adopted by both the successor religions of Judaism, Christianity and Islam, which for fourteen centuries have shared—or rather contested—the Mediterranean world. The three religions have an immense heritage in common—from the ancient Middle East, from Greco-Roman antiquity, from Jewish revelation and prophecy. Yet their mutual perceptions and reciprocal attitudes differ enormously.

The Jewish perception of the religious other is different from that shared by Christians and Muslims, and, in this respect, brings Judaism closer to the religions of eastern and southern Asia—in that, while Jews claim that the truths of their faith are universal, they do not claim that they are exclusive. Judaism is for Jews and those who care to join them. But, according to a well-known Talmudic dictum, the righteous of all peoples and faiths have their place in paradise. The rabbis relate that before the Ten Commandments were given to Moses, there were seven commandments revealed in the time of Noah, and these were for all humanity. Only two of them, the bans on idolatry and blasphemy, are theological; all the rest, including the prohibition of murder, robbery, cruelty, etc., are no more than the basic rules of human social coexistence. Since Judaism makes no claim to exclusive truth, salvation, according to Jewish teaching, is attainable for non-Jews, provided that they practice monotheism and morality. Much medieval Jewish theological and legal writing is concerned with the question whether Christians and Muslims qualify under these headings. It was universally agreed among Jewish scholars that Islam is a monotheistic religion, but the often misunderstood doctrine of the Trinity caused problems for Jewish as well as for Muslim theologians.

Traditional Christianity and Islam differed from Judaism and agreed with each other in that both claimed to possess not only universal but exclusive truths. Each claimed to be the sole custodian of God's final revelation to mankind. Neither admitted salvation outside its own creed. In the fourteen-centuries-long encounter between Islam and Christendom, the profoundest conflicts between the two religions, the most irreconcilable disagreements between their followers, arose not from their differences but from their resemblances. Some other religions would not accept converts. Most, while not rejecting them, did not seek them and felt no mission or duty to cause other men, in other parts, to change their faiths. Christians and Muslims shared the belief that theirs was the sole universal truth and that it was their sacred mission to bring it to all mankind. When Christians and Muslims called each other accursed infidels, each understood exactly what the other meant, because both meant exactly the same thing. Neither the adjective nor the substantive would have conveyed much to a Hindu or a Confucian. More recently, many—though by no means all—Christian churches and theologians have relinquished this claim to exclusive truth and have begun to use the term "triumphalism" to denote and denounce it. There has as yet been no corresponding change among the authorized spokesmen of Islam.

Christendom and Islam were not only major religions; each of them was also, in modern parlance, a considerable power bloc, with universal claims and aspirations and, for most of their shared histories, with their main power bases by or near the Mediterranean. The other great civilizations of the world, India and China, despite their antiquity and their sophistication, were essentially local, regional, almost ethnic. Neither Hinduism nor Confucianism ever made an attempt to become a world religion or a world power. Buddhism, which preceded both Islam and Christianity in ecumenical ambition, had long since abandoned the attempt. Rejected in its Indian homeland, it was, in effect, confined to East and Southeast Asia. Only Christianity and Islam remained—two religions of the same kind, for more than fourteen centuries neighbors, rarely in association, sometimes in confrontation, often in conflict, each claiming to possess God's final dispensation.

But how would the possessor of God's final dispensation to mankind view a rival claimant? Much depends on whether that claimant is previous or subsequent. From a traditional Christian point of view, since Christianity was, so to speak, the end of the process of revelation, anything subsequent was necessarily false and noxious. From a Muslim point of view, since Christianity was earlier, Christianity, like Judaism, was an incomplete, somewhat damaged, and now superseded religion, but not in itself false and not in itself noxious. When Muslims have confronted a subsequent dispensation, like the post-Islamic faiths of the Baha'is or the Ahmadiyya, they have also reacted with something of the hostility which Christians showed to the advent of Islam—a similar situation though, as it turned out, much less dangerous from their point of view.

For both Christianity and Islam, Judaism is a predecessor, yet there is a fundamental difference in the attitudes of the two religions toward the Jews, alike in the extent, the form, and the manner of toleration. Both claimed a world mission, whence the continuing clash between them. For both of them, Judaism as a predecessor was entitled, by the logic of their own beliefs, to a certain, albeit limited, measure of tolerance. But in their actual treatment of Jews there were significant differences deriving from the foundation myths—I mean no disrespect by this expression—of the two religions, reinforced by subsequent experience. The founders of both religions came into conflict with Jews, but in these conflicts one lost, the other won. This made a profound difference to the perception of Jews in sacred history, in the memories enshrined in the scriptures and other writings that formed the core of self-awareness of the two religious communities. Muḥammad won his battle with the Jews, and it was he who destroyed them, not the reverse. His successors therefore felt able to adopt, shall we say, a more relaxed attitude to subsequent generations of Jews.

There is also a difference in their claims. The Christian dispensation claims to be a fulfillment of promises made to the Jews and the accomplishment of Jewish prophecies. Christians retained and reinterpreted the Hebrew Bible, which they called the Old Testament, and added a New Testament to it. In a view only recently and partially relinquished by the churches, God's covenant with the Jews was taken over, and Israel was, so to speak, replaced by the "true Israel," *Verus Israel,* which is the Church. Jewish survival and still more Jewish refusal were thus seen as somehow impugning the authenticity of the Christian dispensation. Muḥammad and his successors made no such claim, and the conversion of the Jews was therefore a matter of little or no concern to them. Muslims abandoned both testaments, which in their belief were replaced, not supplemented, by the Qur'ān. This difference is manifest in the polemical literature of the two faiths. There is in medieval and even in modern Christendom a vast literature of polemics written by Christian theologians to persuade Jews of the truth of the Christian dispensation. The theologians of Islam felt no such need. There are few Muslim polemics against Judaism, and most of them are efforts at self-justification by recent converts from that religion.

This doctrinal difference was confirmed and amplified by important practical differences between the two situations. In Christendom, which until the dawn of the modern era substantially meant Europe, Jews were the only religious minority in an otherwise religiously and to a large extent racially homogeneous society. Their presence and still more their otherness were always clearly visible, and in times of trouble they provided not just the best but the only scapegoat. The Islamic world, in contrast, was international, indeed intercontinental, embracing peoples in Asia, Africa, and Europe and forming a varied and pluralistic society in which Jews were just one among a great many minorities. In Muslim eyes they were for the most part neither the most important nor the most dangerous. They were obviously much less important than the Christians, who were vastly more numerous and who could moreover be accused of treasonable sympathy with the Christian European enemy. No such suspicion attached to the Jewish minorities in Islamic lands.

A religious definition of group identity inevitably raises the question of another kind of otherness, crucial in the history of Christendom, not unimportant in the history of Islam—that of an intermediate status between the believer and the unbeliever: the schismatic, the heretic, the deviant.

Islamic experience, both past and present, shows many groups of deviants who differed from mainstream Islam in belief or practice or both. The major polemical literature of Islam was written by Muslims against other Muslims—between Sunnis and Shi'a, between the different schools and tendencies within each of these, and between mainstream Islam and extremist fringe groups such as the Isma'ilis, the Alawis, and the Druse. These polemics are far more extensive and sophisticated than any directed against Christians or Jews. Deviation was serious; it was dangerous. It represented a real adversary that could threaten the established order. Beginning in early times, it continues to the present day. Yet there is no such thing as either schism or heresy in Islam, in the Christian sense of these terms.

Schism means split. There is no split in Islam like the schism between the Greek and Roman churches, since there is no institutional authority—no popes or patriarchs or councils and therefore no questions of jurisdiction or obedience or submission. Heresy means choice, and therefore, human nature being what it is, it has been specialized to mean a wrong choice. This again hardly arises in Islam because there is considerable freedom of choice in matters of belief, within very widely drawn limits. And so despite frequent deviation and occasional repression, we find few of the legal, theological, and practical implications of heresy that we know from Christendom. One reason has already been mentioned—the absence of an institutional structure, a church. There was no ecclesiastical authority to formulate, promulgate, and direct belief or to define and denounce incorrect belief—to detect, to enforce, to punish. All this, so characteristic of the Christian churches, has no true equivalent in Islamic history. There have been a few attempts by rulers to impose some kind of orthodox creed. Most such attempts were short-lived and ineffectual.

There is another reason for this difference. Correct Islam is defined not so much by orthodoxy as by orthopraxy. What matters is what a Muslim does, not what he believes. According to an oft-repeated Muslim dictum, only God can judge sincerity in belief. What a Muslim does is a social and at a certain point a political fact, and it is this that is of concern to the public authorities. The demand of Islam from the believers is not textual accuracy in belief but loyalty to the community and its constituted leader. This led to a broad tolerance of deviation, ceasing only at the point where it became disloyalty, easily equated with treason, or where it became seditious and subversive, a danger to the existing social and political order. When that happens, the deviant crosses a boundary—not between orthodoxy and heterodoxy, which is relatively unimportant, but between Islam and apostasy. When deviation reaches that point, it becomes an issue of law, a matter for prosecution and punishment.

Have there been wars of religion within Islam, comparable with the great struggles which convulsed Christendom? The answer must be no. There have been many internal wars in Islamic history, and in some of them people on opposing sides professed different forms of Islam, but one cannot speak of wars of religion in the Islamic world, in the sense that this term is used of events in Europe in the sixteenth and seventeenth centuries. There were regional, tribal, and dynastic wars with, shall we say, a religious coloration. There were great power rivalries, as between the sultans of Turkey and the shahs of Iran. One was Sunni, the other Shīʿa, and this difference is reflected in the propaganda, the subversion, and the repression of the two sides, but it would be misleading to describe these as Sunni–Shi'a wars.

In the sixteenth and seventeenth centuries, the agonizing problem for Christians was not that of coexistence with followers of other religions, but of coexistence with fellow Christians of other churches. It was from these bitter conflicts, which devastated so much of Europe, that the modern doctrine that has come to be known as secularism emerged. The notion that religion and political authority, church and state, are different and that they can or should be separated is, in a profound sense, Christian. Its origins may be traced in the teachings of Christ, notably in the famous passage in Matthew 22:21, in which Christ is quoted as saying: "Render therefore unto Caesar the things which are Caesar's; and unto God the things that are God's." This notion was confirmed by the experience of the first Christians; its later development was shaped and in a sense even imposed by the subsequent history of Christendom. The persecutions endured by the early Church made it clear that a separation between the two was possible. The persecutions inflicted by later churches persuaded many Christians that such a separation was necessary.

The notion of the separation of church and state seems to have emerged in the Protestant countries of northern Europe and was first given legal and constitutional force in the United States of America. In John Locke's *Letter Concerning Toleration,* published in both Latin and English in 1689, he concludes that "neither Pagan nor Mahometan, nor Jew, ought to be excluded from the civil rights of the commonwealth because of his religion."[1] In a letter written to a Jewish community leader in Newport, Rhode Island, in 1790, George Washington explained how the new republic embodied this principle:

> The citizens of the United States of America . . . all possess alike liberty of conscience and immunities of citizenship. It is now no more that toleration is spoken of, as if it was by the indulgence of one class of people that another enjoyed the exercise of their inherent natural rights. For happily the government of the United States, which gives to bigotry no sanction, to persecution no assistance, requires only that they who live under its protection, should demean themselves as good citizens, in giving it on all occasions their effectual support.[2]

In these words, the first president of the United States expressed with striking clarity the real difference between tolerance and coexistence. Tolerance means that a dominant group, whether defined by faith or race or other criteria, allows to members of other groups some—but rarely if ever all—of the rights and privileges enjoyed by its own members. Coexistence means equality between the different groups composing a political society as an inherent natural right of all of them—to grant it is no merit, to withhold or limit it is an offense.

For fourteen centuries, the countries of the Mediterranean have been ruled by Christian or Muslim governments whose record at best is one of limited tolerance. Their frequent lapses into intolerance can readily be explained by the long and bitter struggle between them for the domination of their common homeland. In the seventh century, at the time of the advent of Islam, the Mediterranean world was entirely Christian, with only Jewish minorities. In a series of swift and overwhelming victories, the eastern and southern shores of the Mediterranean were permanently wrested from Christendom, and even substantial parts of the European mainland were subject, for many centuries, to Muslim rule. For most of their common history, relations between the two communities were shaped by attack and counterattack, jihad and crusade, conquest and reconquest. The loss of the Levant and of North Africa to Christendom proved permanent, and the attempt in the Crusades to recover the Holy Land finally failed. The reconquest—of Iberia from the Moors, of Russia from the Tatars—grew into a vast new expansion of Christendom into Africa and Asia, where Spaniards and Portuguese at one end of Europe and Russians at the other pursued their former masters into their own homelands.

The last great Muslim assault on Europe, that of the Ottoman Turks, ended with the second unsuccessful siege of Vienna in 1683. With that failure and the Turkish retreat that followed, a thousand years of Muslim threat to Europe came to an end, and three centuries of Christian threat to Islam began.

With the ending of the great European empires and the subsequent collapse of the last of them, that of Russia, this phase too has come to an end. Christians and Muslims face each other across the Mediterranean with old prejudices and new anxieties, but for the first time in centuries without threat or fear of armed invasion. Christian minorities remain in the lands of Islam; new Muslim minorities have been created by migration in the lands of Christendom. And in the eastern Mediterranean, after a hiatus of almost two millennia, the Jews—the eternal and universal minority—have created a third Jewish commonwealth after a second and immeasurably longer Babylonian captivity.

There are now three sovereign religions in the Mediterranean world. To these some would add a fourth—secularism. There is a kind of secularism which flourished especially in eastern Europe, though it has its supporters elsewhere. This kind of secularism seems to have retained the defects, without the merits, of earlier orthodoxies. Its adherents are atheists, but not godless. They have no theology, but they do have a creed. They have no religion, but they certainly have a church, complete with scriptures and dogmas, prelates and hierarchs, orthodoxies, heresies, and an inquisition to detect and extirpate them. This church too, coincidentally, was founded by someone of Jewish origin and background, and it has even been argued that he was to some extent inspired by Jewish prophetic vision and messianism. Fortunately, unlike his predecessors, he did not come into collision with any Jewish establishment, and the Jews are therefore not cast in Marxist sacred history in an adversarial role, as they are in Christian and to a lesser extent in Muslim historiography. In this kind of secular religion, there appears to be little or no room for tolerance, let alone coexistence. At the present time it is manifestly in decline, and offers no current threat.

The secularism that emerged in western Europe in the seventeenth century and was established by the American and, in another way, the French revolutions in the eighteenth century was of quite a different kind. Its purpose was not to establish and enforce irreligion as a new state doctrine but, rather, to preclude the state from any involvement in doctrine and to prevent the upholders of any doctrine from using the coercive powers of the state. After the long and bitter struggles of the wars of religion, Christians gradually came to the conclusion that only in this way would it be possible for adherents of rival or even merely different churches to live side by side in reasonable peace.

This principle—some would say this expedient—is denoted by the French term *laïcisme,* which has also been adapted in a number of other languages, though not as yet in English, where we continue to use "secularism" with a wide range of connotations of which this is one, and "separation" for the constitutional and legal arrangements by which church and state are prevented from interfering with each other. Few modern Western states have followed the American example all the way, and many retain some form of state-established church. But interference, either way, has become minimal in most of the Western democracies, and a situation of de facto separation prevails.

No such problem, and therefore no such solution, arose in Islamic history and culture, or was considered in Muslim theology or statecraft. In pagan Rome, Caesar was God. Christians were taught to differentiate between what is due to Caesar and what is due to God. For Muslims of the classical age, God was Caesar, and the sovereign—caliph or sultan—was merely his viceregent on earth. This was more than a simple legal fiction. For Muslims, the state was God's state, the army God's army, and, of course, the enemy was God's enemy. Of more practical importance, the law was God's law, and in principle there could be no other. The question of separating church and state did not arise, since there was no church, as an autonomous institution, to be separated. Church and state were one and the same.

For the same reason, though Islamic society very soon developed a large and active class of professional men of religion, these were never a priesthood in the Christian sense and could only loosely be described even as a clergy. In the upper house of the British Parliament sit the lords spiritual and temporal, the former being the bishops. As already noted, there were no lords spiritual, no prelates or hierarchs in classical Islam, and nothing resembling such figures as Cardinal Richelieu in France or Cardinal Wolsey in England. It is only in Ottoman times, almost certainly under the influence of Christian example, that an organization of Muslim religious dignitaries was developed, with a hierarchy of ranks and with territorial jurisdictions. The ayatollahs of Iran are an even more recent innovation and might not unjustly be described as another step in the Christianization of Islamic institutions, though by no means of Islamic teachings. As a charismatic religious leader claiming his authority direct from God and as a radical activist subverter and creator of regimes, Khomeini has many predecessors in Islamic history. As a political prelate, however, he has none, though it would not be too difficult to find parallels in the history of Christendom.

It was not only the theoretical and historical basis for separation that was lacking in Islam; it was also the practical need. The level of willingness to tolerate and live peaceably with those who believe otherwise and worship otherwise was, at most times and in most places, high enough for tolerable coexistence to be possible, and Muslims did not therefore feel the imperative need felt by Christians to seek an escape from the horrors of state-sponsored and state-enforced doctrine. The character and extent of traditional Muslim tolerance should not be misunderstood. If by tolerance we mean the absence of discrimination, then the traditional Muslim state was not tolerant, and indeed a tolerance thus defined would have been seen not as a merit but as a dereliction of duty. No equality was conceded, in practice or even less in theory, between those who accepted and obeyed God's word and those who willfully and of their own choice rejected it. Discrimination was structural and universal, imposed by doctrine and law and enforced by popular consent. Persecution, on the other hand, though not unknown, was rare and atypical, and there are few if any equivalents in Muslim history to the massacres, the forced conversions, the expulsions, and the burnings that are so common in the history of Christendom before the rise of secularism.

In our own day, certain self-styled fighters for Islam, who claim to be acting in the name of their faith, have brutally maltreated hostages and other innocent victims, and their claim has not been convincingly repudiated by accredited Muslim authorities. But these are crimes against civility, decency, and humanity, not against non-Muslims as such, and those who have committed them, along with those who direct them, deal as badly or worse with their own coreligionists. Both as tyrants at home and as terrorists abroad, their actions are in violation of Islamic morality and law.

From a Muslim point of view, neither Judaism nor Christianity is a false religion. Both were in origin based on authentic revelations, but both are superseded by the final and perfect revelation vouchsafed to Muḥammad in the Qur'ān. Some go further, and claim that the Jewish and Christian scriptures were distorted and corrupted by their unworthy custodians. However, the principle has always been adopted in Muslim law and usually in practice that Christians and Jews—but not atheists, polytheists, or idolaters—are entitled to the tolerance and protection of the Muslim state. This has meant, in law and in practice, that they were allowed to practice their religions and to form their own communal organizations in which they administered their own laws, subject to the payment of additional taxes and the acceptance of certain social, fiscal, and political restrictions. The severity with which these restrictions were in fact applied varied enormously from place to place and from time to time. It was determined by many factors, perhaps the most important among them being relations with the outside and more particularly the Christian world. In some periods the restrictions were harshly and rigorously enforced; in others they amounted to little more than a token of formal submission.

By a sad paradox, the adoption in the nineteenth and twentieth centuries of democratic constitutions, guaranteeing equal rights for all citizens in the Ottoman Empire, in Iran, Egypt, and elsewhere, on the whole weakened rather than strengthened the position of minorities. On the one hand, it deprived them of the limited but substantial and well-grounded rights and privileges which they enjoyed under the old Islamic dispensation. On the other, it failed to make good the new rights and freedoms offered to them by the newly enacted constitutions which, in this as in many other respects, proved a dead letter. It is easier to be tolerant from a position of strength than from a position of weakness, and in the age of overwhelming European superiority of wealth and power, the Christian and to a lesser extent the Jewish minorities, suspected with some justification of sympathizing and even collaborating with European imperialists, were subject to increasing hostility. After the withdrawal of those imperialists in the postwar period, the surviving minorities were in an exposed and dangerous position.

The first Muslim encounter with secularism was during the French Revolution, which they saw not as secular—a word and concept equally meaningless to them at that time—but as de-Christianized and therefore deserving of some consideration. All previous movements of ideas in Europe had been to a greater or lesser extent Christian, at least in their expression, and were accordingly discounted in advance from a Muslim point of view. The Renaissance, the Reformation, even the scientific revolution and the Enlightenment passed unnoticed in the Muslim world. The French Revolution was the first movement of ideas in Europe which did not appear Christian and which even presented itself, to Muslims at least, as anti-Christian. And Muslims in increasing numbers therefore looked to France in the hope of finding in these ideas the motors of Western science and progress freed from Christian encumbrances. These ideas, and others derived from them, provided the main ideological inspiration of many of the modernizing and reforming movements in the Islamic world in the nineteenth and twentieth centuries.

From the beginning, that is to say, from the first impact of these ideas at the end of the eighteenth century, there were a few who saw that they could threaten not only Christianity, which did not concern them, but also Islam and who, seeing this, gave warning. For a long time they had little influence. The small minority who were at all aware of European ideas were, for the most part, profoundly attracted by them. Among the vast majority, the challenge of Western secular ideas was not so much opposed as ignored. It is only in comparatively recent times that Muslim religious thinkers of stature have looked at secularism, understood its threat to what they regard as the highest values of religion, and responded with a decisive rejection.

In the secularization of the West, God was twice dethroned and replaced: as the source of sovereignty by the people; as the object of worship by the nation. Both these ideas were alien to Islam, but in the course of the nineteenth century they became familiar, and in the twentieth for a while became dominant among the Westernized intelligentsia who at that time ruled many if not most Muslim states. In a nation-state defined by the country over which it ruled or by the nation which constituted its population, a secular state was in principle possible.

Only one Muslim country, the Turkish Republic, has formally adopted the separation of religion and state as law. It has enacted the removal of Islam from the constitution, and the abrogation of the *sharīʿa,* which ceased to be part of the law of the land. One or two other Muslim states went some of the way, and several of them restricted *sharīʿa* to marriage, divorce, and inheritance, adopting mainly Western laws in other matters. There have been some political movements which claim to be secularist, the most remarkable of these being the Baʿath, which rules in Syria and Iraq. In 1990–1991, the secular leader of this party in Iraq, finding himself at war, inscribed *Allahu Akbar* on his banner and, after seeing the Prophet in a dream, proclaimed jihad against the infidels. This suggests an imperfect understanding of what secularism means, or perhaps a perfect understanding of how little appeal it would have.

For some years now, there has been a strong reaction in Muslim countries against these secularizing tendencies, expressed in a number of Islamic radical movements, loosely and inaccurately designated at the present time as fundamentalist. Among these countries are Egypt, North Africa, and, to some extent, even Turkey. These movements share the objective of undoing the secularizing reforms of the last century, abolishing the imported codes of law and the social customs that came with them, and returning to the holy law of Islam and the Islamic political order.

That is what Islamic fundamentalism is primarily about. In one country, Iran, these forces captured power. In several others they exercise growing influence. And a number of governments have begun to reintroduce *sharīʿa* law, either from conviction or as a preemptive strike against the fundamentalist challenge. Even nationalism and patriotism, which, after some initial opposition from pious Muslims, had begun to be generally accepted, are now once again being questioned and even denounced as anti-Islamic. After a long period in which, for example, Arab nationalism was sacrosanct, it is now under attack. In some Arab countries defenders of what has now become the old-style, so-called secular nationalism are accusing the Islamic fundamentalists of dividing the Arab nation.

"You are dividing the Arab nation," they say, "and setting Muslim against Christian," to which the fundamentalists reply that it is the nationalists who are divisive by setting Turk against Persian against Arab within the larger community and brotherhood of Islam and that this division is the greater and more heinous offense.

In the literature of the Muslim radicals and militants, the enemy is variously defined. Sometimes he is the Jew or Zionist—the terms are more or less interchangeable; sometimes the Christian or missionary or crusader, again more or less interchangeable; sometimes the Western imperialist, nowadays redefined as the United States; occasionally—though not much of late—the Soviet Communist. The primary enemy and immediate object of attack among many of these groups are the native secularizers, those who have tried to weaken and modify the Islamic base of the state by introducing secular schools and universities, secular laws and courts, and thus excluding Islam, and so also the professional exponents of Islam, from two major areas which they had previously dominated, education and justice.

In these antisecularist writings, the arch enemy is often Kemal Atatürk, the first major secularist ruler in the Islamic world and the model for all others. Some fundamentalist writers even allege that he was neither a Turk nor a Muslim, but a crypto-Jew, who established the Turkish Republic to punish the Ottoman house for having refused to give Palestine to the Zionists.

The fundamentalist demonology includes characters as diverse as King Fārūq and Presidents Nasser and Sadat in Egypt, Hafiz al-Asad in Syria, Saddam Hussein in Iraq, the shah of Iran, and the kings of Arabia, all lumped together as the most insidious of enemies, the enemy from within who wears a Muslim face and bears a Muslim name and is therefore much deadlier than the open enemies from outside.

At the present time secularism is in a bad way in the Middle East. Of those Middle Eastern states that have written constitutions, only two have no established religion. One is Lebanon, once a shining example of religious tolerance and even coexistence, now a terrible warning of the consequences of their failure. The other, as already noted, is the Turkish Republic, where, while the general principle of separation is maintained, there has been some erosion in recent years, for example, in the reintroduction of religious education in the schools and the maintenance of the longstanding distinction between Turk and Turkish citizen. Turk means Muslim—perhaps an unbelieving or lapsed Muslim, but at least some kind of Muslim. Non-Muslims may be designated and treated as Turkish citizens, but are not called Turks. A similar, or rather parallel, distinction exists in Israel.

Of the remaining Middle Eastern countries, those that possess written constitutions all give some constitutional status to Islam, ranging from the Islamic republic of Iran, which gives religion a central position, to the rather minimal reference in the Syrian constitution, which says the laws of the state shall be inspired by the *sharīʿa*. Of the states without written constitutions, Israel and the Kingdom of Saudi Arabia both accord a very considerable place to religion in the definition of identity and of loyalty. If one may briefly compare the two, Saudi Arabia gives a greater place to the application of religious law; Israel, because of its unique electoral system, allows a far greater political role to the clergy through the parties which they influence or control.

I said a little earlier that historically speaking there are no lords spiritual for Muslims or, for that matter, for Jews, no political churchmen like Richelieu or Wolsey. The first statement, that there are no lords spiritual, is clearly no longer true, either for Jews or for Muslims. I wonder if it is still true, and if so, how long it will remain true, that there are no political ecclesiastics. There is of course the obvious example of Khomeini in Iran, though if one looks for a Christian parallel he was a Savonarola rather than a Richelieu. One may also see, if one looks nearer, other Muslim and Jewish men of religion who, forsaking traditional values, have become both political and ecclesiastical.

Secularism in the Christian world was an attempt to resolve the long and destructive struggle of church and state. Separation, adopted in the American and French revolutions and elsewhere after that, was designed to prevent two things: the use of religion by the state to reinforce and extend its authority and the use of the state power by the clergy to impose their doctrines and rules on others. This is a problem long seen as purely Christian, not relevant to Jews or Muslims. Looking at the contemporary Middle East, both Jewish and Muslim, one must ask whether this is still true—or whether Jews and Muslims may perhaps have caught a Christian disease and might therefore consider a Christian remedy.

Notes

Chapter 1

1. *The Turkish Letters of Ogier Ghiselin de Busbecq, Imperial Ambassador at Constantinople 1554–1562,* translated from the Latin by Edward Seymour Forster (Oxford, 1927), p. 112.

2. Ibid.

3. The quotation is from article 7 of the Treaty of Küçük Kaynarca.

4. Halil Inalcık, "Osmanlı Imparator luğunun Kuruluş ve inkişaf devrinde Türkiye'nin iktisadî vaziyeti üzerinde bir tetkik münasebetiyle," *Belleten,* no. 60 (1951): 629–84, especially pp. 661ff.

5. *Das Asafnāme des Lutfi Pascha,* ed. and trans. Rudolf Tschudi (Berlin, 1910), pp. 32–33, trans. pp. 26–27. See also B. Lewis, *The Muslim Discovery of Europe* (New York, 1982), p. 43.

6. *Tarih al-Hind al-Garbī* (Istanbul, 1142/1729), fol. 66f.; see also B. Lewis, *The Emergence of Modern Turkey,* 2d ed. (Oxford, 1968), p. 27.

7. From an unpublished manuscript, quoted in A. Zekî Velidi Togan, *Bugünkü Türkili (Türkistan) ve Yakın Tarihi* (Istanbul, 1947), vol. 1, p. 127.

8. William Penn, *An Essay Towards the Present and Future Peace of Europe.*

9. Preface to *Relation de l'ambassade de Méhmet Effendi à la cour de France en 1721 écrite par lui même et traduite du turc par Julien Galland* (Constantinople and Paris, 1757). See also Fatma Müge Göçek, *East Encounters West: France and the Ottoman Empire in the Eighteenth Century* (New York and Oxford, 1987), pp. 69–70, 80.

Chapter 2

1. Mīrzā Abū Ṭālib Khān, *Masīr-i Ṭālibī yā Safarnāma-i Mīrzā Abū Ṭālib Khān,* ed. H. Khadīv-Jan (Tehran, 1974), pp. 250–51; see also loose English translation by C. Stewart, *Travels of Mīrzā Abū Ṭālib Khān* (London, 1814), vol. 2, p. 21, cited in B. Lewis, *The Muslim Discovery of Europe* (New York, 1982), pp. 215–16.

2. See Qur'ān 5:87 and the commentary on this text of Fakhr al-Dīn al-Rāzī, *Al-Tafsīr al-kabīr* (Cairo, 1938), vol. 12, p. 71 ("It is clear that just as one may not permit what God forbids, so one may not forbid what God permits").

3. Qur'ān 3:32: "Obey God and the Prophet"; see also 4:59: "Obey God and obey the Prophet and those among you who hold authority." These verses have been interpreted by jurists as giving authentic *ḥadīth* equal authority with the Qur'ān. This leaves the problem of deciding which *ḥadīths* are authentic.

4. Al-Ghazālī, *Al-Iqtiṣād fi'l-i'tiqād* (Cairo, A.H. 1320), p. 107; critical edition, ed. Ibrahim Agah Çubukçu and Huseyin Atay (Ankara, 1962), p. 240. This passage has frequently been cited and discussed by scholars. See, for example, G. E. von Grunebaum, *Medieval Islam,* 2nd ed. (Cambridge, 1957), pp. 291ff.; Ann K. S. Lambton, *State and Government in Medieval Islam* (Oxford, 1981), pp. 110–11; H. A. R. Gibb, "Constitutional Organization," in *Law in the Middle East,* ed. Majid Khadduri and Herbert J. Liebesny (Washington, D.C., 1955), pp. 19–20; David Santillana, *Instituzioni di diritto musulmano malichita* (Rome, 1925), vol. 1, p. 22; David Santillana, "Law and Society," in *The Legacy of Islam,* ed. T. W. Arnold and A. Guillaume (Oxford, 1931), p. 302.

5. See Santillana, *Instituzioni,* pp. 14–24; H. A. R. Gibb, *Studies in the Civilization of Islam* (London, 1962), pp. 141–44; B. Lewis, *The Political Language of Islam* (Chicago, 1988), chap. 5. The whole question of legitimacy and tyranny is examined in depth in Lambton, *State and Government.*

6. I. Goldziher, *Die Zâhiriten: Ihr Lehrsystem und ihre Geschichte* (Leipzig, 1884), pp. 94ff.; I. Goldziher, *Muslim Studies* (London, 1971), vol. 2, p. 78; I. Goldziher, *Introduction to Islamic Theology and Law,* trans. Andras Hamori and Ruth Hamori (Princeton, 1981), p. 48; A. J. Wensinck, *The Muslim Creed* (Cambridge, 1932), pp. 104, 112ff.; J. Schacht, *The Origins of Muhammadan Jurisprudence* (Oxford, 1950), p. 96; J. Schacht, *An Introduction to Islamic Law* (Oxford, 1964), p. 67.

7. For Sunni views, see Muwaffaq al-Dīn ibn Qudāma, *Al-Mughnī,* ed. Maḥmūd 'Abd al-Wahhāb Fā'id and 'Abd al-Qādir 'Aṭā (Cairo, n.d.), vol. 9, pp. 269ff.; Shams al-Dīn Muḥammad b. Aḥmad al-Sarakhsī, *Al-Mabsūṭ* (Cairo, A.H. 1324), vol. 10, pp. 66–68; Shams al-Dīn Muḥammad b. Aḥmad al-Sarakhsī, *Sharḥ al-Siyar al-kabīr* (Hyderabad, 1335–36/1916–17), vol. 4, p. 238; Majid Khadduri, *The Islamic Law of Nations: Shaybānī's Siyar* (Baltimore, 1966), pp. 138–41. For a Shī'ite view, see Abū Ja'far Muhammad b. al-Ḥasan al-Ṭūsī, *Ikhtiyār ma'rifat al-rijāl* (Mashhad, n.d.), p. 344.

8. Ibn Isḥāq, *Sīrat Rasūl Allāh,* ed. F. Wüstenfeld (Göttingen, 1858–59), p. 958; English translation in A. Guillaume, *The Life of Muḥammad* (London, 1955), nos. 644–45; Al-Ṭabarī, *Ta'rīkh,* vol. 1, p. 1567.

9. Al-Sarakhsī, *Al-Mabsūṭ,* p. 928; Khadduri, *Shaybānī,* pp. 193–94; *Al-Fatāwā al-'Ālamgīriyya* (Bulaq, A.H. 1310), vol. 2, pp. 232–34; Sharaf al-Dīn Mūsā al-Ḥujāwī, *Al-Iqnā' fī fiqh al-Imām Aḥmad b. Ḥanbal,* ed. 'Abd al-Laṭīf Muḥammad al-Subki (Cairo, n.d.), vol. 2, p. 49. See further, Santillana, *Instituzioni,* vol. 1, pp. 70ff.; Adel Theodor Khoury, *Islamische Minderheiten in der Diaspora* (Mainz, 1938), pp. 54ff. On the question of Sharī'a jurisdiction in the Dār al-Ḥarb, see also Wahba al-Zuḥaylī, *Al-'Ilāqāt al-dawliyya fi'l-Islām* (Beirut, 1401/1981), pp. 110–12; Ṣubḥī Maḥmaṣānī, *Al-Qānūn wa'l-'ilāqāt al-dawliyya fi'l-Islām* (Beirut, n.d.), pp. 87–88. On the Moroccan embassy reports, see Lewis, *Muslim Discovery,* pp. 117–19, 179–82; H. Pérès, *L'Espagne vue par les voyageurs musulmans de 1610 à 1930* (Paris, 1937).

10. The text of the pact, known in Arabic sources as *Baqt,* is preserved in al-Maqrīzī, *Al-Khiṭaṭ* (Bulaq, A.H. 1270), vol. 1, pp. 199–202, English translation

and analysis in Yūsuf Faḍl Ḥasan, *The Arabs and the Sudan* (Edinburgh, 1967), pp. 22–24.

11. Abū'l-'Abbās Aḥmad ibn Yaḥyā al-Wansharīsī, "Asnā al-matājir fī bayān aḥkām man ghalaba 'ala waṭanihi al-Naṣārā wa-lam yuhājir," ed. Ḥusayn Mu'nis, *Revista del Instituto Egipcio de Estudios Islámicos en Madrid* 5 (1957): 129–91; see also Abdel-Magid Turki, "Consultation juridique d'al-Imām al-Māzarī sur le cas des Musulmans vivant en Sicile sous l'autorité des Normands," *Mélanges de l'Université St. Joseph* (Beirut) (1980): 691–704.

12. Ibn Qudāma, *Al-Mughnī,* vol. 9, pp. 293–95; Muḥammad al-Shirbīnī, *Mughnī'l-muḥtāj ilā ma'rifat ma'ānī alfāẓ al-Minhāj* (a commentary on Nawawi's *Matn al-Minhāj*) (Cairo, 1933), vol. 4, pp. 238–39; Muḥammad Ḥasan al-Najafī, *Jawāhir al-kalām,* (Beirut, 1981), vol. 21, pp. 34–36; 'Alī ibn al-Ḥusayn al-Karakī, *Jāmi' al-maqāsid,* (n.p., n.d.), vol. 3, p. 347. See further Santillana, *Instituzioni,* vol. 1, pp. 69–70, 76–77; L. P. Harvey, *Islamic Spain: 1250 to 1500* (Chicago, 1990), pp. 55ff.; Muhammad Khalid Masud, "The Obligation to Migrate: The Doctrine of *Hijra* in Islamic Law," in *Muslim Travellers: Pilgrimage, Migration, and the Religious Imagination,* ed. Dale F. Eickelman and James Piscatori (London, 1990), pp. 29–49; Rudolph Peters, *Islam and Colonialism: The Doctrine of* Jihad *in Modern History* (The Hague, 1979), pp. 41–42, 48, 57–59, 61–62, 66, 88, 108, 152; Khoury, *Islamische Minderheiten,* pp. 54–60; Fritz Meier, "Über die umstrittene Pflicht des Muslims, bei nichtmuslimischer Besetzung seines Landes auszuwandern," *Der Islam* 68 (1991): 65–86.

13. See *EI*², s.v. "Mudéjar," by P. Chalmeta; L. P. Harvey, "Crypto-Islam in Sixteenth Century Spain," in *Actas del primer congreso de estudios árabes y islamicos* (Madrid, 1964), pp. 163–78.

14. Cited by al-Wansharīsī, "Asná al-matājir," pp. 156ff.

15. For modern rulings, see, for example, Muḥammad Aḥmad 'Ulaysh, *Fatḥ al-'alī al-mālik fi'l-fatwā 'alā madhhab al-Imām Mālik* (Cairo, 1356/1937), vol. 1, p. 375, and the collected *fatwās* of Muḥammad Rashīd Riḍā, ed. Ṣalāḥ al-Dīn al-Munajjid and Yūsuf Q. Khūrī (Beirut, n.d.), especially those dealing with the Muslim lands conquered by Russia and by Austria-Hungary.

Chapter 3

1. The historical works selected for translation are in the main concerned with local (e.g., histories of Qumm, Nishapur, Bukhara and other cities) or with dynastic history.

2. On these, see Moritz Steinschneider, *Die europäischen Übersetzungen aus dem arabischen bis Mitte des 17 Jahrhunderts* (1904–5; reprint, Graz, 1956); Steinschneider, *Die hebräischen Übersetzungen des Mittelalters* (Berlin 1893).

3. The translation, begun on the initiative of the famous Abbot of Cluny, Peter the Venerable, was completed in July 1143. See M. T. d'Alverny, "Deux traductions latines du Coran au Moyen Age," *Archives d'histoire doctrinale et littéraire du Moyen Age* 16 (1948): 69–131; J. Kritzeck, "Robert of Ketton's Translation of the Qur'an," *Islamic Quarterly* 2 (1955): 309–12.

4. The best known example is the Hebrew version of the Arabic *maqāmāt* of al-Ḥarīrī, written by Yehuda al-Ḥarīzī and entitled *Maḥberoth Ithiel.*

5. On these matters, see A. L. Tibawi, "Is the Qur'ān Translatable? Early

Muslim Opinion," *Muslim World* 52 (1962): 4–16; *EI*[2], s.v. "*I'djāz*," by G. E. von Grunebaum, and "Ḳur'ān," by R. Paret.

6. On Persian translations of the Qur'ān, see C. A. Story, *Persian Literature, a Biobibliographical Survey*, vol. 1, sec. 1: *Qur'anic Literature* (London, 1927); the Russian translation by Yu. E. Bregel, *Persidskaya Literatura*, vol. 1 (Moscow, 1972), contains much additional information.

7. A Hebrew translation of the Arabic original has been printed a number of times, for example, B. A. Lichtenberg, ed., *Qoveṣ Teshuvot ha-Rambam ve-igrotav* (Leipzig, 1858), vol. 3, pp. 27a–29a. For a complete English translation, by H. Adler, see *Miscellany of Hebrew Literature* (London, 1872), vol. 1, pp. 219–28, reprinted with minor changes in F. Kohler, ed., *Letters of Jews throughout the Ages* (London, 1953), vol. 1, pp. 208–17.

8. On these, see Johann Fück, *Die arabischen Studien in Europa bis den Anfang des 20 Jahrhunderts* (Leipzig, 1955).

9. On this point, see L. C. Brown, "Color in Northern Africa," *Daedalus* 96 (1967): 471; B. Lewis, *Race and Slavery in the Middle East* (New York, 1990), pp. 56, 69, 125 n.10.

10. Al-Māwardī, *Al-Aḥkām al-Sulṭāniyya* (Cairo n.d.), p. 207, French translation by E. Fagnan, *Les statuts gouvernmentaux* (Algiers, 1915), p. 462 ("le maintien des lois, Kânoūn").

11. For example, by K. A. Fariq, "The Story of an Arab Diplomat," *Studies in Islam* 3 (1966): 66 and passim.

12. E. Westermarck, *Wit and Wisdom in Morocco* (London, 1930), p. 132.

13. On the use of *Ḥurriyya*, see *EI*[2], s.v.

14. Al-Balādhūrī, *Kitāb Futūḥ al-Buldān*, ed. M. J. de Goeje *State* (New York, 1916), p. 317; O. Rescher, *El-Belâdorî's kitâb futûh el-buldân'* (Leipzig, 1917), p. 226, ("Das sind nun eure Rechte und Pflichten").

15. Ibn Hishām's redaction of Ibn Isḥâq, *Sīrat Rasūl Allah*, ed. F. Wüstenfeld, (Göttingen, 1858–60,) p. 341, German translation by Gustav Weil, *Das Leben Mohammeds* (Stuttgart, 1864), vol. 1, p. 250, English translation by A. Guillaume, *The Life of Muhammed* (London, 1955), p. 231. For later versions, see A. J. Wensinck, *Mohammed en de Joden te Medina* (Leiden, 1908), p. 74 ("en hun verplichtingen oplegde en rechten schonk"); W. Montgomery Watt, *Muhammad at Medina* (Oxford, 1956), p. 221 ("gave them certain rights and duties"). On this document and its significance, see R. B. Serjeant, "The 'Constitution of Medina'," *Islamic Quarterly* 8 (1964): 3–16.

16. Abū Shāma, *Kitāb al-Rawḍatayn fi akhbār al-dawlatayn*, 2 (Cairo, 1288/1872), vol. 2, p. 24, abridged German translation by E. P. Georgens, *Zur Geschichte Salahaddins* (Berlin, 1879) p. 28. The Arabic text reads "bi dār da'wa bi-Halab."

17. Al-Jahshiyārī, *Kitāb al-Wuzarā wa'l-Kuttāb*, ed. Muṣtafā al-Saqqā, Ibrāhīm al-Abyāri, and 'Abd alḤafiẓ Shalabī (Cairo, 1938), pp. 40–41.

Chapter 5

1. Edward Gibbon, *Autobiography*, ed. Dero A. Saunders (New York, 1961), p. 67.

2. Ibid., p. 79.

3. Thus, Catholic polemicists accused Calvin of Islamizing tendencies, and Calvinists in Geneva tried to bring the same charge against Servetus. See Aldo-

brandino Malvezzi, *L'Islamismo e la cultura europea* (Florence, 1956), pp. 246ff.; R. H. Bainton, *Michel Servet, hérétique et martyr* (Geneva, 1953), p. 116.

4. See Kenneth M. Setton, "Lutheranism and the Turkish Peril," *Balkan Studies* (Thessaloniki) 3 (1962): 133–68; Dorothy Vaughan, *Europe and the Turk: A Pattern of Alliances* (Liverpool, 1954).

5. S. Ockley, *History of the Saracens* (Cambridge, 1757), vol. 2, p. xxxv, cited in P. M. Holt, *Studies in the History of the Near East* (London, 1973), p. 55.

6. Edward Gibbon, *The History of the Decline and Fall of the Roman Empire,* ed. J. B. Bury (London, 1909–14), vol. 7, p. 135.

7. Ibid., vol. 5, p. 375, n. 119.

8. Edward Pococke, *Specimen Historiae Arabum* (Oxford, 1648–50; reprint, Oxford, 1806).

9. Claude Étienne Savary, *Le Coran, traduit de l'Arabe, accompagné de notes et précédé d'un abrégé de la vie de Mahomet, tiré des écrivains orientaux les plus estimés* (Paris, 1783), preface.

10. *The Koran: commonly called the Alcoran of Mohammed; translated into English immediately from the original Arabic, with explanatory notes . . . to which is prefixed a preliminary discourse,* trans. George Sale (London, 1734).

11. Holt, *Studies in the History of the Near East,* p. 60.

12. *Alcorani Textus Universus ex correctionibus Arabum exemplaribus summa fide . . . descriptus, eademque fide . . . ex arabico idiomate in Latinum translatus; oppositis unicuique capitis notis, atque refutatione. . . .* (Padua, 1698).

13. Gibbon, *Decline and Fall of the Roman Empire,* vol. 5, p. 374 n. 118.

14. Humphrey Prideaux, *The True Nature of Imposture fully Display'd in the Life of Mahomet. With a Discourse annex'd for the Vindication of Christianity from this Charge. Offered to the Consideration of the Deists of the Present Age* (Oxford, 1697).

15. Henri de Boulainvilliers, *La Vie de Mahomed; avec des réflexions sur la religion Mahometane, et les coutumes des Musulmans* (London, 1730; reprint, Amsterdam, 1731).

16. Gibbon, *Decline and Fall of the Roman Empire,* vol. 5, p. 375 n. 119.

17. Prideaux, *True Nature of Imposture,* preface, cited in Holt, *Studies in the History of the Near East,* p. 51.

18. On this work and its influence in Europe, see Massimo Petrocchi, "Il mito de Maometto in Boulainvilliers," *Rivista Storica Italiana* 60 (1948): 367–77.

19. Boulainvilliers, *Vie de Mahomed,* p. 267.

20. Ibid., p. 85.

21. Ibid., p. 225.

22. On this literature, see further Hans Haas, "Das Bild Muhammeds in Wandel der Zeiten," *Zeitschrift fur Missionskunde und Religionswissenschaft* 31 (1916): 161–71, 194–203, 225–39, 258–69, 289–95, 321–33, 353–65; Gustav Pfannmüller, *Handbuch der Islam-Literatur* (Berlin and Leipzig, 1923), pp. 115–206; Pierre Martino, "Mahomet en France au XVIIe et au XVIIIe siècle," in *Actes du XIVe Congrès international des Orientalistes: Alger 1905* (Paris, 1907), pt. 3, pp. 206–41; Martino, *L'Orient dans la littérature française au XVIIe et au XVIIIe siècle* (Pairs, 1906); G. H. Bousquet, "Voltaire et l'Islam," in *Studia Islamica,* fasc. xxviii (1968): 109–26; Djavad Hadidi, *Voltaire et l'Islam* (Paris, 1974). On the history of Arabic scholarship in Europe, see Johann Fück, *Die arabiscben Studien in Europa bis den Anfang des 20. Jabrhunderts* (Leipzig, 1955).

23. Gibbon, *Decline and Fall of the Roman Empire,* vol. 5, p. 375 n. 119.

24. Ernest Renan, *Études d'histoire religieuse,* 2nd ed. (Paris, 1857), pp. 217ff., especially p. 220. The same desire to observe the visible birth of a prophetic religion inspired the historian of antiquity Eduard Meyer and the Islamicist D. S. Margoliouth to study the history of the Mormons.

25. Tor Andrae, *Die Person Muhammeds in Lehre und Glauben seiner Gemeinde* (Stockholm, 1917).

26. More recent scholarship, chiefly in Russia, has questioned the historicity of the Qur'ān and even of Muhammed himself. See N. A. Smirnov, *Očerki istorii izučeniya Islama v SSSR* (Moscow, 1954), English abridgment, *Islam and Russia* (London, 1956).

27. Gibbon, *Decline and Fall of the Roman Empire,* vol. 5, p. 354.

28. Ibid., p. 349. In spite of this, Gibbon devoted considerable attention to the Arabian background of Muhammad's career, drawing, in addition to his classical and Arabic sources, on the accounts of recent travelers, notably Carsten Niebuhr, for information about the geography of Arabia and the way of life of the Arabs. His treatment of this subject is much colored by his general views on barbarian virtue, and might usefully be compared with his discussion of the pre-Christian Germans and pre-Islamic Turks.

29. Ibid., p. 420.

30. Boulainvilliers, *Vie de Mahomed,* p. 343.

31. Gibbon, *Decline and Fall of the Roman Empire,* vol. 5, p. 360.

32. Ibid., pp. 365–66.

33. Ibid., p. 376. This distinction between superstition and fanaticism (sometimes equated with enthusiasm) is derived from David Hume, "Of Superstition and Enthusiasm," *Essays;* cf. *Dialogues Concerning Natural Religion,* ed. Norman Kemp Smith (Indianapolis and New York, 1947).

34. Gibbon, *Decline and Fall of the Roman Empire,* vol. 5, pp. 400–401.

35. Ibid., p. 332.

36. For a fuller discussion of these points, see G. E. von Grunebaum, "Islam: The Problem of Changing Perspective," in *The Transformation of the Roman World: Gibbon's Problem After Two Centuries,* ed. Lynn White, Jr. (Berkeley and Los Angeles, 1966), pp. 147–78.

Chapter 6

1. *New York Times,* 20 December 1986.

2. Pakistan press, spring and summer 1955, especially editorial and news columns in *Morning News* (Karachi), 24 August 1955, and two letters by Sh. Inayatullah, protesting against this campaign, published in the *Pakistan Times,* 1 and 28 September 1955.

3. Muḥammad al-Bahī, *Al-Mubashshirūn wa'l-Mustashriqūn wa-mawqifuhum min al-Islām* (Cairo, n.d. [ca. 1962]).

4. Ibrahim Abu-Lughod, "Al-Sayṭara al-Ṣahyūniyya 'ala al-dirāsāt al-'arabryya fī Amrīkā," *Al-Adab* 12, no. 6 (June 1974):5–6.

5. Raymond Schwab, *La Renaissance orientale* (Paris, 1950). An English translation, *The Oriental Renaissance: Europe's Rediscovery of India and the East, 1680–1880,* trans. Gene Patterson-Black and Victor Reinking (New York, 1984), is so inaccurate as to be unusable.

6. In a discussion of some Islamic terms for "revolution," I began the ex-

amination of each term—following a common Arab practice—with a brief look at the basic meanings of the Arabic root from which it was derived. One passage, introducing the term most widely used in modern Arabic, ran as follows: "The root *th-w-r* in classical Arabic meant to rise up (e.g. of a camel), to be stirred or excited, and hence, especially in Maghribi usage, to rebel. It is often used in the context of establishing a petty, independent sovereignty; thus, for example, the so-called party kings who ruled in eleventh-century Spain after the breakup of the Caliphate of Cordova, are called *thawwār* (singular *thā'ir*). The noun *thawra* at first means excitement, as in the phrase, cited in the *Ṣiḥāḥ*, a standard medieval Arabic dictionary, *intaẓir ḥatta taskun hadhihi 'l-thawra,* wait until this excitement dies down—a very apt recommendation. The verb is used by al-Iji, in the form *thawarān* or *ithārat fitna,* stirring up sedition, as one of the dangers which should discourage a man from practising the duty of resistance to bad government. *Thawra* is the term used by Arabic writers in the nineteenth-century for the French Revolution, and by their successors for the approved revolutions, domestic and foreign, of our own time" ("Islamic Concepts of Revolution," in *Revolution in the Middle East and Other Case Studies,* ed. P. J. Vatikiotis [London, 1972], pp. 38–39.)

This definition, in both form and content, follows the standard classical Arabic dictionaries and would have been immediately recognized by anyone familiar with Arabic lexicography. The use of camel imagery in politics was as natural for the ancient Arabs as horse imagery for the Turks and ship imagery among the maritime peoples of the West.

Said understood the passage differently: "Lewis's association of *thawra* with a camel rising and generally with excitement (and not with a struggle on behalf of values) hints much more broadly than is usual for him that the Arab is scarcely more than a neurotic sexual being. Each of the words or phrases he uses to describe revolution is tinged with sexuality: *stirred, excited, rising up.* But for the most part it is a 'bad' sexuality he ascribes to the Arab. In the end, since Arabs are really not equipped for serious action, their sexual excitement is no more noble than a camel's rising up. Instead of revolution there is sedition, setting up a petty sovereignty, and more excitement, which is as much as saying that instead of copulation the Arab can only achieve foreplay, masturbation, coitus interruptus. These, I think, are Lewis's implications, no matter how innocent his air of learning, or parlorlike his language" (pp. 315–16). To which one can only reply in the words of the Duke of Wellington: "If you can believe that, you can believe anything."

7. Maxime Rodinson, *La fascination de l'Islam* (Paris, 1980), p. 14. The "two sciences" of Zhdanov and his successors and imitators have been variously defined, according to the ideological alignments, the political purposes, and the social or even ethnic origins of the scientists.

8. *New York Times Book Review,* 31 October 1976.

9. Such as, for example, the *Review of the Arab Academy* (Damascus), *al-Abḥāth* (Beirut), the *Review of Maghribi History* (Tunis), and the Bulletins of the Faculties of Arts and of Social Sciences of Cairo, Alexandria, Baghdad, and other universities.

10. For example, the writings of Tibawi and Khatibi, and Najib al-Aqiqi's three-volume Arabic work on Orientalism and Orientalists, surely the most comprehensive treatment of the subject in any language.

11. I may perhaps mention here that several of my own publications, in-

cluding some to which the anti-Orientalists have taken the strongest exception, have been translated and published in the Arab world—in Egypt, Lebanon, Libya, Saudi Arabia, Algeria, and Iraq.

12. Fu'ād Zakaria, "Naqd al-Istishrāq wa'azmat al-thaqāfa al-'Arabiyya al-mu'āṣira," *Fikr* (Cairo) 10 (1986):33–75. An abridged French translation is included in a volume of Professor Zakariya's essays, entitled *Laicité ou Islamisme: les arabes à l'heure du choix* (Paris and Cairo, 1990), pp. 119–66. For other Arabic critiques of anti-Orientalism, see Ṣādiq al-'Aẓm, *Al-Istishrāq wa'l-istishrāq ma'kūsan* (Beirut, 1981), partial English version: "Orientalism and Orientalism in Reverse," *Khamsin* 8 (1981):5–26; Nadīm al-Bīṭār, *Ḥudūd al-Huwiyya al-Qawmiyya* (Beirut, 1982), chap. 6, pp. 153–96: "Min al-istishrāq al-gharbī ilā 'istishrāq 'Arabi." Some of these and others are discussed by Emmanuel Sivan in his *Interpretations of Islam: Past and Present* (Princeton, 1985), chap. 5, pp. 133–54: "Edward Said and His Arab Reviewers." Between 1987 and 1990, the Office of General Cultural Affairs of the Iraqi Ministry of Culture and Education published several volumes entitled *Orientalism,* containing articles and interviews in both Arabic and English. With the exception of Dr. Ṣādiq al-'Aẓm's essay, all of the above appeared after the original publication of this article.

Chapter 8

1. Western Islamologists have sometimes been accused by reformers and secularists of supporting and encouraging conservative and fundamentalist Muslims in their resistance to change. I have often heard such charges, with anger from strangers and with anguish from friends, and I must admit that they are not entirely unjustified, since some of the fundamentalists are clearly of the same opinion. A few of my own writings, condemned by expatriate, mostly non-Muslim Arabs as "anti-Islamic," have been translated into Arabic and published by the Muslim Brothers, in book form or as articles in their journals. One of them was even abridged to pamphlet size and hawked outside the mosques. I picked up my own copy outside Al-Azhar, in Cairo.

The coincidence of views between Islamologists and Islamic fundamentalists is apparent, not real, and the reformers' accusations of complicity in reaction arise from a failure to distinguish between descriptive and prescriptive statements. The scholarly student of Islam—especially if he is not a Muslim—studies Islam as a historical phenomenon, as a civilization with a long and distinguished record of achievement. The evidence he uses is that provided by Muslims—what they have said, written, and done in the course of the centuries. That is, he is concerned with the past and with the ways it can be used to understand the present. It is not his task or his right to change the present or to try and shape the future. This task is for the Muslim—his right, his duty, his exclusive privilege.

The universality and centrality of religion in the Muslim past are surely beyond dispute. Its place in the Muslim future is for Muslims—and only Muslims—to decide.

2. Another proffered explanation of the name Fataḥ is that it represents a reversed acronym for Ḥarakat Taḥrīr Falasṭīn, Movement for the Liberation of Palestine.

3. The *Sovetskaya Entsiklopediya,* though, devotes a long article to discrediting them. A French scholar, Rémy Dor, recently published a remarkable poem that he gathered from the Kirghiz Turks who migrated into Afghanistan from Soviet

Kirghizia. In true heroic style, it celebrates the bitter and unavailing struggle of the Kirghiz against the Bolsheviks (Balchi Beg) and their final defeat in the early 1930s (*Turcica* 8 [1976]: 87–116).

4. Among many Christian Arab intellectuals, now living chiefly in France or the United States, and among the French and American descendants or successors of their former mentors, there is a natural nostalgia for their shared golden age and a quite unnatural assumption that it was a normal and proper condition which would have continued indefinitely had it not been for the malevolent intervention of disruptive alien forces. These malevolent forces can, of course, be identified in whatever way interest or prejudice may indicate.

5. Gamal Abdel Nasser, *The Philosophy of the Revolution* (Cairo, n.d.), pp. 67–68.

6. A different kind of exception is the refusal of some Arab and some other Muslim countries to support Turkey on the Cyprus question. One element in this is residual resentment against former rulers; another is disapproval of the policies of Westernization and secularization pursued by the Turkish republic since its inception.

Chapter 9

1. Ibn Māja, *Sunan, fitan,* i; Dārimī, *Musnad, fitan,* 1. For a discussion, see I. Goldziher, *Introduction to Islamic Theology and Law* (Princeton, 1981), pp. 50–52.

2. See, for example, Bukhārī, *Ṣaḥīḥ, fitan,* 2, and *aḥkām,* 3; Muslim ibn al-Ḥajjāj, *Imāra,* 53. Further references: A. J. Wensinck et al., *Concordance de la tradition musulmane* (Leiden, 1965), vol. 5, p. 129.

3. Niẓām al-Mulk *Siyāsat-nāma,* ed. and translated into French by Charles Schefer (Paris, 1891–97), text 173, translation 268.

4. Tabari, *Tarīkh,* i, 2053.

5. For fuller documentation, see B. Lewis, "Usurpers and Tyrants: Notes on Some Political Terms," in *Logos Islamikos: Studia Islamica in Honorem Georgii Michaelis Wickens,* ed. R. M. Savory and D. A. Agius (Toronto, 1984), pp. 259–67; Lewis, "On the Quietist and Activist Traditions in Islamic Political Writing," *BSOAS* 49 (1986): 141–47.

6. Wensinck, *Concordance,* vol. 1, p. 327. See the discussion in S. D. Goitein, *Studies on Islamic History and Institutions* (Leiden, 1966), pp. 203–4; B. Lewis, *Race and Slavery in the Middle East* (New York, 1990), p. 115 n.30.

Chapter 10

1. Homer, *Iliad,* xii, 243.

2. Horace, *Odes,* ii, 13.

3. On the kind of political benefits a Roman politician conferred on his home province, see Sir Ronald Syme, *Roman Papers* (New York, 1979), vol. 2, pp. 620–22. My thanks are due to Professor Z. Yavetz for drawing my attention to this paper.

4. Al-Juzjānī, *Al-Ta'rīfāt* (Istanbul, 1327), p. 171.

5. For examples, see Gustave E. Grunebaum, "The Response to Nature in Arabic Poetry," *Journal of Near Eastern Studies* 4, no. 3 (1945): 144–46.

6. Al-Jāḥiẓ, "Al-Ḥanīn ilā'l-Awṭān," in *Rasā'il al-Jāhiz,* ed. 'Abd al-Salām Hārūn (Cairo, 1965), vol. 2, pp. 379–412, German translation in O. Rescher, *Excerpte und Übersetzungen aus den Schriften des Philologen und Dogmatiken Gâhiz aus Basra* (Stuttgart, 1931), vol. 1, pp. 488–97. Jāḥiẓ's final example of love of country is the practice which he ascribes to 'the sons of Aaron and the house of David' during the Babylonian captivity. It was their custom, he says, when any one of them died anywhere in Babylonia, to give his body temporary burial, and after an interval to remove his remains and give them final burial in Jerusalem.

7. 'Izz al-Dīn Abū 'Abdallah Ibn Shaddād, *Al-A'lāq al Khaṭīra fī dhikr umarā' al-Shām wa'l-Jazīra,* ed. D. Sourdel (Damascus, 1953), vol. 1, pt. 1, pp. 2–4.

8. Ali Sher Navoy, *Khamsa* (Tashkent, 1960), p. 750.

9. Darwīsh Tawakkul b. Ismā'īl b. Bazzāz, *Ṣafwat al-Ṣafā,* ms. British Museum, Add. 18548, fol. 202a and Or. 7576, fols. 38a-b.

10. Ibn Khaldūn, *Al-Muqaddima,* ed. Etienne Quatremère (Paris, 1858), vol. 1, p. 237; English translation by Charles Issawi, *An Arab Philosophy of History* (London, 1950), 106, and F. Rosenthal, *The Muqaddimah* (New York, 1956), vol. 1, p. 266.

11. Bernard Lewis, *The Political Language of Islam* (Chicago, 1988), pp. 55ff.; Ḥasan al-Bāsha, *Al-Alqāb al-Islāmiyya fi'l-Ta'rīkh wa'l-Wathā'iq wa'l-Athar* (Cairo, 1957).

12. The seventeenth-century lexicographer Francis Mesgnien-Meninski, in his great Turkish–Persian–Arabic Thesaurus, defines *waṭan* in accordance with the classical lexica and gives many examples of its use, none of them political. Interestingly, he cites the above-mentioned saying attributed to the Prophet and cautiously translates it: "Amor patriae est de fide, *aut* ex fide. L'amor della patria é cosa di fede, ò di religione" (Meninski, *Thesaurus,* s.v.).

13. "Ali Efendinin Sefaretnamesi . . . ," ed. Ahmed Refik, in *Tarih-i Osmani Encümeni Mecmuasi* (1329), p. 1459.

14. On *Cumhur* as republic, see EI^2, s.v. "Djumhūriyya."

15. Report published in Ottoman official journal of 21 Dhu'l-Qa'da—1254–1839, reprinted in Mahmud Cevad, *Maarif-i Umumiye Nezareti Tarihçe-i Teşkilât ve Icraati* (Istanbul, 1922), pp. 6–10, English translation in Niyazi Berkes, *The Development of Secularism in Turkey* (Montreal, 1964), p. 105.

16. Turkish text in A. Şerif Gözübüyük and Suna Kili, eds., *Türk Anayasa Metinleri* (Ankara, 1957), pp. 3–5, English translation by Halil Inalcik in J. C. Hurewitz, ed., *The Middle East and North Africa in World Politics: A Documentary Record* (New Haven and London, 1975), vol. 1, p. 270.

17. Mustafa Sami, cited in *Aylik Ansiklopedisi,* no. 5 (September 1944): 152–53.

18. In Ebüzziya Tevfik, ed., *Nümûne-i Edebiyat-i Osmani* (Istanbul, 1296/1878?), p. 239.

19. Şerif Mardin, *The Genesis of Young Ottoman Thought: A Study in the Modernization of Turkish Political Ideas* (Princeton, 1962), p. 210.

20. Cevdet Paşa, *Maruzat,* ed. Yusuf Halaçoğlu (Istanbul, 1980), pp. 114–15; also, in Arabic characters, in *Tarih-i Osmani Encümeni Mecmuasi* (1341), p. 273. Partial English translation in Bernard Lewis, *The Emergence of Modern Turkey,* 2nd ed. (London, 1968), p. 338.

21. On Sheikh Rifā'a's patriotic poetry, see James Heyworth Dunne, "Rifā'a Badawī Rāfi' al-Tahtāwī: The Egyptian Revivalist," *BSOAS* 9 (1937–39): 961–67; *BSOAS* 10 (1940–42): 399–415.

22. *Nafīr Sūriya,* 25 October 1860, cited in Ami Ayalon, *Language and Change in the Arab Middle East: The Evolution of Modern Political Discourse* (New York, 1987), pp. 52–53.

23. *Ibret,* 22 March 1873, reprinted in Mustafa N. Özön, *Namik Kemal ve Ibret Gazetesi* (Istanbul, 1938), p. 265, English translation in Lewis, *Emergence of Modern Turkey,* p. 337.

Chapter 11

1. John Locke, *A Letter concerning Toleration, with the Second Treatise of Civil Government,* ed. J. W. Gough (Oxford, 1946), p. 160

2. Facsimile and edition in David Goldenberg, ed., *To Bigotry No Sanction: Documents in American Jewish History* (Philadelphia, 1988), pp. 56–59.

Bibliographical Appendix

Contacts

1. "Europe and Islam." The Tanner Lectures, presented at Brasenose College, Oxford University, 26 February, 5 and 12 March 1990. Published in Grethe B. Peterson, ed. *The Tanner Lectures on Human Values*. Salt Lake City, 1991, pp. 79–139.

2. "Legal and Historical Reflections on the Position of Muslim Populations Under Non-Muslim Rule." Presented at the seminar "Les Populations Musulmanes en Europe," under the auspices of the Observatoire du Changement Social en Europe Occidentale, Poitiers, 7–9 November 1991. A French translation, without the notes, was published in the proceedings of the seminar: *Musulmans en Europe*. Poitiers, 1992. The English original was published in the *Journal of the Institute of Muslim Minority Affairs,* January 1992, pp. 1–16.

Studies and Perceptions

3. "Translation from Arabic." Presented at the American Philosophical Society, Philadelphia, 23 April 1977. Published in the Society's *Proceedings* 24, no. 1 (February 1980): 41–47.

4. "The Ottoman Obsession." Published in *FMR* (Milan) 5 (1984): 89–99.

5. "Gibbon on Muḥammad." Presented at the colloquium "Gibbon and the Decline and Fall of the Roman Empire," under the auspices of the American Academy of Arts and Sciences and the Istituto della Enciclopedia Italiana, Rome, 1976. Published in *Daedalus,* Summer 1976, pp. 89–101.

6. "The Question of Orientalism." Published in *The New York Review of Books,* 24 June 1982, pp. 49–56.

7. "Other People's History." Adapted from a lecture presented at the inaugural colloquium of the Center for Non-Western Studies, University of Leiden, 29 August 1989. Published in *The American Scholar* 59, no. 3 (Summer 1990): 397–405.

Islamic Response and Reaction

8. "The Return of Islam." Originally published in *Commentary,* January 1976, pp. 39–49. Revised and recast for this edition.

9. "The Shīʿa in Islamic History." Lecture presented at an international conference on Shiʿism, Tel Aviv University, December 1984. Published in Martin Kramer, ed. *Shiʿism, Resistance, and Revolution* Boulder, Colo., 1987, pp. 21–30. Substantially revised for this edition.

10. "Country and Freedom." Published as "Watan," *Journal of Contemporary History* 26 (1991):522–33.

11. "Religious Coexistence and Secularism." Adapted from a lecture presented at the colloquium "Coabitazione tra religioni e laicità dello stato nel Mediterraneo del novecento," under the auspices of Storia Uomini Religioni, Italian translation to be published in the proceedings of the colloquium. The English original was published as "Muslims, Christians, and Jews: The Dream of Coexistence." *The New York Review of Books,* 26 March 1992, pp. 48–52.

Index

Arabic names are indexed in the form in which they are most familiar in the West. Generally, names from earlier periods are indexed under the given or first name, while more current persons are found under the last name. Last names beginning with "al" are alphabetized according to the element following this particle (for example, Hasan al-Bannā is found under Bannā, with the particle "al" retained in front of it).